PRAISE FOR *CIDER PLANET*

"Claude's unique involvement with the international craft cider scene makes him the perfect guide for the rest of us. He takes a deep look at the way that traditional and industrial cider processes have come to differ as much as they do, and he explores the distinct histories of ciders and perries in different countries and the way in which their fruit and climate have influenced their drinks. Along the way, he introduces us to some exceptional cider making personalities worldwide. In the light of the huge revival of interest in craft cider and its differentiation from the mainstream, this book is both timely and fascinating."

— **ANDREW LEA**,
author of *Craft Cider Making*

"In his new guide to global cider, Claude Jolicoeur offers a characteristically thorough overview of regional traditions and emerging trends. His even-handed descriptions of cider styles, fruit selections, and production methods describe the various influences shaping this often-misunderstood drink. What is 'modern' cider? How does it contrast with traditional and more artisanal styles? This is a very helpful and unbiased survey for those planning travel destinations, or are curious to learn where favorite local producers fit within the big picture of the Cider Planet."

— **DAVID BUCHANAN**, owner,
Portersfield Cider; author of *Taste, Memory*

"With what must be one of the best global cider address books, Claude Jolicoeur takes us with him on a fascinating around the world journey, delving deep into cider and perry heritage, culture, and practice as we go.

"In typical erudite fashion, Claude brings his encyclopedic knowledge of orcharding practice, cidery process, and apple and pear varieties with him. Whether it's being transported to Kazakhstan (the birthplace of the domestic apple), wandering the perry orchards of Herefordshire with Tom Oliver, exploring the diversity of apple varieties from North America, or a visit to any of cider's other homes, this is the perfect accompaniment for a fascinating pomologically inspired voyage."

— **SUSANNA FORBES**,
Little Pomona Orchard & Cidery

"*Cider Planet* is a delightfully written how-to, history, and travelogue all rolled into one fantastic read. Over the decades, Claude Jolicoeur has become one of the world's most knowledgeable and articulate cider geeks. If you are a seasoned cider veteran or just getting curious, *Cider Planet* is for you."

— **JOHN BUNKER**, apple historian;
author of *Apples and the Art of Detection*

"A delightful and deeply researched guide to the world's best drink. Required reading for every ciderhead."

— **ROWAN JACOBSEN**, author of
Apples of Uncommon Character

Also by Claude Jolicoeur

*The New Cider Maker's Handbook:
A Comprehensive Guide for Craft Producers*

CIDER
PLANET

Exploring the Producers, Practices, and Unique Traditions of Craft Cider and Perry from Around the World

CLAUDE JOLICOEUR

CHELSEA GREEN PUBLISHING
White River Junction, Vermont
London, UK

Photos of plates from the *Herefordshire Pomona* (pages vi, 46, 81, 184, 220, 291)
courtesy of Cornell University Libraries.

Project Manager: Patricia Stone
Developmental Editor: Benjamin Watson
Copy Editor: Diane Durrett
Proofreader: Angela Boyle
Indexer: Shana Milkie
Designer: Melissa Jacobson
Page Layout: Abrah Griggs

Printed in the United States of America.
First printing September 2022.
10 9 8 7 6 5 4 3 2 1   22 23 24 25 26

Our Commitment to Green Publishing
Chelsea Green sees publishing as a tool for cultural change and ecological stewardship. We strive to align our
book manufacturing practices with our editorial mission and to reduce the impact of our business enterprise in
the environment. We print our books and catalogs on chlorine-free recycled paper, using vegetable-based inks
whenever possible. This book may cost slightly more because it was printed on paper that contains recycled fiber,
and we hope you'll agree that it's worth it. *Cider Planet* was printed on paper supplied by Versa that is made of
recycled materials and other controlled sources.

ISBN 978-1-64502-141-4 (hardcover) | ISBN 978-1-64502-142-1 (ebook)

Library of Congress Cataloging-in-Publication Data is available upon request.

Chelsea Green Publishing
85 North Main Street, Suite 120
White River Junction, Vermont USA

Somerset House
London, UK

www.chelseagreen.com

CONTENTS

Plate I.

Foxwhelp.

Introduction

It is now quite a while since I wrote *The New Cider Maker's Handbook* (which was published in 2013). After its publication, one unexpected side effect was that I started to receive invitations to visit cider making regions all around the world, to participate in conferences and workshops, and to be a judge in competitions. The nice thing is that, as a now well-known author, all the doors were open for me and I have been able to meet many great artisans around our cider planet. Yes . . . Cider Planet—an expression that came up while speaking with my friend and traveling companion Mark Gleonec. We were talking in French about how *la planète cidre* was diverse and accessible when compared to, for example, the wine world. Diverse because one of the amazing things when we look at ciders made in all regions of the world is the huge variability in their styles and flavors, in apple varieties, as well as in the methods used for making them. And accessible because even the most recognized cider artisans are simple, unpretentious people who will readily agree to speak and share their knowledge with visitors.

It then became clear for me that I ought to testify to what I have learned from my travels. The main idea here is to discuss the unique features of ciders and perries from different regions, to see how they are made and what makes them different from those of other regions. In addition to my own experiences, I relied heavily on my collaborators, contacts, and friends from all these regions, who provided me with a lot of important information. Hence, in the present book, I am able to talk about this worldwide diversity of ciders and perries mainly from a maker's perspective. So the focus is on making these beverages, on the apples and pears used to make them, on the different styles, and on good producers. We also talk about the history (how cider and perry appeared and evolved in the regions under consideration), about the relevant literature, and quite a bit about the traditions that exist around the cider and perry scene.

What Is Cider and What Is Craft Cider?

One long-standing question, which is unresolved within the cider community, is that of a good definition of *cider*. First, I'll write here the answer to the question, *What is cider?* given by the European Cider and Fruit Wine Association (AICV) in their document *European Cider Trends 2021*:

> *Cider is an alcoholic beverage obtained only by the complete or partial fermentation of:*
>
> - *the juice of fresh apples, or*
> - *the reconstituted juice of concentrate made from the juice of apple, or*
> - *the mixture of juice of fresh apples and of reconstituted juice of concentrate made from the juice of apple*
>
> *The product will have in general an alcohol content within the range of 1.2% to less than 8.5% alcohol by volume (ABV), and should maintain the character of fermented apple juice. Adding distilled alcohol to cider is forbidden.*
>
> *[. . .]*

In the late 1980's modern ciders were born: ciders containing juice and flavorings began to be produced, alongside traditional ciders. The industry calls these 'flavored ciders', and they can contain, in addition to the apple base, ingredients such as juice of other fruits, extracts, flavourings, etc.

The range of beverages that share the name *cider* (or its equivalent in other languages) is huge. In one extreme of this range, we find small producers who grow their own apples, juice them, and make a cider from the natural fermentation of that juice with no other addition. On the other extreme, we find large multinational industrial facilities that produce alcopop-type cider from water, sugar, glucose syrup, imported apple juice concentrate, and chemical flavorings and additives, but often, no fresh apples at all. According to the website of one of these producers: "Rekorderlig is made by combining the purest Swedish spring water with wild and exotic fruits," which is quite paradoxical when we know that neither water nor wild and exotic fruits are ingredients in traditional cider making.* In some countries (but not all) these two obviously very different products, alcopop-type cider and real cider, may be seen on the shelves of the same store and share the same name: *cider*. Such an absurd situation has been made possible by extremely lax regulations in countries where lobbying from large companies may have contributed to the relaxing of rules. And please, understand me on this: I have nothing against alcopop-type ciders. They exist because there is a demand for them; plus, some of them actually taste good. It is just that I don't think they should be called cider because they are, really, something else. The fact that they share the same name makes it confusing for the customers who may have difficulty knowing what exactly they are buying. Naturally, things would be easier if cider had the same international status as wine, which has a fairly well-accepted definition throughout the world—it is generally well understood that a fermented mixture of water, sugar, grape concentrate, and other chemicals can't be sold as *red* or *white wine* anywhere on this planet. Such drinks do exist, but they are given a different name.

In reaction to this situation, smaller-scale cider makers try to differentiate their product from some of the industrial offerings. One

---

* "About Us," Rekorderlig Cider, updated 2019, www.rekorderlig.com/about-us.

way of doing this is by adding a qualifier to the word *cider*. Some people then talk about *farm* cider, *traditional* cider, *real* cider, or *craft* cider. . . . Let's try to see what these qualifiers really mean:

Farm Cider should be farm-based, which means that it is made from apples that are grown on the farm (or nearby), and all cider making activities are also done on the maker's farm.

Traditional Cider should respect the traditions of the region where it is produced. This would mainly relate to the choice of apple varieties, the cider making process, and the style.

Real Cider should be the product of the fermentation of a must (unfermented juice) obtained from freshly milled and pressed apples, with minimal adjuncts or other ingredients. Hence this is mainly a question of ingredients.

Craft Cider may be seen as the opposite of industrial cider, made on a small scale by a maker who is an artisan. But in a more stringent sense, a craft cider may include all other previous qualifiers and be defined as a farm-based, real cider that respects local traditions.

However good these qualifiers may be, the question remains as to where we draw the line. Some larger producers firmly believe they also produce craft cider, even if they chaptalize (add sugar) heavily and use some apple juice concentrate in their process. They then hijack the word *craft* and use it in the marketing of their product with bucolic images of orchards that let customers believe they are buying something other than what the product actually is. The point is that, unfortunately, these qualifiers don't mean much anymore when they appear on the label of a bottle of cider.

It should be said that this question of the definition of *craft* is not unique to cider. I read recently about this same problem relative to distilled spirits:

> *Moreover, since a clear legal definition of "craft" as well as associated concepts is lacking in most countries, big brands often resort*

*to marketing their (mass-produced) products as "craft" (Johnnie Walker), "handcrafted" (Jim Beam), "handmade" (Tito's vodka) and so on.**

This being said, for the purpose of this book, since I can't find a better qualifier, I will nevertheless call the cider that drives our interest by the name *craft cider*. This is not a perfect solution, of course, as many people have very different perceptions for the meaning of this term. For my part, I see it as the opposite of industrial cider. Hence there is a question of scale of production (craft cider usually being made in small batches), but also, when cider making becomes more akin to a process that is repeated to create exactly the same product batch after batch, it loses the crafty side of it. I would not consider as craft a cider maker who does systematic chaptalization and/or dilution of his ciders or who uses bulk-bought juices or concentrates, because I think craft cider makers should know their raw material (the apples), where they come from and how they have been grown, and work to make the best possible product while respecting the apples they have. I'll close this with the opinions of two good friends of mine. Tom Oliver, a well-known cider maker from Herefordshire, once said: "A craft cider maker has an involvement in every step of the process and can answer any question about the cider," to which he also added that "he gets his hands dirty." On the same order of ideas, Mark Gleonec wrote in his blog:

> *Cider is the product of an orchard.*
> *Cider is the work of a cider maker.*
> *Cider is a cultural marker.*†

---

* L. Cockx, G. Meloni, and J. Swinnen., *The Water of Life and Death: A Brief Economic History of Spirits*, American Association of Wine Economists, Working Paper No. 246, 2020, https://wine-economics.org/wp-content/uploads/2020/01/AAWE_WP246.pdf.

† Mark, "Pour un appel à définir le mot Cidre" [For a call to define the word Cidre], Macgleo [website], August 11, 2008, http://www.macgleo.com/blog/2018/08/11/pour-un-appe-a-definir-le-mot-cidre.

And I think these two quotes taken together say it all. Hence in this book we particularly draw our attention to ciders that are made by cider makers who get their hands dirty and know about the cider they make—from the apples that have ripened in a nearby orchard to their respect for the culture or tradition relative to the region of production.

Cider Regulation and Certification

The only sure methods to ensure that a product conforms to what is written on the label is through legislation or through a certification label. Laws and regulations vary greatly from one country to another. Let's look at a few very different situations:

- In Australia, there is no minimum apple juice content required for a product to be called cider. Hence it is legal to market a beverage as cider that has only some apple flavor added but zero apple juice used to make it.
- In the United Kingdom, the mixture used to make cider or perry must have at least 35 percent apple or pear juice at a specific gravity (SG) of 1.033 degrees or above. And this apple/pear content may be fully provided by juice reconstituted from concentrate (often imported). It is also permitted to chaptalize heavily in order to first produce a cider that contains around 14 percent alcohol, and to dilute this back to about 5 percent alcohol, a process typical of what is done in industrial cideries.
- In France, the cider has to be 100 percent apple juice. However, it is permitted that half of this juice be reconstituted from locally made concentrate.
- In Quebec (Canada), for a product to be labeled as cider, it has to be from 100 percent fresh apple juice. Concentrates and dilution with water are forbidden. And 80 percent of the apples have to be grown in Quebec. However, it is permitted to chaptalize heavily, as cider can have up to 15 percent alcohol content. A product that includes some concentrate or more

than 20 percent imported apples, or that has been diluted with water, would be called cider cocktail.

We can easily see that with such a diversity of laws it becomes unrealistic to even think all countries could adapt their regulations in order to have a common international definition for cider.

Another avenue is through labels of certification and quality marks. For example, in September 2018, in Exeter (United Kingdom), the Small Independent Cidermakers Association had a meeting called Cider 'X', where they agreed that a cider should be 90 percent fresh apple juice in order to obtain the quality mark of the association. In Australia, a similar process is underway with the Cider Australia organization to develop a trust mark for the identification of ciders made with 100 percent Australian-grown fruit. And there are labels for certification of origin that are mostly seen in the European Union (plus one for ice cider in Canada). This is progress, but there is still a lot of work to do.

Certification Labels

The main purpose of these labels is to certify that an agri-food product conforms to certain specifications relative to its origin, composition, or processing. Let's look at some of these labels:

AOC is a French label that stands for *Appellation d'origine contrôlée*. This is the label we are used to seeing on French wines. Many other European countries have an equivalent label. These national labels are now being superseded by the following designations, which are defined by the European Union and are more international in scope.

PDO is the newer European label, equivalent to AOC. It stands for Protected Designation of Origin. In French, this label becomes **AOP** for *Appellation d'origine protégée*. And in Spanish it is **DOP** for *Denominación de origen protegida*.

PGI is a label meaning protected geographical indication. In French this is **IGP** for *Indication géographique protégée*. Usually, the specifications for a PGI are not as stringent as for a PDO.

These labels additionally have the purpose of protecting the name of a product, often by associating the name with its region of production. For example, a red wine that bears a Bordeaux PDO label is immediately associated with that region of France. No wine from other regions can use the word *Bordeaux* in its name. These certifications are usually represented by a logo printed on the bottle or its label. Some certification labels are more stringent than others and may require high standards of quality as well as tasting of the product by a board of experts. It is worth reading the specifications as they provide some very useful information on fruit varieties and on processes. They are easily downloadable from the internet. Other types of certification labels also might be related to organic or biodynamic agriculture, or for certain types of food—for example, there are labels to certify that a product conforms to the vegan way of living.

The Origin and the Future of the Cider Apple: Kazakhstan

Before getting to the heart of our subject, I would now like to say a word about a place one might not expect to see here . . . Kazakhstan. No, this is not a traditional cider country, but I think it deserves to be included in the beginning of our tour of the Cider Planet because this is where our apples originated, and more precisely in the Tian Shan range of mountains that spread between China, Kazakhstan, and Kyrgyzstan in Central Asia. At the foot of those mountains, we find forests of wild apple trees of the species *Malus sieversii* that have grown and evolved naturally for thousands of years. According to some historians, these apples were brought to Europe by the first merchants who made the trip between China and Europe—in effect the ancient Silk Road that crossed the Tian Shan—and no doubt these merchants gathered a good supply of the best apples they could find as they traveled through the forests. They then threw the pips along their route, all the way to Europe. . . . New trees grew from these seeds, produced apples, crossed with some native populations of crab apples of different species, and after a number of generations this process produced a complex hybrid now known as the domestic apple,

Figure 1. Andrew Lea, Ryan Burk, Peter Mitchell, and the author tasting the apples from a wild *Malus sieversii* tree. These apples had a nice bittersweet flavor.

Malus domestica. Most botanists and geneticists who have studied the apple conclude that *M. domestica* is quite close genetically to *M. sieversii*. This species, then, would be the most important gene provider to our modern cider apple.

I had the very special opportunity to visit some of the wild apple forests of Kazakhstan in the late summer of 2017 with three respected colleagues: Andrew Lea, author of *Craft Cider Making* and of numerous scientific publications; Peter Mitchell, founder of the Cider and Perry Academy; and Ryan Burk, head cider maker at Angry Orchard. Pretty good company indeed. We were like kids in a dream playground! Additionally, our little group included my wife, Banou Khamzina, who also happens to be a Kazakh woman, and our hosts, Alexander Thomas and Aizhan Bekzhanova, owners of Apple City Cider in Almaty, Kazakhstan (see chapter 11), who I take the opportunity here to thank gratefully.

We did make some fascinating observations during this visit, and it is interesting to compare the *M. sieversii* wild apples we saw in these apple forest locations with a population of *M. domestica* natural seedlings such as we can find in most countries. Some comparisons:

Figure 2. Many trees of *M. sieversii* have green-yellow fruit.

Flavor. Of the apples tasted (and we tasted quite a number), all had a rather familiar apple flavor, with more or less bitterness, astringency, acidity, and sugar in a rather similar range that we might find in domestic apple seedlings. No strange or unfamiliar flavors were noted, although we were told such odd flavors might sometimes exist.

Size. Most apples were on average smaller than what we might observe from wild domestic apple seedlings. This is no doubt because humans have systematically selected the larger fruits for their consumption and thus have favored the genes responsible for larger size in the domestic apple population.

Skin color. Yellow and green apples seemed to be in relatively higher proportions in comparison to red or red-striped fruits than we would find in domestic apple seedlings, probably because the genes responsible for the red color were favored by humans in the same way as those that are related to size. And we didn't see apples with russet (light tan or brown coloring or netting) on the skin. I was however told there are russeted apples in some other locations that we didn't visit. Interestingly, we didn't see many scabby apples either.

Cider potential. Sure, most of the apples were overly acidic and harsh tasting, just like in any wild apple population, but the fruit from maybe one tree out of ten had a flavor profile that could make it useful in cider making. This means good sugar, low to moderate acidity, moderate tannins, and a nice apple flavor. Interestingly, this ratio is about the same in the populations of domestic apple seedlings that I have seen. We did taste some that could make fine bittersweet or bittersharp cider apple varieties. And if we take the entirety of these forests that contain millions of trees, the potential to discover many superior varieties for cider is phenomenal.

There is a man, Aimak Dzhangaliev, who devoted his entire life to the study and conservation of the wild apple forests in Kazakhstan. Fortunately for us, a good part of his work has been translated and

Figure 3. A row of *M. sieversii* cider apple selections in Dzhangaliev's conservation orchard near the city of Almaty.

published in English in the scientific journal *Horticultural Reviews*.* In the second half of the last century, he identified a number of wild apple trees that produced superior fruit for cider making, fresh eating, juicing, or processing. He then founded, near the city of Almaty, a conservation orchard where these selections were grafted and grown in a more typical orchard environment. We were privileged to be able to visit this orchard, meet the head scientist, Gaukhar Mukanova, and taste the apples as well as juice from selections that showed a wide diversity in appearance and flavor. Some seemed highly promising, and no doubt very fine cider could be made from these apples.

As yet, there is no tangible cider production in Kazakhstan, but it is coming soon. . . . Apple City Cider is a very serious project and is a cidery that will use *M. sieversii* apples in their blends. Possibly, in the foreseeable future, we will be able to taste Kazakh cider. Let's note also that during the 1990s there were a number of scientific expeditions to these wild apple forests, and the scientists brought back some vegetative cuttings and seeds of *M. sieversii*. Now, many trees of that species are growing at the Geneva Experiment Station in New York. In addition, seeds as well as grafting wood have been distributed to many

_____

* Jules Janick, ed., *Horticultural Reviews*, Volume 29 (Hoboken, NJ: John Wiley & Sons, Inc., 2003).

Figure 4. Juice samples produced from selections of *M. sieversii*. It is interesting to note the variations in color and clarity of the different samples.

collectors all around the world. As a result, I expect that some people will soon discover great cider apples within these materials, and that we will be able to see and drink ciders made at least in part from *M. sieversii* apples of Kazakh origin.

About This Book

During this tour of the Cider Planet, we first review some cider making practices used by producers from all regions, highlighting the differences between modern and traditional methods. We examine this in chapter 1 because these practices are fairly similar in all centers of production.

Following, the bulk of our subject is divided into three parts. In part 1 we look at ciders made in European countries that have long cider traditions, and that have established some well-defined cider style families that are very distinct from one another. In effect, some specific regions of the United Kingdom, France, Spain, and Germany will be seen as the four cradles from which cider making has emerged and evolved. This first part has opening text that explores the history of cider evolution in Europe from the beginning of the Common Era, followed by a chapter for each of these four countries.

In a similar fashion, in part 2, we visit the three main production centers of traditional perries in regions of the U.K., France, and Austria. We will examine three very distinct perry styles as well as rich traditions. Perry has evolved in parallel with cider, but there are quite different challenges with perry making, which are highlighted.

In part 3, we explore newer and emerging cider-producing regions. In many cases, cider tradition was brought to these places by Europeans—for example, the Spanish introduced cider to Latin America, while the English introduced it to North America. In this part, we have one chapter for Australia and New Zealand, and another for the United States and Canada—four countries where craft cider has seen incredible development since the beginning of the current century. And in the last chapter, we go around the planet to visit lesser-known regions where some makers are breaking the barriers to establish themselves as craft cider producers.

CHAPTER ONE

Modern and Traditional Cider Making Practices

The words *modern* and *traditional* are two terms you will often see in this book, because the cider industry worldwide is split between two tendencies. These words are used as qualifiers for cider making practices, and additionally, they are used as qualifiers for cider styles in many regions. Although most of the time the modern practices are used to make ciders of a modern style, the opposite is not always true, as there are many producers who make some traditional-style ciders using modern technologies. During our tour of the Cider Planet, we will meet different craft cider makers, some of whom follow modern cider making practices, and others, more traditional practices. I will try here to highlight the differences: The easiest would be to say that traditional practices correspond to the way cider was made a century ago, and that modern practices are those that have been developed since that time.

Table 1.1. Modern vs. Traditional Practices

	Modern	**Traditional**
Orchard	Consumer apple varieties in high-density and high-yield orchards.	Traditional heirloom or cider apple varieties in low-density orchards.
Pressing room	Fast extraction, belt press.	Maceration of the pulp, slow pressing.
Fermentation	Selected yeast inoculation, control of yeast nutrients, rapid fermentation.	Wild or natural yeast, low levels of natural nutrients, slow fermentation.
Final processing	Clarification, back-sweetening, sterile filtration with chemical stabilizers.	Natural stability with residual apple sugar.
Sparkling	Forced carbonation by injection of CO_2.	Carbonation by fermentation (*prise de mousse*).

But there is a little more to it. . . . And since these practices are fairly independent from the region where the cider is made, we will review them here so that we can refer to this section later on instead of repeating similar explanations in every chapter. In fact, we will see that very few cider makers are all modern or all traditional, but rather stand somewhere between these two poles, using, for example, some modern technologies in an overall traditionally oriented process. Table 1.1 gives a summary of the main features of the two types of practices.

If you have read my first book, *The New Cider Maker's Handbook*, you probably noticed I was strongly biased in favor of traditional practices. However, since those days, I have had the opportunity to taste several true craft ciders made with a modern approach, that were excellent. In consequence, in this book I am a lot more impartial on this issue.

In the Orchard

It is well known that good cider needs good apples (and good perry needs good pears—all that is said for apples and cider also applies to

Figure 1.1. An assortment of traditional French cider apples. Their appearance is quite different from market apples. Photo by John Bunker.

pears and perry). There are two elements we need to consider for this topic: the *pommage* and the management of the orchard.

The Pommage

Pommage is a French word to indicate a selection of apple or pear varieties that are used in a certain region or locality, or by a single producer. Let's take as an example the specification of the PDO for *Cidre de Cornouaille* in Brittany: There is a list of about 30 accepted varieties, meaning that a cider maker who wishes to have the PDO label should use varieties that are on the list. This is then the accepted pommage for the PDO, what we might also call the *regional pommage*. In a certain locality, however, it is not all the varieties included in the regional pommage that are traditionally grown, and that locality might have a pommage which is a subset of the regional one. And similarly for each producer, who might grow in their respective orchards different subsets of the regional pommage.

In traditional cider making, producers use special apple varieties that are not usually found in food stores. These may be ancestral varieties, or cider-specific apples that are rich in tannins, or crabs and wild

Cider Apple Classification

In the English-speaking world, we use a classification for the cider apple varieties that was developed in England by Professor B. T. P. Barker of the Long Ashton Research Station in the beginning of the twentieth century. It consists of four classes that are based on the acid and tannin concentration in the juice from an apple variety, after a sufficient number of samples have been analyzed and averaged. The acidity is a property that gives freshness to the juice and cider, while tannins bring astringency, bitterness, mouthfeel, and persistency. The classes are defined as follows:

> **Sharp** for apples that have acidity but little or no tannins. May be **Mild** or **Full** sharp depending on if acidity is medium or high.
> **Bittersharp** for apples that have both acidity and tannins.
> **Bittersweet** for apples that have tannins but little or no acidity. May be **Mild** or **Full** bittersweet depending on if tannin content is medium or high.
> **Sweet** for apples that have little acidity and little tannins.

Naturally, there are variations from year to year, and in reality, some varieties may be borderline between two classes. Typically, apples from different classes would be mixed to make a well-balanced blend characteristic of the cider style. Other countries, such as France and Spain, have slightly different classification systems that contain more categories, and we will see those in their respective chapters.

seedlings, which are all selected and chosen primarily for their good juice properties for the making of cider. By *cider-specific*, I mean that such apples are grown only for the purpose of cider making, as most of these varieties are quite unpleasant to eat fresh and not really suitable for other uses. It is different in modern cider making because it is rather the consumer apple varieties that are used. These are varieties that have been initially selected for and are mostly used as dessert or cooking fruits. Generally speaking, these market-oriented varieties display less acidity and tannins, and they produce lighter ciders than their traditional counterparts. Pommages used in either traditional or modern cider making vary a lot from country to country, and this will be discussed further in each chapter.

Orchard Management

Most cider apple orchards are of one of the three following types:

Traditional orchards are of the extensive type, which means large trees on standard rootstocks, with wide spacing between trees. Such orchards were (and still are, in some regions) grazed by cattle or other animals. There are typically 120 to 200 trees per hectare (about 50 to 80 per acre), and the initial planting costs as well as the maintenance and spraying costs are low because there is minimal, if any, pest management. However, the yield is also low, usually ranging between 5 to 12 tons annually per hectare (2 to 5 tons per acre), and these orchards need a long time (15 years or more) before reaching full production. Such orchards are nowadays seldom planted except for a few regions where they still are popular, and for small cider producers who manage their own orchards.

Modern orchards are of the intensive type, which means small dwarf trees planted at high density (over 2,500 trees per hectare, or 1,000 per acre). Management of the orchards for market apples is aimed to produce the highest possible yields with good sizing and perfect visual appearance. Such orchards require physical support for the trees, irrigation, orchard floor management (typically an herbicide strip in the rows), and strict pest control. Management can be organic or conventional, and might, or might not, follow IPM practices (that is, integrated pest management, consisting of a number of techniques aimed at reducing the use of pesticides while maintaining the fruit quality standards). The initial capital costs and the operating costs are very high. These orchards need to be managed by skilled professionals. Their yield is high, often over 50 tons annually per hectare (20 tons per acre), and they start to produce very young. Such orchards are mainly used for the growing of market apples, but in many regions cider apple varieties are also grown in intensive orchards.

Cider-bush orchards are an in-between class often qualified as semi-intensive. In these, the trees are of an intermediate size, grafted on medium-sized rootstocks such as MM 106 or MM 111. The density may range between 500 to 1,000 trees and the yield between 20 to 30 tons annually per hectare (200 to 400 trees and a production of 8 to 12 tons per acre). These orchards are a very popular option with the craft cider makers, as production costs are reasonable and they can be managed by nonspecialists.

The type of orchard management has an influence on the quality and flavor of the fruit, including the concentration of important components such as sugar, acid, tannin, and nitrogen. Many people believe the traditional orcharding practices yield the best apples for the making of cider, and that the intensive cultural practices that induce maximal productivity may reduce the quality by a dilution effect (more water in big apples), by an increase of nitrogen content in juice because of the fertilization, and by a reduction of the tannin content. The amount of nitrogen in the apple has a particular importance as it is a natural yeast nutrient, and juices with a high content of nitrogen are not as appropriate for traditional fermentation—they require the

Table 1.2. Cider Orchard Management Systems

Type of Orchard	Costs	Skills Required	Yield	Yeast Nutrients (Nitrogen)
Traditional, extensive	Low	None	Low	Low
Cider-bush, semi-intensive	Medium	Some	High	Medium
Modern, intensive	Very high	High	Best	High

Figure 1.2. Good examples of well-maintained traditional and modern cider orchards. *Top,* at Obsthof am Steinberg (Andreas Schneider), near Frankfurt, Germany. *Bottom,* at Black Diamond Cider (Ian Merwin), New York.

cider maker to use modern practices. However, many people firmly believe a well-managed intensive orchard may yield cider apples of just as high quality as a traditional orchard. This debate isn't close to being settled yet! Table 1.2 gives a summary of some pros and cons of the three orcharding management systems.

Fruit Handling and Juicing

Fruit harvest is quite different in the traditional and modern approaches. In traditional cider making, the apples are collected on the ground after they have naturally fallen from the tree, as this favors a maximum of tree ripening. Two or three passes are usually done, and often the trees are shaken just before the last pass. There exist some mechanical tree shakers, directly mounted on a tractor, that rapidly strip the apples still hanging from the tree, without harming it. The collecting itself may be done by hand in small operations, or mechanically in larger orchards. The apples are then brought into a storage location where they will complete their maturation, what is called *sweating* (see figure 3.10 on page 116). One of the arts of the cider maker is to evaluate the best moment for processing the apples, when they have attained perfect maturation without being overripe.

For their part, modern makers use apples that are grown for the market and are tree-picked before they attain complete tree maturity. They are kept in storage until they are needed. It is only then that a sorting occurs: The premium fruit is packed for the market, and the nonpremium fruit is declassified and sold at lower cost for processing into cider. In some cases, the apples are juiced by large processors who deliver juice in bulk to the cider producers. Generally, less attention is given to the maturity of these apples.

The process of extracting the juice from the apples is also fairly different between traditional and modern practices. The main point is in the speed of extraction. In all cases, there is some washing and sorting of the apples, followed by milling to produce the pomace. Most mills are of the grinder or centrifugal type (hammer mill), with the latter being more common in larger systems. In a typical modern installation, the mill output is fed directly to a belt press that extracts the juice in a matter of seconds. This makes a very rapid extraction where there is no time for any sort of chemical transformation within the pomace.

In a traditional installation, the mill discharges to a special container (called a *conquet* in France) that is a sort of buffer where the pomace will macerate for a period of time that may vary between a few hours to a full day, or even more in some instances. This allows for oxidation of the tannins, thus making them less harsh, and for the natural enzymes to start to degrade the pectins and improve the pressing yield. When this maceration is completed, the pomace is then fed into the press. The hydraulic rack and cloth–type press, also called a pack press, is most often seen with traditional medium-size producers. In more recent installations, horizontal pneumatic presses that permit some important reductions of labor cost are used; while the trend of the very small producers is to use hydropresses, as they are relatively inexpensive. Old screw presses are also still in use in many regions. All of these pressing systems have in common a slow extraction of the juice from the pomace, with cycle times that may last from about 15 minutes and up. In Spain, the cycle time may be as long as a few days.

The complete effect of these slow systems for extracting the juice is still not fully understood by scientists, but there are certainly some differences in the properties of the must that is obtained. For sure, some reports claim that the juice from a belt press has more turbidity,

Figure 1.3. A traditional juicing line at Ecomusée de la pomme et du cidre in Normandy, France. On the left side is the apple reception container and a conveyor belt where sorting is done. In green, in the center, is the washer-elevator-mill unit that discharges the pulp in a special container (*conquet*) for maceration, and at the right, a rack and cloth hydraulic press.

and that keeving is more difficult with such juice (although not impossible). Another obvious difference is the color of the juice obtained. With fast extraction, the juice gains very little color and yields a cider that also is quite pale, while juices obtained after maceration and a long pressing will have a deeper brownish or amber color caused by the oxidation of the pulp. With very long pressing times, such as seen in Spain, certainly microorganism activity has time to initiate some biochemical transformations during the pressing cycle, but again it is not clear what the effect might be on the finished cider.

Fermentation

The must that undergoes fermentation may be of a single variety or a blend. In all cases, the acidity should be checked because it has an influence on the microbiological activities. When blending, the cider maker doses different varieties to attain a target acidity and the flavor sought. Single variety fermentations are done on varieties that naturally have adequate juice properties and acidity balance, and these generally are of the bittersharp or sharp classes. Varieties of the sweet and bittersweet classes that have a low content in acids are more rarely used for single variety fermentations as the cider maker needs to chemically raise the acidity to insure a healthy fermentation.

Yeast Inoculation and Nutrition Strategies

A most significant differentiation between traditional and modern fermentations is in the type of yeast used and how this yeast is fed. In a traditional fermentation, no yeast is added by the cider maker: The wild yeast strains that occurs naturally in the orchard and the cidery are what colonizes the must. There is then a succession of yeast and bacteria species and strains during the course of the fermentation that may yield richer and more complex flavors, and also some "funkiness," which may be associated with off-flavors, or with authentic flavors, depending on one's point of view. The cider maker has no real control over which strain is active, and this may induce more variability of flavor between batches. With time, house strains establish themselves in the cidery, and this may give a special character to the ciders of a given producer or even to the ciders of a region—and thus comes the notion of *terroir*. It may be interesting to note that some studies done in Spain have revealed that hundreds of identifiable strains of yeasts could be residing in an old cidery.

The other characteristic of traditional fermentations is that the nutrient level is low. This is because apples from traditional, unfertilized orchards contain much less nitrogen, and also, the cider maker doesn't add yeast nutrients. This results in low yeast populations and slow fermentations. In traditional fermentation, the much lower yeast population is normally able to feed itself from naturally occurring nutrients, and thus the addition of nutrients is not necessary or beneficial.

The strategy is very different for a modern fermentation. First, the wild microorganisms are eliminated, usually by an appropriate dosage of sulfite or by pasteurization. Then a selected yeast strain is inoculated, putting it in position to take control of the fermentation without competition from wild microorganisms that could alter the flavor profile. This yeasting strategy ensures excellent consistency of flavor from batch to batch, and produces a "clean" cider dominated by the fruit, typical of modern style ciders. The yeast nutrition strategy is also quite different in modern fermentations. Since the juice used to make the cider is generally from high-density orchards that are fertilized, it is rich in nitrogen, which is used by the yeast as a nutrient. This produces high populations of yeasts, which in turn need to be fed during the course of the fermentation. Hence the cider maker needs to have a good nutrition regime to ensure the yeast will make a good, strong, and healthy fermentation.

Traditional Fermentation

In its purest traditional form, the fermentation itself is simply a matter of filling clean barrels (or wooden vats of sometimes huge volumes) with the freshly pressed and untreated must, and then letting nature do its thing until the cider is ready. A few different approaches are possible. The barrels may be filled to the top, right at the start, and then during the turbulent phase of the fermentation, the foam is allowed to escape through the bung (and make a mess on the floor). Or the barrels may be only partially filled so the foam stays contained in the barrel, and a racking to a smaller barrel is done after the

Racking

Racking is the action of transferring a cider from one fermentation vessel to another while leaving the lees (sediment) behind in the first vessel. This process may be accomplished with gravity using a siphon for very small volumes; for larger volumes a pump is generally used. When done while there is some active fermentation, a racking will decrease the yeast population and the amount of nutrients, thus slowing the pace of fermentation. Further reduction of the yeast population can be obtained via filtration or centrifugation during the racking. If the racking is done at the end of fermentation, then the aim essentially is to separate the cider from its lees. Rackings may be used in both traditional and modern fermentations.

turbulent phase is completed. These barrels are then filled to the top and an airlock is fitted. A third possibility is to have a spontaneous keeve, which is a method that utilizes a naturally occurring pectin gel (see the next section for more on this). In all these approaches, once the fermentation is going, one or two rackings may optionally be performed to slow things down and help in the clarification. The only other interventions done by the cider maker are to keep the barrels well filled and make sure no oxygen comes in contact with the cider. The fermentation proceeds slowly during winter, and the cider is ready in the spring or beginning of summer. It may then be bottled or served directly from the barrel. I found one good account of this basic traditional cider making process in a book written by Thomas Andrew Knight, in 1811, titled *Pomona Herefordiensis*. It goes as follows:

> *The art of making fine cider and perry is exceedingly simple, when proper varieties of fruit, in a perfect state of maturity, can be obtained. Such fruit should remain in heaps of not more than twelve inches deep, in the open air till it has become perfectly*

Figure 1.4. The contrast between these two fermentation rooms is quite striking. *Top*, at Domaine Kervéguen in Brittany, France, where Éric Baron ferments his ciders in old wood barrels. *Bottom*, at Blake's Orchard and Cider Mill in Michigan, we have variable volume stainless steel tanks.

mellow, and it should then be ground in a mill of stone till the pulp and rind are perfectly reduced, and have acquired a deep and uniform brown colour. The juice is then expressed, and placed in casks to ferment, where it is as soon as possible separated from its grosser lees; and excess of fermentation is prevented by placing the casks in a cool and airy situation, and by drawing off the liquor from one cask to another.

There are nowadays only a few cider makers who manage their fermentations in a truly traditional fashion as described here, and I have met or have heard of some in all the traditional cider making regions. They are usually very small producers who still make their cider the way their grandfather and great-grandfather used to make it. The vast majority of cider producers—and that includes those who are considered traditional cider makers—incorporate some of the modern technologies in their process.

Keeving

The practice of keeving is traditional in France and England. It is also done by a few producers of the traditional-style cider in other regions. The principle is that the pectins present in the apple are partly degraded by an enzyme and combined with calcium to form a calcium pectate gel. This gel rises by buoyancy to the top of the vessel and forms a thick layer with a gelatinous consistency. This gelatin has a light brown color and is called the *chapeau brun* (brown cap). The process yields a perfectly clarified must under the chapeau brun, and this must is racked to another vessel where the fermentation will proceed. The process additionally reduces the amount of natural nutrients of the must, and thus the yeast population remains small. As a result, the fermentation speed is very slow. A selected yeast is normally not added when doing a keeve; these fermentations rely on natural wild yeast. Another advantage with this process is that a keeved fermentation is very easy to stop by a simple racking at the moment chosen by the cider maker to yield a cider that retains some of the natural apple sugars, unfermented. Thus it is possible to produce a stable sweet or medium-sweet cider.

A century ago, the role of enzymes wasn't well known, and keeving relied on the small quantities of enzymes that are naturally present in the apple. The success of the process was irregular and unpredictable. Cider makers had nevertheless understood that they could improve the chances of obtaining a successful keeve by a maceration of the pulp and an addition of some form of calcium, considered as a keeving aid (crushed chalk was often used). It wasn't until the end of the 1980s that the industry was able to provide pectin methyl-esterase enzyme (PME) to cider makers, which, when combined with an addition of calcium chlodire, permits regular success of the keeve process. This is a good example of a traditional process that has been modernized, in this case with the help of recent developments in enzyme technology.

Chaptalization

The word *chaptalization* is derived from the name of Jean-Antoine Chaptal (1756–1832), a French chemist, doctor, and politician under Napoleon Bonaparte, who described the process in a book published in 1801, *L'art de faire, gouverner et perfectionner les vins.*

Chaptalization is the addition of sugar to the must in order to increase the alcoholic strength of the beverage after the fermentation is completed. The original intent is to chaptalize a must only in years when the conditions weren't so good for ripening and the fruits have a lower than normal sugar content. Then, the addition of sugar increases the alcoholic potential to a level comparable to an average year, thus permitting better conservation. In wine making, and in particular for wines that are made under a label of origin certification, chaptalization is strictly controlled and can only be done within the limits described here. This is not the case, however, in cider making: In many production regions, unless there is a label of certification, chaptalization is usually left to the discretion of the cider maker. As a consequence we sometimes see producers who systematically overuse chaptalization to make ciders that have an alcohol level higher than could normally be obtained from a natural apple juice. Chaptalization is more common in modern cider making practices; however low levels of chaptalization may also be seen in more traditional ciders.

Modern Fermentation

Nowadays, in all cider making regions, modern fermentation is done in stainless steel, fiberglass resin, or plastic tanks (all materials that were developed during the twentieth century). Wood barrels are not used in modern fermentations, but we may still see some used for the maturation of cider. The modern fermentation practices normally ensure a good repeatability of the flavor profile from batch to batch, which is a desirable trait for modern-style ciders. The following operations and steps are usually seen:

- Pre-fermentation clarification, a process also called *débourbage*, by adding a pectic enzyme to the juice as it exits the press, and then letting it rest between 12 to 48 hours. Sometimes a fining agent is added to increase the sedimentation. The must might not be perfectly clarified, but there would be a good deposit in the bottom of the tank. The must is then transferred to another tank where the fermentation will take place.
- Elimination of the wild microorganisms and inoculation of a selected yeast strain as described previously.
- Control of yeast nutrients.
- Temperature regulation to ensure the yeast will perform at its optimum conditions.

When the right conditions are met, the fermentation then proceeds to dryness (until all the sugar is fermented) in a matter of a few weeks, compared to months in a more traditional way. Rackings are normally not done during the fermentation, but may be done once it is completed (or almost completed), before storing the cider for maturation.

Maturation

Once the alcoholic fermentation is completed, many producers (both of modern or traditional inclination) let the cider age for a period of time before further processing. During such maturation many biochemical transformations may occur even if there is no more fermentation per se. In particular, we note some smoothening of the cider, due in part to the action of some lactic acid bacteria. This maturation may be *sur lies* ("on the lees"), if the producer prefers to let the cider age in the presence of the lees that were produced by the alcoholic fermentation. This gives a special flavor from the decaying dead yeast cells. In other cases, the cider is transferred to a new vessel and thus separated from the lees before maturation.

We often see cideries that use wood casks for the maturation of their ciders. This may modify the flavor of the cider as it picks up some tannins from the wood. Also, if the cask was previously used to store some other beverage, the flavor of the cider may reflect it. For example, in the United States, ex-bourbon barrels are often used for this.

Final Processing

The final processing operations described here are done after the fermentation and maturation are completed, and are the last steps in the fabrication of the cider. The objectives here are to ensure that the cider has the flavor wanted, is well clarified, and has long-term stability once packaged and shipped.

Clarification

In traditional cider making, post-fermentation clarification is not normally done. The cider maker simply waits long enough for the cider to clear naturally before further processing. Traditional ciders may be slightly hazy as a result, which is considered acceptable for such ciders. Modern-style ciders on the other hand are generally expected to be perfectly clarified. For this, the cider maker first proceeds with a fining if the cider is very hazy, and follows with filtration. The clarified cider may be stored while awaiting further processing or blending.

Blending

In modern operations, blending of different batches once the fermentation is completed is important to ensure the cider that is sold under a certain brand always has a consistent flavor profile batch after batch. Traditional cider makers also often blend their ciders to give a good balance among the acids, tannins, and sugars. For some producers, however, there may be a lot more involved in blending. For example, Andy Brennan is a cider maker in New York State who makes his ciders from wild apples. He collects samples from each of his barrels, and tastes and evaluates them during the course of a whole month before making his final blending decisions. He wrote: "Blending cider is an art, not a recipe. Yes, you must be formally skilled in the craft, and yes, you need to master your palate, but even so, the final decisions during the act of blending are entirely dependent on intuition."*

Residual Sugar and Back-Sweetening

Residual sugar is the sugar that remains in the cider at the moment of drinking. It is normally expressed as grams of sugar per liter of cider (g/L). A cider that has zero residual sugar would be qualified as bone dry. We don't often see such ciders as they may be quite harsh. Some residual sugar helps to balance the acidity and the tannins of the cider, making it more appealing to the consumer's palate. Depending on the balance obtained in the finished cider, the level of residual sugar is most often indicated by a qualifier such as dry, off-dry, medium, semi-sweet, or sweet (whose definitions are not standardized and may change from one country to another).

In traditional cider making, either the cider is left dry or the desired level of residual sweetness is achieved by some process such as keeving or successive rackings, which permit a control of the fermentation such that the nutrients that are essential for yeast activity become exhausted and the fermentation cannot proceed further and stops, leaving some unfermented sugar. In modern cider making, the cider is usually fermented to dryness, and the desired quantity of sugar is added at the time of bottling, a process called back-sweetening. The quantity added may thus vary between 5 grams of sugar per liter for an off-dry cider, and to over 40 g/L for a sweet cider. The sweetening agent used is highly variable: It may be normal table sugar (sucrose), or it may be other sugars such as glucose or fructose, or fresh or

* Andy Brennan, *Uncultivated: Wild Apples, Real Cider, and the Complicated Art of Making a Living* (White River Junction, VT: Chelsea Green Publishing, 2019).

concentrated apple juice, ice cider, honey, maple syrup, or some non-fermentable sweetening agents such as saccharin or sucralose. Naturally, after the addition of fermentable sugar to the cider, the maker needs to take measures to stabilize the cider and prevent this sugar from fermenting, unless the cider is to be drunk quickly. This is also the reason nonfermentable sweetening agents are used by some, as there is then no risk for such a restart of the fermentation.

In modern operations, it is also possible to stop the fermentation before it reaches dryness to preserve some of the unfermented sugars, resulting in a flavor that's closer to what may be attained with the traditional approach. This is done by cold shock: The cider is refrigerated to near the freezing point, and a good part of the yeast then deposits itself on the bottom of the tank. The cider is then racked, filtered, and transferred to another vessel. This process improves the flavor and reduces the alcohol content of the resulting cider by approximately 0.6 percent ABV per 10 g/L of unfermented residual sugar.

Stabilization

Stabilization is an operation by which the producer renders the cider an inert beverage, meaning that it will not biochemically evolve once it is bottled because the microorganisms are either killed or removed. Hence this process is clearly in the modern philosophy of cider making. In particular, stabilization prevents refermentation of the sugar in ciders that have been sweetened. It also prevents any change in flavor due to the action of other yeasts or bacteria. On the other hand, unstabilized ciders are often considered by their producers as a live beverage that still contains living microorganisms, and thus these ciders are more capable of evolving over time. Traditional unstabilized ciders can keep well in a cool cellar, but generally they will not travel well and risk turning bad if subjected to high temperatures.

Three different approaches are used for stabilization of ciders: thermal, mechanical, and chemical. The thermal method is pasteurization, where the cider is heated to a sufficiently high temperature to kill the yeast and bacteria present. The mechanical method involves a very fine filtration, which removes yeast and bacteria cells. This is called *sterile filtration*. The chemical method consists of adding some preservatives that inhibit microorganism proliferation. This usually entails adding sulfite along with potassium sorbate. Very often, chemical preservatives are added after sterile filtration.

Bottling and Packaging

Cider is packaged in glass bottles or aluminum cans for home consumption sales, while in bars, restaurants, or pubs, it may be sold in larger containers such as kegs, if sparkling, or as a bag-in-box of up to 20 liters for still cider. More often, cans are used for modern-style ciders, as well as for lower-cost, mass-produced ciders, while traditional producers prefer to use bottles, which also normally carry a higher price tag—but this is in no way universal, and we can find many exceptions.

To bottle cider, there is a very wide variety of equipment for filling, closing, and labeling the bottles. Equipment can range from simple, rudimentary manual gravity fillers with manual fitting of the closures and label application up to entirely automatic bottling lines that can fill, close, and label thousands of bottles in an hour. For their part, canning lines are reserved to larger-scale operations and are not as well adapted to small production.

For smaller producers, manual bottling and packaging of the cider is very labor-intensive, and the investment for an automatic bottling or canning line might be prohibitive. In many regions, there are contractors that perform these operations, as well as the back-sweetening and stabilization processes, according to the specifications given by the cider maker.

Sparkling Ciders

Nowadays a large proportion of the cider production is made effervescent (pétillant, which is a mild effervescent, or sparkling), and some additional processing is required to produce them. Such ciders contain some carbon dioxide (CO_2) gas in solution, and they are kept in a pressurized container (bottle, can, or keg). There are numerous techniques to obtain the effervescence. These are sometimes called method, a word often seen in French writing (*méthode*), as it is used a lot for the marketing of champagne: The *méthode champenoise* is universally recognized as a standard for very high-quality (and expensive) sparkling wines from the region of Champagne in France. In cider making, the following described methods are most often used. Except for the last one (injection method), all produce the required CO_2 gas by fermentation, a process called *prise de mousse* in French. When this fermentation occurs inside hermetically closed bottles, the cider is often labeled as bottle conditioned, a term that, unfortunately, doesn't have the same exact definition in all regions. In general, the methods that produce the sparkle by prise de mousse, although cider makers often use modern technologies at some point during the process, are considered more traditional than the injection method, which is definitely a modern process.

Basic Method

The most basic bottle conditioning method simply consists in letting the cider ferment to dryness, and when it's ready to bottle, some sugar is added so that the fermentation of this sugar inside the hermetically closed bottle will produce the desired sparkle within a few weeks. The quantity of sugar addition varies between 6 and 15 g/L for a pétillant to fully sparkling cider. Optionally, some yeast and nutrients may be added with the sugar. Normally this method produces completely dry ciders. However, if the in-bottle fermentation is interrupted by pasteurization of the bottles, then it is possible to obtain a cider with some residual sweetness. This basic method is also called *bottle conditioning*, although the term can be used for the ancestral method, which is described later in this section. The basic method is not used in modern cider making, as it leaves a sediment in the bottle that may be objectionable when the cider is offered for sale. It is however popular with small craft cider makers and also with hobbyists, as it is easy to do and doesn't require any special equipment.

Traditional Method

This method is the same as the méthode champenoise used for the making of champagne in France. Since the word *champenoise* is reserved for champagne, all other sparkling wines and ciders made with this method then use the naming traditional method or *méthode traditionnelle*. In

Spain, the term *cava* is used with the same signification. Legend says the method was invented by Dom Pérignon (his true name was Pierre Pérignon, 1638–1715) for conditioning the wines of the Champagne region. In reality, while Pérignon did make some contributions, the true origin of the method is most likely in England, in the years that followed the invention of strong glass bottles in the 1630s.* Some authors rather think Pérignon took the inspiration from the wines of Limoux, which at that time were processed with the ancestral method. Additionally, an important step of the method, the *dégorgement* (disgorgement), was invented in France about a century after Pérignon's death. The development of this method thus spanned over almost two centuries, and quite a number of cider and wine makers contributed to what it is today.

The traditional method starts with a base cider that is fermented to dryness. At bottling, a *liqueur de tirage* is added. It contains sugar, yeast, and, optionally, yeast nutrients and a fining agent (also called a *riddling aid*) that helps in obtaining compact lees, and it's all mixed with the fermented cider. The sugar addition might be as much as 20 g/L to produce up to 6 bars (87 psi) of internal pressure. Bottling is done in full weight champenoise bottles, closed with a crown cap, to which one may add a *bidule* in the neck (this is a small plastic cup that collects the lees). Once the in-bottle fermentation is completed, the cider may be left on its lees for a varying period of time; the longer the time, the more it will get a flavor from the contact with the lees, a flavor often described as biscuity. Following this maturation, the producer proceeds to the riddling (*remuage* in French), which consists in bringing the lees to the neck of the bottle. In more traditional cideries, the bottles are placed on a *pupitre* (a wooden rack) that permits changing the angle gradually until the bottles are in a vertical position, upside down. The bottles are also regularly shaken lightly so the lees move toward the neck. In large

---

* The process to make sturdier glass bottles was invented in England during the early 1630s. This development is often credited to Sir Kenelm Digby, a founding member of the Royal Society, but quite a few other people were involved. Before that time, glass bottles existed but they were not strong enough to sustain an internal pressure. From the 1630s up to the 1660s, there are many written accounts in England of cider and wine made sparkling inside such bottles, sometimes with the addition of a "walnut of sugar." Pérignon's involvment with Champagne wines only began around 1670.

modern operations, the riddling may be done mechanically: The bottles are stacked in a metallic cage and shaken automatically.

The final operation is the disgorgement, which is done in one of two ways. The first is *à la glace*, where the necks of the bottles are frozen in a special bath, then the bottle is decapsulated and the lees are ejected with a frozen slush; or the second is *à la volée*, without freezing, where the crown caps are removed with a special tool during a rotation movement from upside down to right side up. When a bidule is used, the lees then accumulate in it, thus making their elimination easier at disgorgement. A *liqueur de dosage* is then added, which might contain sugar if a non-dry cider is made. Additionally, this dosage may contain a chemical stabilizer. The bottle is finally topped with dry cider and closed. Most of the time a mushroom-type cork is used with a wire cage, but some producers may use a crown cap or a plastic mushroom closure. Nowadays, it is also possible to add the yeast in an encapsulated form at bottling time, a process that insures all the yeast is removed when doing the disgorgement. When doing so, the producer has to do a sterile filtration at bottling to remove all remaining yeast in the cider. In the United Kingdom, ciders and perries conditioned with this method are said to be bottle fermented.

Figure 1.5. Ernest Gasser of Union Libre Cidre & Vin (Quebec, Canada), in front of his pupitre for the riddling of the traditional method cider.

Figure 1.6. Mechanical riddling machine at Cidrerie Michel Jodoin, Quebec, Canada.

Ancestral Method

The ancestral method is the simplest method to obtain a sparkling cider or wine, as no addition is required at bottling time. This method was probably the first to have been done in the history of fermented beverages. Its advantage over the basic method is that no sugar is added, and in historic times sugar was expensive and not always easy to obtain. It will also yield a cider with about 0.5 percent less ABV than with the basic method, this difference being caused by the absence of added sugar that would produce additional alcohol during fermentation.

The ancestral method essentially consists of bottling the cider before the fermentation is completed so that the fermentation will terminate inside the hermetically closed bottles and thus produce the required CO_2 gas to make the sparkle. A drop of specific gravity of 2 to 8 points inside the bottles will produce a slightly pétillant to fully sparkling cider, but generally cider makers will aim for a drop of 4 to 5 points, sufficient to obtain a nice foam at pour. Somewhat different procedures may be followed depending on if a dry cider is made, or if the cider is to retain some of its natural sweetness after the process is completed. To obtain a dry cider, the producer bottles the cider while it is still in fermentation, when the quantity of remaining fermentable sugar is just enough to produce the desired sparkle. For example, if the cider maker expects the fermentation to be completed at a specific gravity of 0.998, then bottling when the cider has reached 1.003 would ensure a drop of 5 points in the bottle for a good sparkle. For semidry to sweet styles, the cider is bottled at a higher specific gravity that varies between 1.010 and 1.025, and it will ferment about 4 to 5 points lower in the bottle before the fermentation stops. The maker needs to take steps to prevent complete fermentation inside the bottles, which would result in overcarbonation and possible bottle explosions. One way is to pasteurize the cider in the bottles when the desired level of carbonation is obtained. The other way is to use the ancestral method in combination with the keeving process. Since the keeved cider has exhausted the supply of nutrients as the fermentation nears completion, it can then be bottled and the fermentation finishes inside the bottles and stops, leaving some unfermented residual sugar.

The ancestral method is thus mostly used by producers who keeve their ciders, and it is the primary method used in France among craft producers. These ciders are often called *cidre bouché*. In the U.K., the ciders produced with the ancestral method are said to be bottle conditioned, which may cause some confusion as the term is also used for the basic method. A new name that has started to become popular for this method is *pét-nat*, which is short for *pétillant naturel* (roughly translates to "naturally sparkling").

There are two major inconveniences with the ancestral method when it's used for ciders that retain some natural sweetness. The first is the control of the effervescence level. It is quite difficult to predict at precisely what specific gravity the fermentation will stop, and this uncertainty may cause the cider to be more or less sparkling than anticipated. Traditionally, success relied mainly on the competence and experience of the cider maker. To help in making a more accurate prediction, it is possible to count the number of yeast cells per mL of cider and adjust accordingly. In-bottle pasteurization is another way to make sure there is no excessive sparkle.

The second weakness of this method is the lack of stability of the ciders. Because they contain some sugar and the lees are still in the bottles, these ciders are prone to a restart of the fermentation or of some activity by spoiling microorganisms if they are kept at too warm a temperature. Transportation and exportation of such ciders is a highly risky enterprise. I have myself drunk French ciders in countries such as Australia or the United States that had badly turned. But the same ciders kept in a cool cellar and drunk at the farm were perfect. They are ciders that do not travel well. . . . To solve this, some producers now process these ciders by riddling and disgorging. Hence this becomes a hybrid method, where the ancestral method is used for the beginning, and part of the traditional method process is used for the finishing. Another solution is to use the transfer method, which is described later in this section.

Charmat Method

The Charmat method, also called closed-tank method (or *cuve close*, in French), was patented in France by Eugène Charmat in 1907. It was, however, mostly developed in Italy, where it is used to produce prosecco wines. Its principle is similar to bottle conditioning except that this conditioning is done in large tanks instead of in bottles, and thus the method could be viewed as tank conditioning. These brite tanks, as they are usually called, are made of stainless steel and are built stronger than normal fermentation tanks to sustain internal pressure. Either a cider that still has some unfermented sugar, or a dry cider to which fermentable sugar is added, may be used as a base. Optionally, yeast, nutrients, and a fining agent may also be added. The tank is then hermetically closed. The fermentation process then produces CO_2 gas, which remains in solution as the pressure builds up. Once the prise de mousse is completed, the cider is filtered to separate the lees and remove the remaining live yeast cells, and it is bottled using a counter pressure filler, which permits filling the bottles with minimal loss of the CO_2 in solution. The Charmat method is mainly used by larger commercial cideries, as it requires quite a large investment for the brite tanks and the equipment for filtration and bottling. The cider obtained is very stable with a good quality of foam. It may be noted that for some PDO labels the specification requires the prise de mousse to be done in the bottles. Consequently, ciders made with the Charmat method may not bear such PDO labels.

Transfer Method

Two variants of the transfer method are better known and used for cider. For the first variant, the cider is fermented to dryness and prepared as for the traditional method so that the prise de mousse proceeds inside the bottle. The second variant is known as the *méthode dioise* and is used for the production of sparkling white wines, such as the famed Clairette de Die of the Rhône Valley. A cider produced with this method still has some unfermented sugar when bottled, in a similar fashion as for the ancestral method. With either variant, once the prise de mousse is completed, the transfer process is performed: The cider is pumped out of the bottles and filtered to remove the lees and yeast cells. Simultaneously, the bottles are rinsed and sanitized. Then the bottles are refilled with the cider, corked, and wire cages are fitted over the cork. Optionally, a liqueur de dosage may be added to sweeten the cider. All this transfer process is done automatically in a special machine that is pressurized to prevent the CO_2 gas from escaping. The

Figure 1.7. Charmat tanks at François Séhédic, Brittany, France.

resulting cider is comparable in terms of quality and stability to what may be obtained by the traditional method, with reduced labor costs (which are quite high for the riddling and disgorging operations).

The transfer method is not yet widely used in cider making, but in recent years it has been successfully trialed in Brittany, and a few installations have been completed. The equipment is quite expensive, however, and so it is reserved to larger cideries or operations that are cooperatively owned by a group of producers. One important advantage is that the ciders are allowed to bear a PDO label because the prise de mousse is effectively done inside the bottles.

Injection Method (Carbonated Cider)

The injection method is the most widely used method in modern cideries to produce a sparkling consumer-grade cider. In this method, the cider is carbonated by using food-grade pressurized CO_2 gas. Two methods are most often used to inject the gas into the cider:

- On-line carbonation, where the CO_2 is directly injected in the cider while on its way to the bottle filler. This is the method used in the soft drink industry. It usually produces coarser bubbles, but the technology has improved and some ciders carbonated this way have finer bubbles. This method is very fast, and it only requires adding the carbonator to the bottling line.
- Carbonation in a brite tank is a longer process. The cider is left under CO_2 pressure until it has absorbed the desired quantity of the gas. In most installations the CO_2 is injected through a "stone" that sits in the bottom of the tank; this way the gas is provided in zillions of very small bubbles that are easily absorbed by the cider. The cider may have to stay in the brite tank anywhere from a few hours to a few days depending on the pressure level and how much sparkle is desired. As a general rule, a longer stay in the brite tank results in finer and better-quality bubbles.

A variant of this method is used in Spain, where the injected CO_2 gas comes from the main fermentation of the cider (see chapter 4).

Industrial Cider Making

Although this book is not about industrial cider making, it may be useful to highlight here some of the practices used in the industry, if only to compare them with the practices used in craft cider making.

Preparation of the fermentable mash. The mash is from a mixture of water; sugar/glucose syrup; fresh apple juice (optional—it may come from cider apples and/or culinary and dessert apples, grown in intensively managed orchards); reconstituted apple juice from concentrate (may be locally produced concentrate or imported); and the possible addition of other ingredients.

Chaptalization. In some legislations where chaptalization and dilution are both permitted, it is possible to heavily chaptalize by the addition of sugar or glucose syrup and fermenting the cider to a high alcoholic strength—around 14 percent ABV is fairly typical. And, after completion of the fermentation, this strong cider is diluted with water in order to lower the alcoholic strength to the desired level for the finished product, thus permitting a reduction of the cost of the raw material (less fruit is used to obtain the same quantity of cider) and also a reduction in the size of the fermentation tanks.

Rapid fermentation to dryness. Many cideries use a proprietary yeast strain, with controlled nutrition and temperature.

Final processing. The process consists of clarification and/or filtration, back-sweetening to desired levels, stabilization by pasteurization or sterile filtration and chemical additives, carbonation, and bottling. Some concentrated fruit syrup or other type of flavoring or extract may be added at this stage if the cider is to be a fruit or otherwise-flavored cider.

Naturally, not all industrial cider producers are alike. Some make a quality product that includes a much higher proportion of apples, and less chaptalization and dilution. However, others such as the "white ciders" in the U.K., or ciders that are destined to become flavored ciders, may have only a very small proportion (if any) apples in their constituents. The legislation in the country where the cider is produced often determines the relative proportions of the raw ingredients, as well as some of the processes.

Plate LXXVII

1. Rouge Bruyère.

2. Bramtot.

3. Médaille d'or.

4. Bédan-des-parts.

5. Michelin.

6. Argile grise.

7. de Boutteville.

8. Fréquin Audièvre.

G. Severeyns, Chromolith. Brussels

Edith E. Bull del.
for The Woolhope Club.

PART I

TRADITIONAL CIDERS

In the following four chapters we take a look at ciders from selected regions of Europe that have a long tradition of growing cider apple trees and making cider: the West Country of England and other regions of Great Britain; Brittany and Normandy in France; Asturias and the Basque Country in Spain; and some regions of Germany and other German-speaking countries. I've selected those specific areas based on a number of factors that I think define a traditional cider making region:

- Each of these regions has special *pommages*, or collections of cider apple varieties, that are local to the region. Naturally, their cider is mostly made with these cider apples and not with general market varieties of apples intended for dessert or culinary uses.

- The cider apples are grown in orchards that are managed specifically for cider production. On the same farm, we normally don't see cider apple orchards and dessert or cooking apple orchards.
- Cider making has been going on without interruption for a few centuries at least, and it has always represented an important activity in the region.
- Cider making techniques have gradually evolved from the ancestral methods.
- In each of these broad regions, there is a homogeneity in the flavors, tastes, and aromas that permits us to talk about a family of related cider styles.

One thing that I find extraordinary with these ciders is how easy it is to recognize them once you have tasted a few samples. On a blind tasting with a cider from Herefordshire in England, Normandy in France, Asturias in Spain, and Hesse in Germany, just by a smell over the glass one can fairly easily identify which is which. In fact, I find that a good cider of those countries has some teleportation properties.... Closing my eyes while sipping, the cider makes me travel instantly to that region—it is almost as efficient as a transporter in Star Trek! So the question arises: What is it that gives such a special character to these ciders and makes them so easily recognizable? To answer this, we need to look at the pommages of each of these regions, the acidity and tannin balance for the typical blends (see also appendix A), and the cider making processes. There is something else that gives a unique character to a cider, and this is what we may call the terroir, which includes the soil, the climate, the local flora of microorganisms, and probably other factors that are more difficult to identify. But the truth is if, for example, you are in North America, grow French cider apple varieties, and use the same process as used in France, you can get pretty close to the style, but there is very little chance that the cider you make will fool an experienced taster.

It is interesting to look at how cider making started and evolved in those regions under consideration. This history may help us understand the cider traditions we still see today. The origin of human's consumption of fermented alcoholic beverages is not really known for sure. Because fermentation happens spontaneously in any mash that contains sugar or starch, this fermentation certainly happened during prehistoric times, and studies show that such beverages could have been first produced intentionally about 7,000 years ago. These might have been grain-based, such as the rice wines of Asia and the *cervoise* of the Celts (the ancestor of beer); fruit-based, such as wine, cider, and perry; milk-based, such as the *kumis* in central Asia; honey-based, as is mead; or other sources of fermentable mash. In the antique northern Europe, it is thought that most people would have mainly consumed grain-based beverages, such as cervoise or beer, but there are also clear indications that these people consumed the fruit of the European native crab, *Malus sylvestris*, since prehistoric times, as apple seeds have been found in early human settlements. No doubt they learned to make a primitive "cider" that most probably would have been a maceration of water with crushed apples that fermented naturally. They could also have used dried apple slices for this. We have no clue, however, as to how important this cider would have been for these people. And we have no real indication of what sort of tools they could have used to produce this drink, but we may assume they simply used stones or wood to crush the apples, which were mixed with water and left to ferment. Filtering this fermented mash with moss or straw would then yield some rough cider. We don't know if they had presses, but they could well have developed some primitive ways for pressing this mash and thus increase the yield, for example by treading with their feet, or simply by pressing with a flat stone and increasing its pressing force with the help of a lever—all systems that existed in antiquity. However, if such systems were in use to make cider in northern Europe at that time, no archaeological remains have yet been found.*

It is the Romans, as they conquered most of Europe in the beginning of the Common Era, who most likely introduced more efficient fruit presses and technologies to make wine and, as a side effect, cider. The principle of the screw was known by the Romans, and it has been used in presses since the second century CE. It is believed the Romans

---

* For example, I was reading recently that archaeologists discovered remnants of wine presses in Iraq that were close to 3,000 years old. Nothing of the sort is known for pressing apples in Europe.

also introduced cultivated varieties of apple trees in the regions they occupied, and grape vines where the conditions were favorable. These apple varieties were no doubt of a quality vastly superior to the native European crab, as they were of the *M. domestica* species, hybrids descending from *M. sieversii* of Kazakh origin.

There is evidence that the Romans knew about wines made from apples and pears quite early. Pliny, in his *Naturalis Historiæ* (77 CE), briefly mentions their existence, suggesting these were the drinks of some other peoples—without specifying who those peoples were, however. We may only speculate they were of the northern countries, as these drinks certainly weren't consumed by the Romans (who were drinkers of grape wine) nor by the peoples around the Mediterranean Sea. Such apple or pear wines were called *pomaceo* and *piratium*, or in other references *pomorum* and *piraticum*. From that period we also find references to a beverage called *cicera* or *sikera*, a word of Greek origin that in turn might be from the Hebrew *sekar*, and from which the words *cider*, *cidre*, and *sidra* are derived. One has to be very careful, however, with the interpretation of texts from ancient times, as the translations often are not very precise. For example, *pomorum* could have had a much broader signification than just *cider*, as it may have meant a beverage made from any sort of fruit. Similarly, *sekar* and *sikera* could have meant any intoxicating beverage other than wine made from grapes. One of the oldest known texts, which leaves no possibility of wrong interpretation, is by the Roman author Palladius, in his *De re rustica*, written by the end of the fourth or beginning of the fifth century. He wrote:

> Vinum de piris fit *[To make wine from pears]*, si contusa *[crush them]*, et sacco rarissimo condita ponderibus comprimantur *[put in a fine mesh bag and compress]*, aut prælo *[or use a press]*. Hieme durat *[it will last during winter]*, sed prima acescit æstate *[but in spring becomes acetic]*. . . .
>
> Vinum et acetum fit ex malis *[Wine and vinegar made from apples]*, sicut ex piris ante præcepi *[is the same process as indicated for pears]*.

There is no question here that Palladius was effectively describing the process of pressing pears and apples to obtain a beverage that will last during winter. Fermentation is not explicit, but in such circumstances it is inevitable. And then by spring or the beginning of summer it becomes sour and acetic, which is perfectly normal in the absence of good measures to keep the cider from contact with air.

Between the fifth and the eighth centuries, the Frankish Merovingian empire covered most of northern Europe, with king Clovis and his wife, Clotilde, being among the better-known figures of the period. It is during that era that the Roman Catholic religion became dominant, and many important abbeys, monasteries, and other religious constructions were built. It is in those monasteries that monks developed the concept of organized orchards. The monks played a crucial role in the development and conservation of fruit varieties as well as of beer, wine, and cider making technologies through the Middle Ages.

There exist some documents dating to the years 800 to 1000 CE that attest cider and/or perry was being made at that time and possibly earlier in the Kingdom of Asturias in northern Spain and in some unspecified locations of the Carolingian Empire (which then covered large parts of central Europe, but some people think it might mostly relate to Germany or France). The oldest known document clearly mentioning cider in Normandy is from 1082, and others from Asturias are quite older. Thus it is assumed Asturias, Normandy, and possibly some region of Germany would be among the first centers of cider production in Europe. It is quite possible that cider was also made elsewhere, but in those days, cider and perry were probably not widely consumed by the people. Cider and perry consumption seems to have been confined to monasteries and was mostly used for medicinal purposes. Another possible reason that could explain the lack of documentation on cider during those early days is that cider would have been the drink of the poor and ordinary people, and so was not considered worthy of writing about.

Apparently there would have been some contact between the Asturians in northern Spain and the Carolingian Empire during that early period, but there is no clear evidence that one would have influenced the other as far as cider and perry making are concerned. Many authors have written that, from around the twelfth century, the Basque or Breton sailors introduced cider making technologies and cider

Figure 1. Illustration of a wheel crusher and lever press from the *Encyclopédie* by Diderot and d'Alembert, published 1751–1782. Photo courtesy of the ARTFL Encyclopédie Project, University of Chicago.

apple varieties from northern Spain to Brittany and Normandy, and eventually these reached the British Isles. However most often these texts do not hold against more rigorous historical research. Still, there is an obvious relationship in cider apple varieties, particularly bitter-sweet varieties, which are found in Spain, France, and England, but not in Germany. There are a few French cider apple varieties whose origins are documented to be related to northern Spain, and there are also many in England that were originally brought in from France, but this is pretty much all that can be said with certitude.

The pressing technologies would have seen important developments around the twelfth to thirteenth centuries, which permitted an increase in cider production. It is estimated the circular troughs where the apples were crushed by a large horse-drawn stone or wooden wheel appeared at that period. These had the capacity to process much larger quantities of apples compared to hand crushing. Such wheel crushers remained the principal way to prepare the pomace for pressing up until the Industrial Revolution (mid-nineteenth century), and they are still common but most often nowadays as decorations. The presses also got bigger during that period to accommodate the increased output from the crushers, and large lever-type presses (looking like giant nutcrackers) were developed. It is also interesting to observe that this ancient press design is very similar in all regions, thus indicating either a common origin, or some transfer of knowledge between them. The horse-drawn wheel crushers, however, were not in common use in Asturias or the Basque Country, where they kept on crushing the apples by hand until mechanical systems were invented.

Obviously some sort of turning point around the twelfth to thirteenth centuries occurred: Before that time, cider would have had a relatively minor role as a beverage. Some democratization then occurred with the development of more efficient crushers and presses, and the introduction of better apple varieties. Cider could finally become a major beverage, with the potential to be consumed by a large percentage of the population. During the centuries that followed, cider effectively was in competition with beer, wine, and mead as the main drink for the people of a given region. Quite a few factors had an influence on the outcome of this competition, among which the most important is the climate. In more southern regions with warmer

Figure 2. Hand crushing of the apples was the main method during antiquity and the Middle Ages. This photo is of a demonstration at the Cider Museum in Astigarraga, Spain.

temperatures, wine was the preference of people. And in fact, in regions where both the grapevine and the apple tree thrived, wine was almost inevitably considered to be the primary drink while cider took a second or third position. This means only poorer people would drink it, or else it served as backup in years when the grape crop failed. Hence beer and cider for their part mostly gained the favor of people in more northern and colder regions where the grapevine would not produce reliably. Beer was often preferred in urban areas, and cider was considered the drink of rural people. It has also been argued that a given area planted with apple trees would yield more cider than the same area planted with barley would for beer. Plus, to make beer one additionally had to provide heat for boiling the wort, hence wood or some other fuel was needed, which may at some times have been scarce or expensive.

It should be noted that all this is not static. Global cooling occurred from approximately 1300 to 1850, and peaked during the 1600s and 1700s. This period has been called the Little Ice Age by climatologists. So, there are districts where the grapevine was doing well during the warmer medieval period but failed during this Little Ice Age, and thus grapevines were replaced by hardier apple trees. As a consequence, people of these regions, which are nowadays among the main cider production centers (for example, Hesse in Germany and Normandy in France), shifted their drinking habits from wine to cider.

Other historic events had an influence on who drank what. For example, periods of famine have had the effect of favoring cider, because all the grain was then required for food and very little was available for making beer. Wars also had some influence, sometimes by devastating orchards, other times by encouraging apple production: During the First World War, for example, apple alcohol was used in large quantities for the manufacture of gunpowder. And one factor that has always been in favor of beer is the speed at which people could start harvesting a crop: With grain, one sows in spring and harvests in late summer; whereas with apple trees, a wait of 15 years or more is required before a sizeable crop is available from a newly planted orchard.

One historic event that had a major influence on many aspects of the modern cider scene is the great phylloxera outbreak that destroyed most of the European vineyards during the second half of the nineteenth century. The phylloxera is an insect native to North America whose larvae attack the roots of grapevines and kill the plant. The European grapevine species, *Vitis vinifera*, is very susceptible to the insect, but most of the American grape species are resistant or tolerant to some degree. The insect was probably first introduced to England during the 1850s by botanists who collected hardier American grapevines to evaluate them in the climatic conditions of England, which were too harsh for the European grapevine. The epidemic was first detected in France by the mid-1860s, and by the end of the 1880s it had devastated approximately three-quarters of vineyards in all parts of Europe, causing shortages in wine supply and cost increases. The answer came by replanting the vineyards with European grape varieties grafted on rootstocks of American vines that were resistant to the insect. However, some of the destroyed vineyards were replanted with apple trees, causing a shift from wine to cider in some regions, and cider production compensated for the loss of wine production. Thus, this phylloxera epidemic was an important factor that contributed to cider's golden age in continental Europe that lasted approximately from the mid-1800s to the early 1900s.

CHAPTER TWO

The United Kingdom
Cider

We will start our journey with English cider and its relatives, the Welsh and Scottish ciders. The United Kingdom may claim to be the most important producer of cider. The total annual cider market in the U.K. is estimated at 800 to 900 million liters depending on which reference we look at, and most of it is produced in the south of England. This makes some 12 to 13 liters *per capita*. It should be understood, however, that an important part of this production is of some industrial cider that would not have the right to be called "cider" in many countries of the world due to differences in regulations and legislation (as mentioned in the introduction), and this makes the comparison of cider production among countries quite difficult.

Historically, the British have been beer and cider drinkers more than wine drinkers, although many enjoy drinking wine and the British have for a long time imported large quantities from continental Europe. The U.K. conditions never were as favorable as on the continent for successful large-scale culture of the grapevine, and thus the production of wine has been rather marginal. Some wine was produced in ancient times, but then came the Little Ice Age, and by the fifteenth or sixteenth century, it was too cold for the grapevine to be grown anymore, thus causing a shift to beer and cider.

It is generally assumed cider making began in England around the eleventh century, after the conquest by the Normans, who would have introduced some cultivated apple varieties. However, written references to cider prior to the thirteenth century are practically nonexistent, and still quite scarce in the centuries that followed. Obviously during that period there were orchards and cider was made, but this remained mostly undocumented. It is only by the seventeenth century that we can see an important development of cider, and that we find good documentation on the orcharding and cider making practices. The Royal Society, which was founded in 1660, then brought together some of the greatest minds of the time. Interestingly, among the founding members of the Society, we find a number of scientists who were interested in apples and cider and wrote on the subject. Two well-known books of that period are John Evelyn's *Pomona* (included as an appendix to his *Sylva*, 1664) and the *Vinetum Britannicum: or a Treatise of Cider*, by John Worlidge, first published in 1676, where we find some of the most-often reproduced of all ancient cider-related illustrations. The depth of these books clearly indicates the importance cider had in those days.

Let us mention here Lord John Scudamore, a Herefordshire nobleman who was a crucial figure in the history of English cider during the seventeenth century. He is credited for being among the first to experiment with a method to produce sparkling ciders by a second fermentation in glass bottles, a precursor to the now universally known traditional method (and probably in fact closer to the ancestral method).* He is also credited for having raised the famous Redstreak

---

* An excellent historical account of the development of sparkling cider and wine is given by James Crowden in *Ciderland*, (Edinburgh: Birlinn, 2008). A number of English gentlemen and scientists got involved in this effort, which began during the 1630s, among which we may mention John Beale, Paul Neile, Christopher Merret, and Kenelm Digby, in addition to Scudamore.

cider apple about which Thomas Andrew Knight wrote in his *Pomona Herefordiensis* (1811): "The Redstreak appears to have been the first fine cider apple that was cultivated in Hereforsdhire, or probably in England." Lord Scudamore was ambassador to France from 1635 to 1639, and as the story goes he was impressed by the quality of the cider apples there, which were far superior to what was then known in England. Although there is no sure documentation about this, some people think he might have brought cider apple pips back from France to raise on his estate in Herefordshire, and that the Redstreak would thus be of French origin. Maybe . . .

We may consider the seventeenth century and beginning of the eighteenth as the first golden age of cider in England. After that, there is a fairly eventless period where cider would have been in decline (in favor of beer) for various reasons, including some quality and taxation issues. Let me mention the publication of *A Treatise on Cyder-Making* by Hugh Stafford in 1753. Then came Thomas Andrew Knight (1759–1838), horticulturalist and botanist from Herefordshire, and a wealthy landowner. He did some breeding of fruit trees and vegetables, and introduced a number of new apple varieties. Knight is the author of *A Treatise on the Culture of the Apple & Pear, and on the Manufacture of Cider & Perry*, first published in 1797, and the aforementioned *Pomona Herefordiensis*, two major contributions to the cider literature of that time.

The subsequent noteworthy events in English cider history happened by the end of the nineteenth century, first with the work of Dr. Robert Hogg and Henry G. Bull, who did a survey of the apple and pear varieties under the sponsorship of the Woolhope Naturalists' Field Club. This work permitted the publication of their famous *Herefordshire Pomona* between 1878 and 1884, a reference that is still useful nowadays and has been recently republished. And then there was the founding of the Bulmers cidery by Henry Percival (Percy) Bulmer in 1887 in Hereford. Bulmer was the first to industrialize the process of cider making in England, which before then had only been made on a relatively small scale on farms. His cidery eventually became the largest in the world, making hundreds of millions of liters a year, and has had a great influence worldwide. The Strongbow cider, which is still the largest-selling cider with a worldwide market share of about 15 percent, is a product of Bulmers. Bulmers has also been active in the breeding, selection, and importation (from France) of new cider apple varieties, and in the modernization of orcharding practices.

As we got to the end of nineteenth and beginning of twentieth centuries, cider making started to be more formally studied by scientists, and hence begins the modern era of cider. Of particular importance in the U.K. is the founding of the Long Ashton Research Station (LARS) near Bristol in 1903, which throughout most of the twentieth century was a leading force in cider research with a worldwide influence. The number of useful papers published by their researchers is countless. They worked in close relationship with cider producers to develop easy-to-implement methods to modernize and improve the quality of the production. Unfortunately, at the beginning of the 1980s, the aims of the station were redirected to other topics and the divisions that did cider- and apple-related research were shut down. The station finally closed in 2003, exactly a century after its creation. We may get a good summary of the work that has been done at the station from a write-up made by my collaborator Andrew Lea and available from his website.[*] Also, a book edited by Ray Williams, *Cider and Juice Apples: Growing and Processing*, contains many articles written by scientists at LARS.[†]

The cider picture has evolved considerably during the twentieth century in the U.K. In the first part of the century, large industrial producers used regionally grown cider apples and applied traditional cider making techniques to large batches. But during the course of the century, as a consequence of the economic optimization of the cider making process, many started to use more and more imported concentrated juice and less fresh cider apples. This, combined with heavy chaptalization, dilution with water, and a reduction of fermentation times, reduced costs and increased productivity. Some of these large-scale producers went on to become huge multimillion-liter industrial plants where the cider making techniques have just about nothing in common with tradition. Some purists will say the products these producers make also have

---

[*] Andrew Lea, "Long Ashton Research Station—A Personal View," http://www.cider.org.uk/LARS_view.html.

[†] Ray Williams, *Cider and Juice Apples: Growing and Processing* (Bristol: University of Bristol, c. 1988).

very little in common with true cider, as the real cider apple content may be quite low and practically nonexistent for some brands.

This evolution occurred in the U.K. in part because of very lax regulations that permit the use of the name *cider* for products that are made from only 35 percent apple juice, even permitting this 35 percent to come from reconstituted juice made out of imported concentrates—a situation that would not be tolerated with wine, for example, and is not permitted in many other European countries where cider is traditionally made. Some data published by the European Cider and Fruit Wine Association (AICV) in their document titled *European Cider Trends 2019* gives a good illustration of this. We see there that in the U.K., 7,000 hectares (17,500 acres) of cider apple orchards are used to produce some 800 to 900 million liters of cider annually. This means that from each hectare of orchard, the industry can produce an average of about 120,000 liters of cider. Now, we may ask how many tons of apples (or how many liters of juice) we might get each year from a hectare of orchard. This depends a lot on the type of orchard and on management practices, and may in general vary between 10 and 50 tons. So let's take a good average at 30 tons, and an extraction of 75 percent; this would give some 22,500 liters of pure juice per hectare of cider apple orchard, from which the industry would manage to produce 120,000 liters of cider. This data certainly gives a quite clear indication of the very low average content of English cider apple juice in the total cider production of the U.K. In all, it works out to less than 20 percent.

According to the data published in 2018 by the National Association of Cider Makers (NACM), there are more than 500 cider producers in the U.K.* It should be noted that in this country there is an important fiscal advantage (tax exemption) for a producer maintaining production volume under 7,000 liters annually, and as a result, more than three-quarters of the cider makers do keep their production under this level. Another 15 percent have production volumes between 7,000 and 100,000 liters. And it is interesting to note that the 10 largest producers among the members of the NACM have, when taken together, a share of 85 percent of all the cider produced in the U.K. Some of these have production well above 100 million liters. It is also

* From their website (https://cideruk.com/uk-cider-market/), as of February 2018.

interesting to note that many of the very large cideries in the U.K. have been bought in recent years by multinational beer companies: HP Bulmer is now owned by Heineken, and Aspall by Molson Coors.

Another interesting fact about English cider is that, according to the *Westons Cider Report* of 2019, 36 percent of the cider volume sales is said to be "on trade," which means it is bought and consumed in a pub, bar, or restaurant, while the rest is consumed at home (off trade).* A large part of on-trade cider is thus delivered in bulk packaging, which would be bag-in-box, or kegs if sparkling, to be served as draught cider. This report also reveals that some of the most sold brands in the U.K. are in fact fruit-flavored ciders that contain very little if any apples, some of which are imported from Scandinavia.

We will not discuss here the industrial cider from the leading brands much further. Instead, we will now concentrate our attention on the ciders produced by small and medium-size producers who make their ciders with real apples and who use more traditional techniques in their processes. A fascinating book about some of these English craft cider makers is James Crowden's *Ciderland* (2008).

———

The U.K. holds a good number of events, fairs, and competitions that are related to cider. The most important is certainly the Royal Bath & West Show, which is a large agricultural fair with an important section for cider, held annually at the end of May or beginning of June near Shepton Mallet in Somerset. The British Cider Championships take place during the Show. It is the most prestigious cider competition in the U.K. and highly respected worldwide, with a special section for international ciders. Some additional cider competitions are the International Cider Challenge, the Big Apple Cider and Perry Trials (also known as the Putley Trials), the Three Counties International Cider & Perry Competition, and the Hereford Cider Museum's International Cider & Perry Competition. And by the way, this Cider Museum in Hereford is definitely a place a cider lover ought to visit.

* *Westons Cider Report* is published annually by Westons Cider and contains data about the cider market in the U.K.

Figure 2.1. This display of old (mostly eighteenth century) fine cider glassware is a highlight at the Cider Museum in Hereford. Such quality glassware clearly indicates that cider was consumed among the wealthy and the nobility, and was not only a drink for the common people.

Cider Making Regions

Cider is present in most parts of the island of Great Britain, although the greater part of it is produced in the south of England. Cider is also produced in Northern Ireland, which is part of the United Kingdom, but I have rather chosen to combine Northern Ireland with the Republic of Ireland in a write-up that appears in chapter 11.

The Southwest (West Country)

The most renowned traditional cider making regions are found in the southwest of England. Though the whole region is often called the West Country, strictly speaking, the West Country should only include the counties of Somerset, Devon, Dorset, and Cornwall, which form the extreme southwestern tip of England. Other important cider making counties—Herefordshire, Worcestershire, and Gloucestershire—are for their part in another administrative region, the West Midlands, and make a group familiarly called the Three Counties. And the Welsh Marches is recognized by some as a distinct region, it being the area along the border between England and Wales. The southwest of England (and in particular Somerset and Herefordshire) is home to most of the well-known large cideries of the U.K., such as Bulmers, Westons, and Thatchers. These distinctions having been made, I will sometimes use the name West Country in this book to mean all these southwestern cider making regions.

What is known as English-style cider (or sometimes English traditional style) originated in those West Country regions. This style is often said to be austere and usually is still or lightly pétillant, with relatively low residual sweetness and high in tannins, which gives it an intense mouthfeel with astringency and a little bitterness. Acidity is also present. It is produced from traditional cider-specific apple varieties that are typical of the region, mostly of the bittersweet and bittersharp classes. There is only very little (if any) dessert or culinary apple varieties used in the making of this cider style. Depending on the producer, it may have a clean aroma but sometimes can be quite funky after going through natural malolactic fermentation (a transformation of malic acid into lactic acid due to lactic acid bacteria). An aroma familiarly called old horse is quite traditional in the region, and for some consumers is necessary for the cider to be considered genuine. Such rough unfiltered and still farm ciders are often called *scrumpy*.

There is quite a bit of variability in the flavor of English ciders. One reason is that many producers make some single-variety (or varietal) ciders, thus highlighting the characteristics of individual cultivars. And a producer may then offer a large number of ciders, each made from a different variety. There are also some historical stylistic differences within the subregions, with the ciders from the Three Counties being slightly more acidic, those from Somerset being more tannic, and those from Devon sweeter. These differences are subtle, and nowadays tend to be less noticeable.

The Southeast

We find a cider of quite different nature in portions of the Home Counties (Kent, Sussex, and Essex) and East Anglia (Norfolk and

Suffolk), which are in the eastern and southeastern parts of England. Although the cider making techniques are fairly similar, this cider differs from that of the southwest region in that it is mostly made from low-tannin dessert and culinary apples varieties. Hence this is a lighter cider, more acid-forward, where the freshness and fruitiness are favored. This cider is often called English eastern–style. The best-known large cidery of the region is Aspall in Suffolk, which dates back to 1728 and has seen nine generations of Chevalliers since it was founded by Clement Chevallier.

In John Evelyn's *Pomona*, there are references to cider being made in the surroundings of London from dessert and culinary apple varieties. Thus we can speculate the cider in the seventeenth century would have been fairly close to what we now know as the English eastern–style, and that there was already some differentiation with the cider made in the West Country, where more tannic, cider-specific varieties were used. The historian Richard Stone wrote a chapter in the book *Finding Good Cider* (by his father, Alan Stone) in which he provides an explanation: The distance to the main market of London would be the most important factor explaining the difference in the varieties grown in a specific location and used for cider making, as both apples that are richer in tannins and the cider made from such apples would keep and stand the transportation to London more easily.* Hence, in counties near London, there would have been no need to use apples that were richer in tannins.

Wales

Cider culture is very important in Wales, where we find many small craft cider makers but no large industrial producer. They united in 2001 with the founding of the Welsh Perry & Cider Society, which has been particularly active in the rediscovery and valorization of heritage Welsh cider apple and perry pear varieties, and also in defining a Traditional Welsh Cider, which has been officialized in a PGI

---

* Richard Stone, "Finding Good Cider in the Age of the Scientific Revolution," in *Finding Good Cider: A Year in the Life of a West Country Cider Lover* by Alan Stone (Shepton Mallet, U.K.: Somersethistory.co.uk, 2016).

(protected geographical indication) label. The cider is fairly similar to the traditional English style, as the regions are neighbors and share pretty much the same cider making practices and apple varieties— although there is now a tendency among the Welsh makers to use more of their local apple varieties.

Scotland and the North of England

In the northern parts of England and in Scotland, there are very few cideries, although the people there do drink good quantities of cider. Hence most of it is brought in from the south. In Scotland, there are some 15 cider producers, all but one of them being very small with productions below the tax exemption mark of 7,000 liters per year. As for cider style, it mostly depends on the producer: Some make a cider closer to the English eastern–style while others use tannin-rich cider apples to make a cider more related to the West Country type. Some cider makers in Scotland claim to be among the most northern commercial producers in the world.

The Channel Islands

The Channel Islands, which include Jersey, Guernsey, and a number of smaller islands, have an ancient cider tradition borrowed in good part from France. Some 100 to 300 years ago, apples were the main crop on these islands, with cider production being a very important activity. A search on the internet yields many articles and pictures of old mills and presses, which are however now mostly found in museums or used as ornaments. We can get an overview of the evolution of the cider industry on the island of Jersey from a publication of 1806, *A Treatise on the Cultivation of Apple Trees and the Preparation of Cider. Being a Theoretical and Practical Work for the Use of the Inhabitants of the Island of Jersey* by Rev. Francis Le Couteur.* We can read that by the middle of the fifteenth century, cider began to be an object of rural economy on

---

* This is a translation from French that was published as an appendix to William Pitt's *A General View of the Agriculture of the County of Worcester: With Observations on the Means of Its Improvement* (London: Richard Phillips, 1810).

this island, and before that time, mead was the main drink of the people there. Le Couteur presumes it was the Normans who introduced the idea of cultivating the apple tree and making cider. In 1734 the island had been described as a "sea of cider," and between that date and 1800, the production increased by another 50 percent. Le Couteur estimates their production at 30,000 to 35,000 hogsheads (approximately 300 liters each), of which about 3,000 were exported. This would amount to some 9 to 10 million liters. Le Couteur mentions the population of Jersey was then about 24,000 inhabitants, hence we obtain a number close to 400 liters *per capita*. So for sure, the description of a "sea of cider" was well deserved! Nowadays however this production has pretty much completely stopped as there are only a few craft makers keeping the tradition alive. Anecdotally, Clement Chevallier was a resident of the island of Jersey before founding the Aspall cidery in 1728, and as the story goes he brought apple trees from his native Jersey to plant in Suffolk.

Figure 2.2. A traditional cider orchard at Ocle Pychard, Herefordshire.

Collaborators

This chapter was written with the invaluable help from my collaborators:

Tom Oliver owns Oliver's Cider and Perry in Ocle Pychard, a bucolic village in Herefordshire. Tom is certainly one of the better-known figures among the traditional English craft producers. His ciders and perries are exported and highly regarded in many countries. A lot of people even say of him that he is the best perry maker in the world, a compliment he always refuses to accept. His cidery has a production of about 100,000 liters annually, split between perry and cider production. The Oliver's farm does have a cider apple orchard, but its production isn't sufficient for the cidery's needs, and Tom buys a good percentage of his fruit from other growers in the vicinity. He does maintain a good relationship with his growers, and in particular they agree on orcharding practices that ensure optimum quality of the fruits. Tom has also collaborated in the section on Herefordshire perry in chapter 6.

Andrew Lea is the cider scientist of our community of cider makers, having earned a PhD in food science, on the study of tannins in apples and cider. He worked for a number of years at the Long Ashton Research Station until the Cider Section's closure in the 1980s. He is the author of *Craft Cider Making*, an excellent book on the making of English-style cider. He has also authored a great number of scientific publications, and he maintains a website on cider making, The Wittenham Hill Cider Portal. Andrew has a small cider production from his backyard orchard near Oxford: Harp Hill Cider.

Mike Penney is my main collaborator for Welsh cider. Mike runs a small cidery in Monmouthshire named Troggi Seidr, which he

Figure 2.3. Mike Penney showing the mechanism of his 1890 Workman and Sons twin screw press, which is still in perfect working condition.

founded in 1984, in the early years of the Welsh renaissance of cider and perry making. His annual cider production may vary between 4,000 and 6,500 liters, with roughly equal proportions of cider and perry. He specializes in bottle-fermented cider using the traditional method. Troggi's cider (*seidr*) and perry (*perai*) have won numerous awards over the years. Mike Penney is a founding member of the Welsh Perry & Cider Society.

In addition, I wish to thank the following people who helped in one way or another: Simon Day (Once upon a Tree), Suzanna Forbes (author and co-owner of Little Pomona Orchard & Cidery), Mike Johnson (Ross on Wye Cider & Perry Company), James Marsden (Gregg's Pit Cider & Perry), Ryan Sealey (Caledonian Cider Company, Scotland), and Christian Stolte (The Wee Scottish Cider Company).

The Orchard

By the late nineteenth century, it was estimated there were over 50,000 hectares (120,000 acres) of cider orchards in the West Country, while current estimations run at about 7,000; that is, one-seventh of the former area is still cultivated as cider apple orchard. A century ago these were traditional, low-density orchards with standard-size trees, about 120 to 160 trees per hectare (50 to 65 per acre), similar to the one shown in figure 2.2. Such orchards continued to be planted and maintained during the first half of the twentieth century, but this stopped during the 1970s as bush orchards started becoming the norm, and many of the old orchards got grubbed out and replaced by more profitable crops. Nowadays, we still find some traditional orchards, but they are becoming rare and those that remain are quite old. Their contribution to the total tonnage of cider apples may be considered marginal at best. Most apples now come from bush orchards, which are more productive. During the 1970s and '80s, the large cider companies encouraged farmers to plant these orchards under contract in order to secure their supply of cider apples. The trees use intermediate-size rootstocks (mainly the MM 106), and when they were planted, their life expectancy was estimated to be about 30 years. However, Mike Johnson of Ross on Wye Cider & Perry Company in Herefordshire has told me that even those that had attained that age in his orchards are still very productive and as yet show no sign of senescence.

Orchard management for the bush orchards often follows IPM (integrated pest management) practices. Very few bush orchards are fully organic, but most traditional orchards are completely unsprayed, and those could be considered as organic.

It is sad to say, but current tendencies are not encouraging for the English orchard. There are surpluses of cider apples and as a consequence the prices are very low. This situation is not sustainable for many apple growers, and we can expect that some bush orchards will be grubbed out in the coming years. The problem comes from the fact that large industrial makers are selling more and more fruit and flavored ciders, which are made with concentrates and don't require cider apples. The smaller craft makers still use cider apples, but the demand from them is much less than the current production.

Figure 2.4. A mature bush orchard at Ross-on-Wye, Herefordshire, which is still very productive nearly 40 years after planting.

Apple Varieties

Certainly a few hundred recorded traditional cider apple varieties may be found in the orchards of the country. An excellent modern reference book on English varieties is *Cider Apples: The New Pomona* by Liz Copas (2013), where we find the full descriptions of 134 of them, plus descriptions of 29 modern introductions that were bred in the Long Ashton Research Station during the 1980s, and are familiarly referred to as "The Girls." There are many other good pomological references for English cider apples, among which I mention here: the *Pomona Herefordiensis* and the *Herefordshire Pomona* that were previously introduced, also the *Bulmer's Pomona*, published by HP Bulmer Ltd in 1987, and *The Apple & Pear as Vintage Fruits* by Dr. Robert Hogg and Henry G. Bull in 1866.

The choice of English varieties for someone who wishes to plant an orchard is huge, with approximately 150 cider apple varieties once offered by the nurseryman John Worle only (now retired, however). Many growers may have more than 30 varieties in their orchards. In the West Country, the largest percentage of the trees would be of the bittersweet class with varieties such as Dabinett, Chisel Jersey,

Michelin, Harry Masters Jersey, Tremlett's Bitter, and Yarlington Mill among the most popular. Varieties of the sharp and bittersharp classes are also always well represented with the Brown's Apple, Foxwhelp, Stoke Red, Porter's Perfection, and Kingston Black. In addition to these varieties, which are ubiquitous in all of the West Country, a grower would typically add some lesser-known local varieties and a few of his personal favorites. Younger orchards planted in the last 15 years or so would also include some of the modern "Girls" varieties. To obtain the flavor balance typical of West Country ciders, most growers and cider makers would have in their orchards about 40 to 60 percent of trees of bittersweet varieties, 20 to 30 percent each of bittersharp and sharp, and maybe 5 percent of sweets, if any.

For the English eastern–style cider, among the most used varieties are Cox Orange Pippin, Egremont Russet, Ashmead's Kernel, Katy, Bramley's Seedling, and Jonagold, which are mainly in the sharp class. In Wales, most cider apple varieties are the same as in the neighboring English county of Herefordshire. There are a few varieties known in the West Country that are of Welsh origin, for example Breakwell Seedling or Frederick, and there are also some good native Welsh varieties that were almost forgotten and are now being revived through the work of the Welsh Perry & Cider Society, such as Perthyre, Pig Aderyn, Twyn y Sheriff, or Kennedy's Late. The Society published in 2018 *The Welsh Pomona of Heritage Cider Apples & Perry Pears* describing many heritage varieties.* In Scotland, cider makers use some English varieties mixed with natives. Of the Scottish apple varieties used in cider, the best known is certainly James Grieve, which is also grown in England. Others that are used in cider making include Arbroath Pippin, Bloody Ploughman, East Lothian Pippin, Galloway Pippin, Hawthornden, Orkney, Scots Dumpy, Scrog, and White Melrose.

If we now go back to the West Country, it is interesting to note that by the end of the eighteenth century and beginning of nineteenth, there apparently weren't that many of the low-acid and

---

* *The Welsh Pomona of Heritage Cider Apples & Perry Pears* (2018) may be downloaded from the link: https://docs.wixstatic.com/ugd/741924_45d8b0c ca6204c0b98b1c0d783aacc71.pdf.

tannin-rich bittersweet apple varieties that are nowadays so characteristic of the region. In the old texts of the seventeenth and eighteenth centuries, the cider-specific apples were often described as harsh and/or rough, and were said to be unpleasant to eat fresh. We can probably assume this indicated a very high content of tannins, with associated bitterness and astringency, but it could also indicate very high acidity or possibly a combination of both (that we would call bittersharp in modern nomenclature)—the authors in those days seldom made the distinction. But for sure, the flavor of modern milder bittersweet varieties such as Dabinett or Yarlington Mill can't in any way be described as harsh or rough. We can only find a couple of references to an apple called Bitterscale, whose name is thought to be a synonym for bittersweet. Some of the better-known cider-specific varieties of that period include the Foxwhelp, Redstreak, Forest Styre, Dymock Red, Cowarne Red, and Hagloe Crab. Most were described by Knight in his *Pomona Herefordiensis*, but unfortunately he seldom gave an indication of the acidity level of the juice, and it is difficult to assess from his descriptions how the apple would have been classified in modern nomenclature (bittersweet, sharp, or bittersharp). In fact, he doesn't describe any variety whose characteristics and flavor clearly correspond to anything like the milder bittersweet varieties that are nowadays so important, except for a now forgotten one, the Yellow Elliot, for which he writes: "It is very astringent and harsh, though not very acid, apple; and it afforded a cider which grew soft and mellow with age." From other authors, however, and in particular from Hogg and Bull's *The Apple & Pear as Vintage Fruits*, we may deduce that most of the early cider apples were sharps or bittersharps with relatively few that would have had a bittersweet flavor. There is the Redstreak, which according to some could have been the first bittersweet in English cider making history, but this is not for sure as neither Knight nor Hogg and Bull mention anything along those lines. So it appears that the pommages by the nineteenth century and earlier could have consisted mainly of bittersharp and sharp varieties, with milder bittersweets playing a lesser role compared to what we see nowadays. It is then quite plausible that the blends in those days would have been higher in acidity than what we now see, and probably had similar or even more tannin.

A number of bittersweet varieties apparently appeared as native seedlings during the nineteenth century, and cider makers started using them more and more in their blends. Added to that, some French bittersweet varieties were introduced during that century (see the plate from the *Herefordshire Pomona*, page 46). Some of these, such as Michelin, Médaille d'or, or Vilberie which are still popular in England, have kept their original French names while others were renamed—for example, Argile grise was grown in England under the name Brown Thorn. Sometimes the word *Norman* was used as an indication of their origin, as for the White Norman, which apparently could be the Blanc mollet of the French, or the Bulmer's Norman, which was imported as an unnamed variety (or maybe the name tag was lost). Some others that were originally given the name Norman could have been native seedlings, possibly named that way because they had a flavor similar to that of Norman varieties—but those were mostly renamed as Hereford varieties by the end of the nineteenth century (see the plate on page 220).

The case of the Jersey apples is worthy of some further discussion. This is an important family of cider apples that share some common features: a small to medium size with a characteristic conical shape often with a "nose" at the calyx, and a bittersweet flavor with a good concentration of tannins. According to the literature, the Jersey apples would have originated in Somerset and are considered typical of that county. Among the better known in the family, let's note the Yarlington Mill Jersey, Chisel Jersey, and Harry Masters Jersey. And some lesser-known ones are, for example, Ashton Brown Jersey, Coat Jersey, Stable Jersey, Stembridge Jersey, and White Jersey. These are all in the bittersweet class. Most of these appeared around the turn of the twentieth century, but the Chisel Jersey is apparently older: in 1886, Hogg and Bull in *The Apple & Pear as Vintage Fruits* mention only the Chisel Jersey plus another, now forgotten variety, the Jersey Flenier. And in an earlier work by Hogg, *British Pomology* of 1851, the previous two don't appear, but we find a Jersey apple described as a "small cider apple of conical shape, red color, and in use during November and December. A bitter-sweet." Let's note here the conical shape and that it is clearly identified as a bittersweet. Possibly this apple could have been the first of the family. And with time, as new varieties arose in Somerset, when they showed the typical characters of that original Jersey apple, they were named accordingly—up until now, where we have a whole family of apples sharing common features.

Because of the name, the origin of the Jersey apples has been the subject of controversy: Would the first have been brought in from the island of Jersey? And if not, why the name Jersey? Some authorities think the Jersey apples are native seedlings of Somerset and that the name is from the old word *jaisy* in the local dialect, which was used to indicate it was a bitter apple. Others think a variety could have been named Jersey because it showed similarities with apples grown on the island; or that it originated directly or indirectly from the island. The eminent pomologist Liz Copas wrote about this, and although she doesn't believe the varieties grown on the island were directly imported, she leaves the door open: "So our 'jerseys' may have come to us indirectly from the Channel Isles. It is reasonable to think that they began as seedlings grown from the pomace waste thrown out after pressing imported fruit, and were brought up as natives." We do know that some 200 years ago, the island of Jersey had a flourishing cider industry, and by its proximity to the Cotentin Peninsula of Normandy, shared many cider apple varieties with the French. We can read in

Figure 2.5. Yarlington Mill apples have the typical shape of Jersey cider apples.

Le Couteur's book of 1806 (see page 66): "There are many at present, who give the preference to the Frequen, the Romeril, the Lucas, and the Lamey. These are all varieties of sweet and bitter apples peculiar to the island." This clearly indicates bittersweets were then the preferred varieties in Jersey, with the Frequen (or Fréquin, a very old family of French bittersweet varieties that incidently share some common characters of shape and flavor with the Jersey varieties) being the first mentioned. So yes, there is definitely a possibility that Jersey apples could originally have been linked to the island of the same name, but there is no clear written documentation that I know that would confirm this.

By the beginning of the twentieth century, the pommages of the West Country had taken shape, with contributions from native varieties intermixed with imported ones, and more modern introductions that could carry genes from both native English and French varieties. Some of the varieties described in the following list are nowadays extensively planted and grown in many cider making regions of the world. The English cider apple varieties are without doubt those that have seen the most success internationally. We can find them in Australia, New Zealand, Canada, the United States, and also in many regions of northern Europe.

> **Ashmead's Kernel** (sharp) is mostly considered a variety for fresh eating and culinary purposes. It is popular in cider making for the English eastern–style cider, and it is also well regarded in North America. The apple is medium size and entirely russeted. It has strong and rich flavor, with low tannin, high sugar, and very high acidity. The ripening season is late. This variety is triploid* and originated in Gloucester in the early 1700s.

> **Bloody Ploughman** is a Scottish apple known since the late 1800s, of nice red color, good size, and with deep ribs. It is well regarded by Ryan Sealey of Caledonian Cider Company in the Highlands,

---

* Most apples are diploid, i.e. have two sets of genes. A few varieties are triploids, and this usually gives more vigor to the tree but makes its pollen sterile, so one needs to have trees of an additional variety for pollination.

Figure 2.6. Ashmead's Kernel apples as grown in the author's orchard.

who told me: "It's a fabulous looking apple. Mid sharp / sweet with an intensely red skin that stains the flesh—and the cider if given a long enough maceration. Aromatically it's all about the raspberries and red berries."

Bramley's Seedling (sharp) is the traditional English cooking apple. As the story goes, it came from a pip planted in 1809 in Nottinghamshire, and began being commercially distributed by the mid-1850s. For cider, it is used mainly in the southeast of England. In the West Country, we sometimes see them used in blends for increasing the acidity of the must. Also worth mentioning is that these apples are grown a lot (accounting for about 25 percent of consumer apple production in the U.K.) and there is a surplus of them; hence they are available at low cost to cider makers. This is a late-ripening apple, triploid, big and mostly greenish with some red, and very acidic in flavor.

Figure 2.7. Bloody Ploughman Scottish apple. Photo by Ryan Sealey.

Brown's Apple (sharp) is a vintage-quality English cider apple that began to be known in Devon during the 1920s. Since then it has gained popularity in most cider-producing regions to become one of the most highly acclaimed of the sharp English varieties. The juice has medium sugar content, medium to high acidity, and low to medium tannin. It should be noted that the tannin content of a sharp cider apple is normally higher than that of a dessert apple, but still not high enough to classify it as a bittersharp. The tree is hardy and has good resistance to scab, but it may be susceptible to canker. It is relatively productive, but its tendency to produce fruit in alternate years may be difficult to control. The apples ripen mid-season, are of medium size, and of a nice striped red color.

Cox Orange Pippin (sharp) is the emblematic dessert apple of the English. Its flavor is considered by some as the most complex, aromatic, and rich of all apples. It is said to be a seedling of Ribston Pippin, possibly crossed with Blenheim Orange in 1832. The Cox

Figure 2.8. Brown's Apple as growing in the author's orchard.

Orange Pippin tree will not grow well and be productive every-where, however. It prefers a humid and oceanic climate and will not tolerate very cold winter temperatures. Its culture is considered to be difficult. For cider, the fruit is generally seen as too expensive to grow in large enough quantities, but in the regions where the conditions are favorable, it is excellent. It is used in England for the English eastern–style cider.

Dabinett (bittersweet) is one of the most highly praised bittersweet cider apples all around the world. It is possibly a seedling of Chisel Jersey, discovered as a chance seedling in Somerset. The Dabinett tree is not very vigorous, which makes it well adapted to the more intensive orcharding practices that we see in modern bush orchards where it is particularly productive. No grower or cider maker would go without it. Copas (2013) writes: "It holds top place for the most popular and highly esteemed variety today." The Dabinett apple is small to medium in size, and of a deep red color. The high-quality

Figure 2.9. Dabinett apples from the orchard of Henry of Harcourt in Australia.

juice is medium to high in sugar and has low acidity and medium tannins, yielding full-bodied cider with soft astringency.

Foxwhelp (sharp to bittersharp) is an old and famous variety that dates back to the seventeenth century. We aren't sure if the original Foxwhelp still exists, but some of its many descendants are still grown, the better known of them being Broxwood Foxwhelp and Bulmer's Foxwhelp (recent DNA testings indicate these two names could in fact be for the same variety). These are both classified as vintage-quality medium bittersharp apples. In the *Herefordshire Pomona*, we find descriptions and illustrations for many other apples that are related to the Foxwhelp: Rejuvenated Foxwhelp, Bastard Foxwhelp, Red Foxwhelp, and Black Foxwhelp. The original Foxwhelp was famous for its very high acidity. (See the illustration on page vi. The illustration also shows that the variety is sensitive to scab.)

Figure 2.10. Plate 45 of the *Herefordshire Pomona* features the Kingston Black along with other cider apples that were popular at the time. Photo courtesy of Cornell University Libraries.

Frederick (sharp) is the favorite Welsh cider apple of my collaborator Mike Penney. It is one of the best known of the Welsh varieties, most of which are still not known outside of their region of origin. It was widely grown in Monmouthshire during the nineteenth century, and later there were some limited plantings in the southwest of England. Mike particularly appreciates the aromatics of this apple, which is small to medium in size and of a nice flushed, dark red color.

Kingston Black (bittersharp) first appeared in the beginning of the nineteenth century in Somerset. This apple is often regarded as the perfect cider apple, one that may yield an excellent and ideally balanced cider without blending. And as such it is probably the variety most often used for making single-variety ciders. The juice has a high sugar content combined with medium acidity and moderate tannin. It has some drawbacks, however, as the tree has the reputation of being capricious: It doesn't succeed well in all locations and may be difficult to grow and be unproductive if the conditions aren't suitable. The apples ripen late, are medium size, and flushed dark red. Although a true cider apple, it is quite palatable to eat fresh, being rich in flavor and well balanced.

Michelin (bittersweet) is an apple of French origin that was obtained by a M. Legrand in Normandy by 1870. Nowadays it is grown primarily in the West Country, where it was introduced in 1884 with a number of other French varieties. Michelin is mostly appreciated for its good and reliable productivity, and it has been one of the most planted varieties during the second half of the twentieth century. The apple is small to medium in size, of a rather conical shape, and green. It yields a juice with medium sugar content, low acidity, and medium tannins that are rather soft. In some locations, the tree may be prone to canker.

Porter's Perfection (bittersharp) is a classic late-season cider apple that yields a juice that is relatively high in acidity with medium tannins. It dates back to the nineteenth century, but it started being known and propagated only around 1907. This variety has the peculiarity of often producing pairs of fused apples.

Stoke Red (bittersharp) is a vintage-quality cider apple. It originated in Somerset around 1920. Stoke Red is generally well appreciated in England, where it is often used for making single-variety cider. It is also grown in other countries. This variety leafs out much later in spring than any other apple, and many people joke about it, saying the Stoke Red still looks dead while most other varieties are already blooming. The juice is very well balanced, with medium values for its concentrations in sugar, acid, and tannins.

Vicky (bittersweet) is a new variety that was bred at the Long Ashton Research Station and released in the late 1990s. This was from a program whose objective was to produce earlier-maturing cider apple varieties for the industry. Most of the apples released within this program have been given the name of a woman (Angela, Betty, Fiona, Lizzy . . .), hence the whole group of these apples is often familiarly called "The Girls," even if a few of them were given unrelated names (for example Prince William or Three Counties). As with most varieties released from this program, Vicky apples ripen early, by mid-September, and the trees perform well in more intensive, high-density orchards.

Yarlington Mill (bittersweet) is another member of the Jersey family, its full name being Yarlington Mill Jersey, but that is a bit long, so the last word is usually dropped. The variety is from a chance seedling that appeared near a mill at Yarlington in Somerset, in the late 1800s. This is another English bittersweet variety (along with Dabinett) to be universally acclaimed across the Cider Planet. It is mostly appreciated for its smooth tannin and the characteristic flavor it gives to the cider. The tree adapts well to many situations, being also very hardy. It is, however, sensitive to fire blight, which does limit its use in some locations, and although productive, it shows some tendency toward biennial bearing in production. In England, the apples ripen late, but interestingly, many growers in North America have reported that it ripens much earlier for them. The apples are quite nice-looking, medium size, and mostly red in color.

Cider Making

Cider apples are mostly collected on the ground in two or three passes, either mechanically (in larger operations) or manually. Tree shaking is usually done before the last pass. Most often, the different varieties of apples are mixed before processing to yield a well-balanced juice. For example, most cider makers making a English-style cider would like to see in their blends approximately equal amounts of low- and high-acidity apples, and between two-thirds and three-quarters of apples that are rich in tannins. Naturally there are some variations in the proportions from each class of flavor between producers, and from year to year depending on the production from each variety. Some producers, however, have a different approach. For example, Mike Johnson of Ross on Wye Cider & Perry Company prefers to make many small single-variety batches, which may be bottled as varietal ciders or blended after fermentation is completed.

The traditional cider making process in England is quite straightforward. After a period of maturation, the apples are washed, sorted, and milled. They are then left for a maceration period and pressed. The rack and cloth press is the most common, usually hydraulic, but we see many twin screw presses, often dating from the Victorian era and rebuilt. The hydropress type is also very popular among the smaller producers. Larger producers may use a horizontal pneumatic press or a belt press.

There is usually no elaborate pre-fermentation processing. The must is simply put in fermentation, either after a normal sulfite dosage and yeast inoculation, or the cider maker omits the sulfiting step (or reduces the dosage) and lets the natural wild yeasts do their work. Racking is done as the cider approaches dryness. It is then transferred to a second vessel where air is eliminated, for a maturation period that can be for varying periods of time depending on the producer and the circumstances. The fermentations are mostly carried at ambient exterior temperature, which are quite cool in winter. As a consequence, the fermentations are rather slow. Partial cider freezing has been seen during exceptionally cold winters, but this is without consequence as the fermentations regain vigor after thaw.

Small farm producers rarely use filtration, and their ciders may sometimes be slightly hazy. They rely on the maturation period for the

Figure 2.11. An old restored twin-screw press at James Marsden's Gregg's Pit Cider & Perry in Herefordshire. Photo by Andrew Lea.

clarification to happen naturally. Once it is completed, some blending may be done, and the final processing to obtain a still cider usually consists of back-sweetening, bottling, and pasteurization. Back-sweetening may be done with plain sugar or some nonfermentable sweetener. The amount of added sugar determines the sweetness: dry, with up to 8 g/L of sugar for a specific gravity (SG) under 1.004; and medium, with approximately 15 to 30 g/L of sugar for an SG under 1.015. The sweet category is rarely seen in craft ciders, but it is more common for industrial ciders. A variety of bottle types are used, most often with a crown cap closure. A popular format is 500 mL in clear glass. Pasteurization is done in bath pasteurizers that are often homemade.

To obtain a pétillant cider, either the cider maker will let the prise de mousse happen before pasteurization, or the cider will be carbonated. There are many small producers who do not wish to handle the bottling process themselves, and they prefer to use the service of a specialist for all the final processing, thus insuring optimal sanitation, stability, and quality. Such contract bottlers may do a sterile filtration rather than a pasteurization to ensure stability of the product.

Another widely used packaging in England is the bag-in-box, for still ciders only. These are suitable for deliveries to pubs or festivals. Back-sweetening is, however, tricky as the bag-in-box cannot be easily pasteurized. Hence, unless a dry cider is desired, either a nonfermentable sweetener is used or the cider has to be consumed quickly, before the sugar has time to start refermenting. Bulk packaging for a pétillant or sparkling cider would be in kegs.

Not all producers follow this basic procedure. There is nowadays a small but growing number who are reviving the tradition of keeving, which was quite popular in England during the early- to mid-1900s but mostly abandoned thereafter, to produce ciders that retain part of their natural sweetness. Such ciders are made pétillant or sparkling with the ancestral method and packaged in 750 mL champagne-type bottles. These ciders are usually labeled as bottle conditioned. The other process used to obtain a premium sparkling cider is the traditional method (described in chapter 1, page 35). These ciders are said to be bottle-fermented, and they are also presented in champagne-type bottles.

Figure 2.12. A simple bath pasteurizer at Ross on Wye Cider & Perry Company in Herefordshire.

Figure 2.13. A display of bottles at Once Upon a Tree, where we can see, *from left*, wine-type bottles for still ciders, champagne-type bottles for bottle-fermented ciders, then two bottles of ice cider (which yet isn't a traditional style in England), and crown-capped 500 mL bottles for pétillant carbonated ciders. The bottles were set on a counter that is used for the laboratory analyses at the cidery, hence the miscellaneous equipment in the background.

Certification of Origin Labels

There are three cider PGI (protected geographical indication) labels in England, all for the Three Counties: Herefordshire Cider, Worcestershire Cider, and Gloucestershire Cider. And there is in Wales a PGI label for Traditional Welsh Cider. Interestingly there are no PGI labels in some important production counties such as Somerset or Devon.

The specifications for the three English PGIs are very similar and not very stringent. They do control the source of the fruit used, but they give a lot of latitude for the processes used. For example, a producer could take a juice with an SG 1.045 off the press, chaptalize to SG 1.070, proceed with fermentation to dryness, and then dilute the cider back to maybe 4 or 5 percent ABV, and finally add more sugar for back-sweetening. This means the actual sugar source could be as low as 60 percent from cider apples and up to 40 percent from other sources such as cane, beet, or corn. Also, as long as the juice is from local cider apples, it can be concentrated for storage and subsequently diluted for using in cider making. The specifications permit pasteurization and carbonation of the cider. In fact, these specifications correspond to the process that some of the larger cideries like Westons use. It must be said, however, that the non-PGI cider produced by some other industrial cideries is even more diluted than this.

The Welsh PGI is a lot more stringent. The addition of dilution water, of chaptalization sugar (an exception is given for dosage sugar needed for in-bottle fermentation), of concentrated apple juice, of nonfermentable sweetener, and of fining agents is forbidden. Additionally, processes such as filtration, carbonation, and pasteurization are also forbidden. In fact, the only additives permitted are yeasts and sulfite, enzyme and calcium salt for keeving, and yeast nutrients, sugar, and riddling aids for in-bottle fermentation. The Traditional Welsh Cider PGI permits the production of three forms of cider: still, bottle conditioned (ancestral method), and bottle fermented (traditional method).

Figure 2.14. A Herefordshire PGI cider from Gregg's Pit Cider & Perry. Note the deep amber color of this great cider, which is made according to far more stringent standards than what the PGI specification allows.

CHAPTER THREE

France
Cidre

Nowadays, most French cider is made in Normandy and Brittany, in the northwest of France, and in this chapter we will concentrate our attention to these two regions. By the end of the nineteenth century, cider was also produced in large quantities in quite a number of other regions, but today these contributions remain small. At present time, the average national production is on the order of 100 million liters (give or take 10 million liters, depending on the reference we look at) and this is split in nearly equal parts between Normandy and Brittany. Another 40 million liters of cider equivalent is produced as distilled apple *eau-de-vie* (Calvados, in Normandy, and Lambig, in Brittany) and as fortified cider (*pommeau*). This production level has been relatively stable for the last decade, and about 10 percent of it is exported. Some 80 percent of the cider production is from a few cooperative industrial producers such as Agrial and Les Celliers Associés, the two largest and better known, who sell their ciders under many different brands—for example, Kérisac, Loïc Raison, Val de Rance, and others. These producers get their apples from a large number of apple growers, generally under contract. There are 500 to 600 commercial cider producers in the country, and according to the UNICID (*Union nationale interprofessionnelle cidricole*), an estimated 15,000 people were involved in cider apple growing and cider making activities in 2020.

The French ciderland is divided into many subregions. In Normandy, we have Upper and Lower Normandy, Upper Normandy being the territory more to the north and east. And then these are further subdivided into smaller terroirs. The best known are Pays de Caux and Pays de Bray in Upper Normandy, and Pays d'Auge, Perche, Cotentin Peninsula, Bessin, Suisse Normande, and Domfrontais in Lower Normandy. In Brittany, we find Cornouaille (in the southwest), Pays de Rennes, Côtes d'Armor (on the north), Pays de Nantes, and Pays Vannetais. And in addition to the two main production regions of Normandy and Brittany, we find craft cider making in most of the northern half of France: the Pays d'Othe, east of Paris; the Pays de la Loire, south of Normandy; and the northern departments between Upper Normandy and Belgium. There is also the French Basque Country (Pays Basque), more south along the border with northern Spain, but the cider produced there is of a completely different nature, being similar to the Spanish ciders. We will cover this family of cider styles in chapter 4.

Northern France, and in particular Normandy, is one of the most ancient cider making regions of Europe. The oldest known mentions in writing of apple trees and cider in Normandy date back to the tenth and eleventh centuries, but it is quite likely that cider was made earlier than that—it's just that nobody wrote about it. In Brittany, cider appears in the literature around the thirteenth century, where it is called *sistr*. Those who have read the adventures of Asterix the Gaul are well aware that cervoise was the drink of the people of Brittany during that time, but it is not known for sure how and when cider appeared in that region. We know, however, that up to the sixteenth century, cider kept a rather low profile in France: It was made and consumed, but in relatively small quantities, and was pretty much confined to religious communities—the main drinks of the people were wine, beer, and cervoise, depending on the region.

France certainly has the most extensive cider literature of all countries. A fascinating book, *Le Cidre: Bibliographie exhaustive* by Jacques Jubert (2010), is entirely devoted to a huge bibliography that lists pretty much all important publications on the subject, over 1,000 titles by nearly 500 authors, in some 400 large-format pages. According to Jubert, the cider literature starts with the *Journal* of Gilles de Gouberville, a *gentilhomme campagnard* (French equivalent of "gentleman farmer") who had his domain between Cherbourg and Valognes in the Cotentin Peninsula of Normandy. This is a manuscript diary, which covers the years 1549 to 1562, that describes the quite extensive apple- and cider-related operations at the domain, including the raising of seedling trees, selection of new apple varieties (which were classified as sweet, bittersweet, or acidic), grafting, pressing equipment, and details of the cider making process, including the blending of varieties from the different classes.

The first important book to be essentially devoted to cider is *De vino et pomaceo*, written by Julien Le Paulmier, published in Latin in 1588 and a year later in French (translated by his collaborator Jacques de Cahaignes) under the title *Traité du vin et du cidre*. Le Paulmier was a medical doctor in Normandy and strongly believed in the curative virtues of cider. And while his *Traité* covers both wine and cider, the main part (over 100 pages) is on cider, also with a chapter on perry and one on beer. It is interesting to note that he describes no less than 65 varieties of cider apples that were then considered the best, many being clearly identified as bittersweets, and of which quite a few are still known and grown today. Of that period, let me also mention *Le théâtre d'agriculture et mesnage des champs* from Olivier de Serres, first published in 1600, a huge and famous work of over 1,000 pages that covers all aspects of rural life, including cider making, and would see over 20 subsequent editions in the following two centuries.

It is during the period of 1550 to 1600 that cider started to become the main drink of the people in the north of France. Until the sixteenth century, vineyards occupied large surfaces in Normandy, and wine was produced. However, by the second half of that century, vineyards and wine making were in decline, no doubt because the climate was becoming too cold for the grapevine to produce reliably (this was the time of the Little Ice Age). Another cause for the decline of wine is that taxation made it too expensive. Thus apple orchards were planted as replacements. The movement began in the Cotentin Peninsula of Normandy, and gradually spread to the other regions. We can also read in the book by Le Paulmier that 50 years earlier (that would bring us to the 1530s) it was beer that was most commonly drunk in the city of Rouen and in the surrounding countryside. But at the time of writing (1588), cider had replaced beer as the main drink. Hence we can see that period as a turning point, where cider was to take first place in front of wine and beer as the main drink of the people in these regions.

Very few noteworthy publications appeared in the following 150 years, essentially only new editions or rewritings of the titles noted previously. Nevertheless, cider was then getting well established as the main drink in the north of France. In the 1770s, some poisoning due to altered ciders started to happen. This was called l'Affaire des cidres (the cider affair) and triggered intense research by the most prestigious chemists of the time, including Antoine Lavoisier, in order to devise some techniques to analyze the ciders for detection of illegal alterations. This resulted in a tremendous increase in the level of knowledge on cider chemistry. Then came the French Revolution (1789–99), which as a side effect, fragmented the large estates into much smaller lots, and in particular, downsized the cider making equipment, which prior to that consisted of huge lever-type presses that could be 8 to 10 meters long, and with 4-meter-diameter troughs for horsedrawn crusher wheels. This also meant that a lot more people got to make cider, and the number of publications on the subject exploded. Jubert mentions that in the 16 years between 1795 and 1811, twice as many titles were published than during the three preceding centuries. The most significant work of the early nineteenth century is probably the *Traité de la culture des pommiers et poiriers et de la fabrication du cidre et du poiré* by Pierre-Joseph Odolant-Desnos, published in 1829. This is a 267-page book whose first part is on the cultivation of the cider apple and perry pear trees, and whose second part is on the making of cider and perry. It contains the most extensive list of apple varieties published at that time, with some 300 varieties described from all regions of Normandy (though it doesn't include varieties from

Brittany). It is also the first book to describe smaller and modern mills and presses (even a hydraulic press) in addition to the old-style large equipment. On the making of cider, we can see there is a good comprehension of the chemistry of cider. The main thing lacking really is the understanding of the role of the yeast, which came with the works of Louis Pasteur by the 1860s.

The second half of the nineteenth century and the beginning of the twentieth (up to 1914, the beginning of the First World War) was a period of intense cider activity in France. New books were published every year. And the articles in publications such as the *Bulletin de l'Association française pomologique* and *Le Cidre et le poiré* make a total of some 50,000 pages during that period! Congresses were organized in a different town every year, and there were various competitions for fruit, ciders, and new equipment such as mills and presses—all this permitted very fast progress in all fields of cider making. Let's remember also that this is the period where the phylloxera epidemic destroyed most vineyards in France, and the cider production had to compensate for the loss of wine production. It is not possible to note here all the important books that were published during that period (see Jubert's book *Le Cidre: Bibliographie exhaustive* for that), but I will mention a few that I have found particularly inspiring or useful for my own research. There is *Le Cidre* by Lucien de Boutteville and Achille Hauchecorne (1875), a landmark as it was the first truly scientific monograph on cider. It shines because it gives analysis results for sugar, acidity, and tannins for all the varieties described. This book is generally considered one of the most important ever published on the subject. Then from 1890 to 1893 we have from Georges Power: *Traité de la culture du pommier et de la fabrication du cidre*, whose three volumes are respectively on the culture of the cider apple tree, on the making of cider, and on the best cider apple varieties. The book includes beautiful color plates.

I'd like to say here a word about the two most prolific authors whose writings have had a great influence on modern cider making: Auguste Truelle and Georges Warcollier. To give an idea of their influence, 47 pages in Jubert's book are dedicated to the contributions from these two men. Truelle was a pharmacist at Trouville-sur-Mer, where he had a laboratory to make analyses on samples of cider apples to determine their properties. He was active from 1870 until his death in the mid-1920s. He was a firm believer that the best cider apples should yield juice with high sugar concentration, and he has had a great influence on the selection of the best varieties and the rejection of low-quality ones. Of all his numerous books, my favorite is his *Atlas des meilleures variétés de fruits à cidre* from 1896.

Warcollier for his part was the director of the Station Pomologique de Caen, and his publications appeared from 1902 to 1940. His most important book was first published under the title *Pomologie et cidrerie* in 1909, reedited in 1920, and for its third edition was split into two parts, *Le pommier à cidre* in 1926, followed by *Cidrerie* in 1928. These books are so complete and well written that they are still sought after by cider makers today. An English translation was done by Vernon L. S. Charley and published in 1949 under the title *The Principles and Practice of Cider-Making*. Warcollier was the first to scientifically study and describe the process of keeving, and a good part of his research was for obtaining a stable cider that retained its natural sweetness. He was also an ardent promoter of hygiene in the cider house.

While all this scientific activity was taking place, French cider production and consumption was also in constant increase, and by the beginning of the twentieth century had reached fabulous levels. Warcollier, in the 1920 edition of his book, reported that in 1900–1910, the average annual production ran at around 1.6 billion liters, which is 16 times more than nowadays. Of this, 38 percent was from Normandy, 32 percent from Brittany, and 30 percent from the other regions of France. The all-time record high was in 1904, with a total production of more than 3.6 billion liters. That year, the department of Ille-et-Vilaine in the northeast of Brittany reported a production of 600 million liters for a population at the time of about 600,000 people. That would make 1,000 liters per head. (Let's just try to imagine numbers like this today!) Naturally, such a production would not have all been drunk that same year or in that region. When another region had a lower production, some of the surplus would have been exported. Also the cities, and in particular Paris, were an important market. In years of abundance a good part was distilled, as it kept better in the form of a spirit. The context also favored such high production levels, in particular because the rivers were often polluted, potable water was

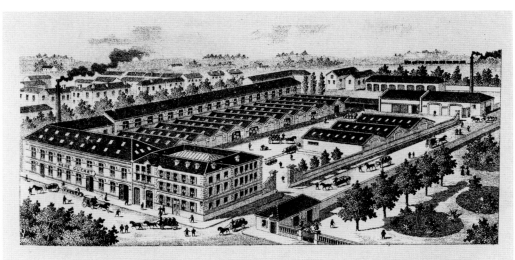

GRANDE CIDRERIE MODÈLE DE LA VALLÉE D'AUGE

René Guéret à Lisieux (Calvados)

Figure 3.1. The René Guéret cidery in Lisieux, in the heart of the Pays d'Auge, was established in 1885. It is considered as the first French industrial cidery and was one of the most important and modern in Normandy. It was sold in 1913, modernized, and became Établissements Saffrey Frères. The annual production was initially around 1 to 2 million liters, and reached 6 million liters after the modernization of 1913. This cidery was destroyed by Allied bombings in June 1944. From the illustration, we can appreciate the size of the installation. The rightmost building was the distillery, and the chimney on the left was for a 50 HP steam machine that provided power for the plant. This illustration is from a post card from the beginning of the twentieth century (private collection, S. Main), © Région Normandie - Inventaire général: Pascal Corbierre.

scarce, and wine was too expensive for ordinary people. Cider was a safe and affordable drink for the working people and could be drunk with all meals, including breakfast. It was low in alcohol, and it was even given to children (although often in a diluted form). Every farm had its orchard and cider production facility, and there were some large industrial production plants in many cities.

This cider golden age lasted until the First World War (1914–1918). During the war, a good part of the cider production was diverted to produce cheap apple alcohol that was used in the making of gunpowder. After that, production never recovered to prewar levels. According to Paul Labounoux (*Le Pommier à cidre et le cidre*, 1949), French cider production during the years 1920–1940 ran at an average of about 180 million liters, with a high of 345 million in 1938. Then there was the Second World War (1939–1945), which gave another strike to cider production. And during the postwar period, the government subsidized the removal of apple trees in order to promote modern intensive agriculture of more valuable crops, resulting in a further decline of cider production during the 1950s and '60s. Commercial production stopped completely in many regions, and it is only in some parts of Normandy and Brittany that small commercial production was kept alive. After a low during the 1970s, the profession started to revive during the 1980s, and growth has been continuous ever since.

In Brittany, it was the rise of the tourist industry at the end of 1970s that helped in the rebirth of cider. Restaurants and *crêperies* were offering rustic meals accompanied with local cider. The profession started to get organized with the foundation of the CIDREF (Comité Cidricole de Développement et de Recherche Fouesnantais et Finistérien) in 1980, and a fight to obtain a certification label for the *Cidre de Cornouaille*, which finally succeeded in 1996—simultaneously with the *Cidre du Pays d'Auge* in Normandy, which followed a quite similar path. In more recent years we have also seen the appearance of a growing number of small producers in other regions that formerly had important cider production, such as Picardie and the northeast, the Pays de la Loire, the Pays d'Othe (the whole of northern France really), and the Pays Basque on the border with Spain. In these areas, we are now seeing a comeback and the producers are reviving the ancient cider traditions of their respective regions.

There is an important center for cider research and development, the IFPC (Institut Français des Productions Cidricoles) in Sées, Normandy. Their team is involved in most domains related to cider and apple production, and a good part of their work is transferring knowledge to the producers. The website of the organization contains a lot of very useful documentation.* One of their scientists, Rémi Bauduin, is the author of an excellent booklet on traditional French cider making, *Guide pratique de la fabrication du cidre* (2006).

There are a great number of cider events in Normandy and Brittany, which are mostly small and local *fêtes du cidre et des pommes*

---

* Visit their website: www.ifpc.eu.

(cider and apple festivals) that feature different activities and sometimes cider competitions. One of the better known of these local festivals is in Fouesnant and hosts a cider competition created in 1905—one of the oldest. I had the chance to be a judge at this competition in 2016, and it was a great experience. Two regional cider competitions that are important are the Saint-Jean des cidres in Normandy, and the Concours régional de Bretagne. The main national competition is within the prestigious Concours général agricole in Paris, which has a section for cider and perry. Worth a mention here is a recently founded event, CidrExpo, which features a tasting salon and some conferences. The first CidrExpo was in February 2020 in Caen, and the organization has the ambition to make this a major international cider event. For travelers, there is a Route du cidre in Normandy, mostly around the town of Cambremer in the heart of Pays d'Auge, and one in Brittany, in the region of Cornouaille, which is managed by the CIDREF.

I have traveled quite a bit in the French ciderland as I was writing a French adaptation of my first book, titled *Du pommier au cidre* (2016). I thus had the opportunity to meet and interview a number of producers to make sure the book accurately reflected the French cider making practices. After the publication, I also went there once more for a promotional tour of the book! As a result, I now have many friends and acquaintances among the French cider producers. I will first say a special word for my friend and travel companion Mark Gleonec—author, storyteller, musician, cider taster, and currently president of CIDREF in Brittany—who introduced me to many producers and was the first reader of this chapter. Mark also traveled with me, visiting cideries in Germany, England, the United States, and Canada. Thus you will see quite a number of photos from him in this book. I would also like to thank the following cider people in France that I have visited, discussed or drunk cider with, and who have contributed to my understanding of French cider making: Régis Aubry (Cave de la Loterie), Éric Baron (Domaine Kerveguen), Pierre Brisset (Ferme du Vey), Jean-Marc Camus (Cidrerie de la Baie), Éric Bordelet, Christian Daniélou (Cidre François Séhédic), Guillaume Desfrièches (Le Père Jules), Hervé Duclos (Domaine Duclos-Fougeray), Gilles Goalabré

(Pressoir du Bélon), Vincent Godefroy (Écomusée de la pomme et du cidre), Claude Goenvec and his family (Cidrerie de Menez-Brug), Michel Legallois (Ferme de la Sapinière), Jean-François Leroux (Domaine du Ruisseau), Benoît Lesuffleur, Gilles Michaudel (Ferme du Chêne), Benoit Noël, Philippe Robert-Dantec, Brieug Saliou (Vergers de Kermao), Jen Scouarnec and Nicolas Mazeau (Cidre de Rozavern), Dominique and Nathalie Plessis (Cidrerie Traditionnelle du Perche), Hervé Seznec (Manoir du Kinkiz), Valérie Simard (CIDREF), Jean-François Vaultier (Ferme de la Commanderie), Guillaume Vauvrecy (Ferme de Billy), and Cyril Zangs (Cidre 2 Table).

Cider Styles and Certification Labels

Traditional French cider as a style is quite unique for its balance point of sweetness, acidity, and bitterness. It is the cider of all extremes: French ciders are in general lowest in acidity and highest in residual sweetness and in bitterness. Hence the balance is more between tannins and sweetness. Contrast this to the ciders from the rest of the world where the balance is rather between acidity and sweetness (see appendix A for a more elaborate discussion of acidity–tannin balance). The French balance point is a result of the pommages, which in France don't include many sharp or bittersharp varieties, and of the traditional cider making process, which produces an incomplete fermentation, thus leaving some unfermented residual sugar. This gives a characteristic natural fruit aroma that is different from what would be obtained in a cider fermented to dryness and then back-sweetened. The aroma may occassionally have strong funky notes, depending on the producer, but it always bears this particular aroma brought by bittersweet apples. The color of the traditional French ciders is normally quite pronounced, often of a deep amber with more or less of orange. This color is brought by the high tannin content from the apples. Another characteristic of French ciders is a lower alcoholic strength, due to the incomplete fermentation.

While most of the French ciders do correspond to this traditional style, there are a few distinct exceptions:

- The Pays d'Othe was an important cider production region in the beginning of the twentieth century that is currently seeing a revival of its cider tradition. The particularity here is that they have pommages that contain mostly sharp apples with little tannins. This results in a cider style that is very different, with less color, and a flavor that is rather acidulous.
- In the department of Morbihan, south of Brittany (the Pays Vannetais), there is a cider made with the apple variety Guil-levic, which is borderline between the sharp and bittersharp classes. This results in a cider that is sharper and less bitter than the mainstream production, and very light in color. Single-variety Guillevic ciders often bear a *Label Rouge* to certify the origin. These ciders are called Royal Guillevic.

And in recent years, we have seen the emergence of other cider styles in France, often influenced by trends that are popular in North American cider making, such as rosé ciders and flavored or hopped ciders.

Both PGI and PDO labels exist for French ciders. Let us first look at the PGI labels which are attributed to the two main regions of production: *Cidre de Normandie* and *Cidre de Bretagne*. These are fairly general labels, and they ensure the origin of the apples while giving a lot of latitude to the producer for processes and variety selection, most of the modern and industrial processes being permitted. In fact these PGI labels are perfectly adapted for large-scale industrial cider production. The cider produced under these PGI labels accounts for about 50 percent of the national production. The PDO labels for their part are more oriented toward craft cider making. These are exclusively for some well-defined subregions. In Normandy there are *Cidre du Pays d'Auge*, *Cidre du Cotentin*, and *Cidre du Perche* (this last one was just obtained in 2020: Jean-François Leroux, who is a producer from Perche, emailed me to tell the news as I was writing this chapter). There is also *Cidre du Pays de Caux*, which is currently in the process of obtaining the label. And in Brittany there is *Cidre de Cornouaille*. The two first regions to obtain the label in 1996 were *Cidre du Pays d'Auge* and *Cidre de Cornouaille* (at the time these were AOC labels). These PDOs have more stringent specifications than the PGIs. For example, carbonation and pasteurization are permitted under a PGI label, but forbidden under the PDO, which only recognizes in-bottle refermentation. Also, each of these PDOs has a specified pommage that restricts the varieties that may be used. These pommages include some varieties that are local to each particular region as well as some that are grown in all regions. The PDO specifications additionally have rules for orcharding practices, densities of planting, and yield. The amount of cider produced under these labels accounts for less than 10 percent of the total cider production.

Within the different PDOs of Normandy, there are but subtle differences in style and flavor. To be frank, one needs to be quite a good taster to be able to differentiate, for example, a *Cidre du Perche* from a *Cidre du Pays d'Auge* in a blind tasting. It is, however, easier to identify a *Cidre de Cornouaille*, as the Breton cider would normally be more bitter.

The Orchard

The French cider orchard is the largest in the world in terms of surface area. It covers about 9,000 hectares (22,000 acres) and the average production is on the order of 250,000 tons, which means there is an annual production of some 28 tons of apples per hectare (11 tons per acre). These are specialized cider orchards, mostly intensive or semi-intensive and professionally managed, operated by about 2,000 growers for whom cider apple culture is a significant part of their income. To this we need to add traditional, smaller and less productive, generally extensive orchards, for which there may be more than 10,000 part-time growers. The output from these isn't accounted for in the statistics just provided. The production from these part-time growers may vary from year to year and there are no official statistics, but we can easily assume they produce another 20,000 to 50,000 tons annually. These numbers are quite consistent with the current production of cider, fortified cider, and apple eau-de-vie, which require about 150 million liters of must: If we assume a yield of 700 liters of must per ton, we would then need 210,000 tons of apples to fulfill these needs. Another 60,000 tons is used for fresh apple juice, thus leaving up to 30,000 tons available for export in good years, mainly to Spain and England.

Figure 3.2. This beautiful traditional orchard is at Le Père Jules, in Pays d'Auge. The name is in honor of Jules Desfrièches who founded the cidery. When I visited, I met Jules's son, Léon (then 88 years old and still active in the cidery), grandson Thierry, and great-grandson Guillaume who now runs the business.

In my opinion, some of the most beautiful and bucolic orchards that may be seen on our planet are in Normandy. This region is also known for the quality of its milk, cream, and cheese. Many cider producers have a mixed farm where they also raise some grazing animals. Hence the traditional orchards are designed for both purposes of apple production and providing grazing land. The combination is for the benefit of both: The animals profit from the windfalls and the rich grasses and herbs, while the soil and the trees profit from the animal droppings. Plus the fact that windfalls are rapidly eaten is good for destroying insect larvae in the fruits.

Figure 3.3. A new plantation of high-stem trees at Cidrerie de Rozavern in Brittany. The graft for the fruiting variety can be seen on the leftmost tree.

The French orchard is quite unique in that a substantial percentage of the cider apple production is from traditional extensive orchards with standard size trees, and the French still plant such orchards on a significant scale. They are called *vergers haute-tige*, which means "high-stem orchards." These trees are produced with three sections by the nurseries: first is the root, provided by a standard-size rootstock, on which a special vigorous variety (often Président Descours) is grafted as a second section so a strong stem is quickly built, and then the fruiting variety is grafted at a height of 1.8 to 2 meters (6 to 6.5 feet) and provides the third section of the tree. One reason for this height is to accommodate the grazing animals. The trunks need to be high enough so the lowest branches are out of reach. The French also believe these lower-yield orchards produce higher-quality apples that are richer in sugar and in tannins. In fact, the specifications of the PDO labels require that a certain percentage of the orchards be of high-stem trees in low density plantings.

Naturally, not all the orchards follow this traditional model. Like everywhere else, semi-intensive bush orchards have been planted since

Figure 3.4. A mature semi-intensive orchard at Ferme de Billy near Caen in Normandy.

the 1980s. Most of them use the MM 106 rootstock at densities of 600 to 800 trees per hectare (240 to 320 per acre). These are called *basse-tige* or *demi-tige* (meaning "low stem" or "half stem"). The larger, industrial cideries get most of their apples from these higher-density orchards, but most smaller artisans who produce under a PDO label have at least part of their orchards as haute-tige, and quite a good number have exclusively haute-tige orchards.

For the traditional orchards, management is kept to a minimum, and on many there is no spraying at all. It is widely accepted that these orchards maintain a natural wildlife equilibrium that prevents catastrophic infestations. Thus there are a good number of producers who are fully organic (although not always certified). The more intensive orchards, however, need more management, and many producers follow IPM practices. At harvest time, the apples are collected on the ground, usually in three passes with some tree shaking before the last pass. Larger orchards use mechanical shakers and harvesters, while on smaller operations, the apples may be brought to the ground either by hand-shaking small trees or by using poles with a hook to shake branches in higher trees, and then the apples are collected by hand.

Apple Varieties

The French cider orchard is certainly one of the richest in terms of the number of varieties. In the book *Pommiers à cidre: Variétés de France* (1997), the authors Jean-Michel Boré and Jean Fleckinger give complete descriptions for 342 varieties, and they additionally refer to the names of about 800 more in the appendix. Considering that this book doesn't include many local varieties that I have seen at producers I have visited, we can only speculate about the total number of varieties that may be found in French orchards. Other useful pomological references include the works from nineteenth-century authors such as Truelle, Power, and de Boutteville and Hauchecorne, who I mentioned in the beginning of this chapter. For Brittany, an important work is by J. Crochetelle with his *Pomologie du Finistère* (1905) where nearly 500 Breton varieties of cider apples are described, and I will mention a recent book (2019) by my friend Mark Gleonec, *Pommes et cidre de Cornouaille*.

The French have a classification system for their apples that is quite similar to the English one:

> **Douce:** low acidity and low tannins, equivalent to *sweet*.
> **Douce-amère:** low acidity and medium tannins, equivalent to *mild bittersweet*.
> **Amère:** low acidity and high tannins, equivalent to *full bittersweet*.
> **Acidulée:** medium acidity and low tannins, equivalent to *mild sharp*.
> **Aigre:** high acidity and low tannins, equivalent to *full sharp*.
> **Aigre-amère:** medium to high acidity and medium to high tannins, equivalent to *bittersharp*. (Sometimes we also see **acidulée-amère** as a class with slightly less acidity.)

To make the following text easier to read, we will use the English equivalent class names.

The great majority of the French apple varieties are in the low acidity classes (sweet and bittersweet), which make up the most important part of the blends. Some sharp varieties are used to increase the acidity of blends, but bittersharps are very seldom seen (this is a major difference with the pommages in the English West Country, where some of the most highly praised apples are bittersharps). The relative proportion of different types of apples used varies between the different regions of production. In a typical Norman orchard, we could find 15 to 20 percent trees of sharp varieties, 65 to 70 percent of sweet and mild bittersweet varieties, and 10 to 15 percent of more bitter varieties (full bittersweet). In comparison, a typical orchard in Brittany would have less sharps (5 to 10 percent of the trees) and more of the strongly bitter varieties (30 percent or even more). This produces a noticeable difference between the ciders from the two regions. In general, the ciders from Brittany, and more particularly those from the region of Cornouaille, have more bitterness and less acidity than those from Normandy.

Within Normandy also there are variations in the relative amount of the different classes, with the ciders from Cotentin, Pays d'Auge, and Perche each having their own specificity and recommended pommages. It must be said, however, that a recent tendency is to increase the number of trees of sharp varieties in the orchards, as a way to reduce both the pH of the musts and the occurrence of the *framboisé* cider disease. In effect, typical musts often have a high pH in excess of 4.0, and some research shows that with a pH lower than 3.8 the framboisé does not occur anymore.

A limited number of varieties are considered national, and they are seen in all regions of Normandy and Brittany. These include Douce moën and Douce coët ligné, respectively a mild bittersweet and a sweet, and the two most popular and widely planted varieties. Other important ones include the bittersweets Kermerrien, Bisquet, Binet rouge, Fréquin rouge, Bedan, Marie Ménard, and the sharps Petit jaune, Judor, and Avrolles. These base varieties are usually grown side by side with local varieties that are characteristic of each specific region.

It is not really known how and when the first bittersweet varieties appeared in France. We know that already by 1550, Gilles de Gouberville had some varieties that he classified as bittersweet. And in 1588,

Julien Le Paulmier described a number that were grown in Normandy, including the Fréquin and the Bedan (respectively spelled Freschin and Bedengue in his book), as well as the Muscadet, Marin Onfroy, and a few others that still exist. There is some speculation that the first bittersweet varieties could have been imported from northern Spain, and there is some evidence that sustains this theory. There are old Norman varieties whose origin is quite clearly related to that region, for example the Bisquet that has as a synonym Biscaye—an ancient name given to the Basque Country—or the Marin Onfroy. Also in Le Paulmier we can read about a Monsieur de Lestre (whose actual name was Guillaume Dursus), who originated from Navarre but had a domain near Valognes in the Cotentin Peninsula of Normandy where he grew apples and made cider. Around the year 1500, this gentleman brought from northern Spain varieties such as Barbarie de Biscaye, Épicé, and the then famous Greffe de Monsieur variety, which apparently were superior to the existing varieties in the region. However, all this is only a small percentage of the Norman varieties, and we don't know how influential these imported varieties have been. We can't exclude the real possibility that most good bittersweet varieties would have appeared in France as natural seedlings and would have been selected and propagated by the people; and that these would have been complemented by a few introductions from Spain.

In Brittany, there is less documentation on the origin of ancient local cider varieties. Some old documents indicate that at the Abbaye de Landévennec, monks made variety selections by the fourteenth century. The pommages nowadays include very bitter varieties that are characteristic of Brittany and particularly of Cornouaille. Several dozens of these have within their name the word *c'hwerv* (meaning "bitter" in the Breton language, and also seen written as *c'hwero, chuero, fuero*). In a similar way as for Normandy, some authors have written these varieties came from northern Spain, but in this case it is harder to believe: First because such highly bitter apples aren't common in Spain, and second because in Brittany we don't find a documented relation between these varieties and Spain, of the sort just noted. I was once discussing the matter with Claude Goenvec (of Cidrerie de Menez-Brug near Fouesnant), who has done quite a bit of research on the Breton apples. He reckons this question is quite a mystery and will probably remain so. He is simply thankful that his region has such a rich heritage of apple varieties that are so unique.

Many relatively modern varieties were raised and introduced during the years 1850 to 1900. While during that period the scientists were busy with their research and publications, nurserymen also played an important role in the development of new, superior cider varieties. Pips were sown and the young trees selected for maximum sugar content and optimal chemical properties. Prizes were given to those nurserymen who produced the best. One such seedling that had been obtained by a M. Godard, a nurseryman near Rouen, won a gold medal in 1873 for its very high sugar content, and thus the new variety was named Médaille d'or. Other well-known and important varieties obtained during that period include Bramtot, Bedan des Parts, and Michelin from M. Legrand in Yvetot. Another nurseryman in Yvetot, M. Dieppois, for his part obtained the Reine des hâtives and Grise Dieppois. Many of these varieties were introduced to England during the 1880s and some, for example Michelin, became very popular there, while they never attained such popularity in France.

More recently, some controlled breeding was done during the 1950s by the INRA (Institut national de la recherche agronomique) in the course of a program to develop new apple varieties for processing. The following were introduced by the mid-1980s: Cidor, a bittersweet, and the sharp Judaine, Judeline, Judor, Juliana, and Jurella. Each name was chosen beginning with "Ci" or "Ju," depending on if the variety was destined to cider or fresh juice production. Interestingly, cider makers decided otherwise, and it is the sharp varieties Judor, Judaine, and Judeline that have been the most planted in cider orchards.

I list and describe here some of the best known of the French cider apple varieties, and will also include a few local ones that are characteristic of their respective region. Naturally, this will be only a very small subset of the pommages, and one of the references listed previously should be read for a more thorough coverage. It should also be noted that the French varieties have not been grown outside of Europe as much as the English ones, but we do find a small number of them in Australia and North America.

Avrolles (sharp) is a variety that originated in the Pays d'Othe. It is a typical traditional variety of that region that produces acidulous ciders with low tannin content, and it is certainly the best known from these pommages. Nowadays it is grown quite a lot in Normandy where it is used to add acidity to the musts. It is also called Pommate d'Avrolles, the word *pommate* being used in the naming of the sharp apples of the Pays d'Othe. The apple is small to medium in size and greenish-yellow with red stripes, and it ripens late. The acidity of the juice is very high at 10 to12 g/L (as malic acid) on average, while the tannin and sugar concentrations are respectively low and medium.

Bedan (bittersweet) is among the oldest varieties. It was described by Le Paulmier in 1588 under one of its numerous synonyms, which include Bedangue, Bec-d'âne, Bédane, and others. Apparently some mentions of this apple are even in old archives dating back to the 1360s. Naturally, as for all very old varieties, there may be variants of it, and it is not certain that the Bedan grown nowadays is identical to what was described in the ancient texts. Back in 1875, de Boutteville and Hauchecorne wrote the following: "Ancient variety whose origin is unknown, grown and highly praised in all departments of Normandy, Brittany and Picardie." The Bedan is still considered a fundamental variety for Normandy and is found in all the cider making regions. It is a mild bittersweet, with medium to high sugar content, medium tannins, and low acidity. The apple is mostly yellow when well ripe. It ripens late, and it is normally harvested by mid-November. A distinct variety, Bedan des Parts, was introduced in 1874 and might be a seedling of Bedan, as the two varieties have some characters in common.

Binet rouge (sweet to mild bittersweet) is an emblematic variety of Normandy. There is a family of Binet apples, which include Binet blanc (or doré), a few variants of Binet gris, and Binet violet. These are all relatively small apples, classified as sweets or bittersweets, which ripen late. Nowadays, the Binet rouge is by far the most common. It is a small red-on-green apple that produces a flavorful juice rich in sugar, low in acidity, and with medium tannin of relatively mild bitterness.

C'hwerv-brizh and **C'hwerv-ruz-mod-kozh** (bittersweet) are emblematic varieties of the Fouesnant region of Brittany, which will always find their way into the blends for the *Cidre de Cornouaille* PDO ciders. The C'hwerv apples are very important in Cornouaille. Mark Gleonec in his book *Pommes et cidre de Cornouaille* (2019) describes 48 of the most important varieties, of which 20 are C'hwerv. C'hwerv-brizh (the name means "bitter and striped") trees are hardy, large, and vigorous, and tend to drop their fruit a bit early. Thus the variety requires perfect timing from the cider maker for harvest and processing. When ideally ripened, the apples are among the best, with good sugar content, low acidity, and a marked bitterness. There are a few variants: The one that is more widely grown and known under this name was called C'hwerv-brizh-bras in older references, but apparently it lost the *bras* at some point (which indicated this was the larger variant). There is a C'hwerv-brizh-bihan, which is smaller, and a C'hwerv-brizh-ruz, which is redder. The C'hwerv-ruz-mod-kozh (this could

Figure 3.5. C'hwerv-ruz-mod-kozh apples waiting to be processed at Cidrerie de Menez-Brug in Brittany.

translate as "genuine" or "authentic red bitter" apple) is also a mid-season, full bittersweet apple, red with a conical shape. It adds to the color and structure of the cider. For making the traditional *Cru de Fouesnant* cider, these two varieties are often blended with Dous-bloc'hig, Trojenn-hir, and Avalou Beleien.

Clos Renaux (sweet to mild bittersweet) is one of the popular varieties with my friends in Normandy. This is a relatively modern variety, appearing by the 1930s in Upper Normandy. Clos Renaux would be borderline between the sweet and bittersweet classes: Most references classify it as a mild bittersweet, but some years and in some locations, the tannin concentration may be lower and the properties correspond to the sweet class. The sugar concentration is medium and the acidity is low. The ripening is late mid-season, and the apple is small to medium size, colored red on yellow.

Figure 3.6. Douce coët ligné apples. Photo by Mark Gleonec.

Douce coët ligné (sweet), also called Dous-Koed-Lignez or Dous-Koat-Lignez in different Breton dialects, is a variety that came from a natural seedling tree found in the department of Morbihan in the south of Brittany. It is currently one of the most planted in all regions of France, representing 11 percent of modern basse-tige (low-stem) orchards (second after Douce moën). It is appreciated for its good hardiness and that it facilitates the obtaining of a naturally sweet cider. The apple is quite large for a cider apple, mostly yellow, and ripens mid- to late season. The juice has a high concentration of sugar, is low in acidity, and is low to medium in tannin.

Figure 3.7. Douce moën apples.

Douce moën (mild bittersweet) was, according to Boré and Fleckinger (*Pommiers à cidre*), the most planted variety in all regions of France during the 1990s, representing about 12 percent of all plantings. Douce moën originated from the *terroir de l'Aven* in the south of Brittany, near the town of Quimperlé. It started to be spread in the area around the years 1880 and eventually was propagated in all regions of Brittany before gaining popularity in the whole of France. Within all my contacts among the cider making community in France, this variety is the most often recommended for planting when starting a cider orchard. The Douce moën apple is rather small, with a characteristic barrel shape, making it one of the easiest varieties to identify. The tree has medium vigour and excellent productivity, although in traditional orchards the trees may produce in alternating years. The blooming and the ripening seasons are medium-late, and the apples keep well. The juice is very nice, sweet, colored, and perfumed. The analyses show a high concentration of sugar, low of acid, and medium of tannins.

Fréquin rouge (full bittersweet) is the best known and most grown of the Fréquin family of French cider apples. They have a characteristic conical shape, a small to medium size, and a bitter-sweet flavor with marked bitterness. These are very old: Already in 1588 Le Paulmier described a *Pomme de freschin, douce-amère qui fait excellent cidre* (bittersweet that makes excellent cider), which might be the original from which the whole family originated. Various Fréquin, Friquet, Fraisquin, or Fréquet apples are mentioned or described in old texts, making this family of apples the most important in France. There are also reports that Frequen (Fréquin) apples were among the most grown in Jersey by 1800. Boré and Fleckinger mention in their book more than 40 varieties whose names contain the word *fréquin*. More specifically on Fréquin rouge, de Boutteville and Hauchecorne wrote in 1875 that it was an old variety of unknown origin, grown in all regions of Normandy and Brittany, but more particularly in the area of Yvetot in Upper Normandy. Fréquin rouge is an emblematic variety for Antoine Marois, an excellent craft maker in Pays d'Auge.

Guillevic (sharp) is an emblematic variety in the south of Morbihan (the Pays Vannetais) in Brittany, and is also popular in Cornouaille. It is often used to add a bit of acidity in the blends, which in these regions consist mostly in sweet and bittersweet apples. But its main fame comes from its use for making an excellent single-variety cider. It is one of the few apples to have a perfect balance, thus yielding a must that doesn't need to be blended. The tree is appreciated for its hardiness, and it has a good and regular production. The season for bloom and harvest is medium to late. The apple is a medium to large size, is greenish-yellow, and keeps well. The juice has almost no color, is rich in sugar and acids, and has low to medium tannins.

Judor (sharp) is a variety that was introduced in mid-1980s by the INRA. It is an open-pollinated seedling of Douce moën. Although it was first destined for fresh apple juice production, cider makers have adopted it as a high-quality apple to add acidity to their blends. It is currently the third most planted in modern bush orchards. No doubt its popularity is related to the recent tendency to increase the acidity of French ciders, which gives them more

Figure 3.8. Kermerrien apples from the author's orchard.

freshness and also resistance to spoiling microorganisms. This variety is mostly seen in Normandy but is also grown to a lesser extent in Brittany. The Judor tree is very vigorous and productive, quite maintenance-free, and relatively resistant to most pests. The apple is small to medium in size and ripens late, being usually harvested at the beginning of November. The juice has a nice fruity flavor, medium sugar concentration, medium to high acidity, and low tannins.

Kermerrien (bittersweet), also called Kêrmerien, is a Breton variety. It originated near Clohars-Carnoët in the south of Cornouaille by the middle or end of nineteenth century as a natural seedling, most probably from one of the numerous Fréquin varieties. One of its first known descriptions is from Truelle in 1893, who claims it is of the same group as the Fréquin rouge. It was also described by Crochetelle in 1905, who had a very high opinion of its quality. In those days, Kermerrien was considered a new variety of high merit. It would apparently have been named and propagated in the early 1890s by a M. Pilorgé, who had orchards in Quimperlé. From its very local status a century ago, the Kermerrien has now become one of the base varieties in the whole of Brittany and has even gained a place in Normandy orchards. It is planted a lot in modern, more intensive orchards. The apple is medium size and has the characteristic conical shape of the Fréquin apples. The color is yellow and pale red, with some russet around the stem cavity. The juice has typical bittersweet properties, with average sugar content, medium to high tannins, and low acidity.

Marie Ménard (full bittersweet) is an important and popular Breton variety that is now also grown by some producers in Normandy. The variety is famous for its marked bitterness that gives good structure to the ciders. It is from a natural seedling that was discovered on the farm of a lady named Marie Ménard, in the Côtes d'Armor, and began being propagated in the beginning of the twentieth century. The variety is triploid, ripens mid to late season, and shows little sensitivity to scab. The apples are of relatively large size. The juice is rich in sugar and tannins, with low acidity.

Marin Onfroy (mild bittersweet) is a variety mostly grown in the Bessin region of Normandy. According to old stories, this variety was brought to this region during the sixteenth century from the Basque Country by Marin Onfroy, a gentleman who was Seigneur de Saint-Laurent-sur-Mer et de Véret (*Seigneur* is similar title of nobility as a Lord). Truelle described it in his *Atlas* of 1896 and wrote he was pretty sure to have found its origin in the Macasgor-rya Basque variety. Marin Onfroy is an emblematic variety for Michel Legallois of Ferme de la Sapinière, a cidery at Saint-Laurent-sur-Mer (just by Omaha Beach) that I visited a few times. Michel told me that one historical reason he cherishes the variety is because Onfroy was the Seigneur of his village. The apple is medium to large in size, of orange-red color, and ripens late. The

Figure 3.9. Marie Ménard apples waiting to be processed at Cidrerie de Menez-Brug in Brittany.

juice is medium to high in sugar concentration, low in acidity, medium in tannins, and according to Michel, is relatively rich in nitrogen.

Mettais (full bittersweet) is from a seedling tree that was either raised or discovered around 1880 (we can read one or the other version in the literature) by Albert Mettais in Upper Normandy. It was first named Adrienne in honor of Mettais's daughter. This variety was highly praised by Warcollier, who in a paper published in 1935 noted its juice was among the slowest to ferment, thus facilitating the production of ciders that retained part of their natural sweetness. This is due to the naturally lower content of nitrogen in the juice when compared with other varieties. War-collier also noted the juice colored rapidly in contact with air, an indication of a high concentration of tannins, which change color by oxidation. This is a rather small apple, mostly red, that ripens mid- to late season. The juice has very high sugar concentration, is low in acid, and has bitter tannins. Nowadays it is mostly grown in Upper Normandy and the northern part of France, and also in Belgium.

Petit jaune (sharp) is an apple that is grown in all cider districts but is seen more often in Normandy. It originated in east Brittany (Pays de Nantes) and was described in 1866 in the proceedings of the *Congrès pour l'étude des fruits à cidre*. The variety is very productive and well adapted to modern, higher-density orchards. As its name claims in French, the apple is small and yellow. The crop is harvested by the end of October and may be processed up to the end of December. The juice has medium-high acidity, average sugar content, and low tannins. In addition to cider, Petit jaune is very popular for making fresh apple juice. In cider it is generally recommended not to exceed 10 percent in the blend.

Cider Making

Traditionally in France, the apples are left for a long period of sweating after harvest. However, modern mechanical harvesters tend to damage the apples, and so they don't keep as well. As a result, in order to minimize the losses, producers now tend to leave the apples for longer on the orchard ground, and press them quickly after collecting. Those producers that still collect by hand do, however, maintain the longer sweating period. This sweating may be in bins or in bags, or sometimes the apples are simply left in piles.

Figure 3.10. Sweating the apples, *from left to right*: in open piles at Pierre Huet in Normandy, in bags at Cidrerie de Menez-Brug in Brittany, and in wooden bins at Domaine Kervéguen in Brittany.

The pressing operations usually start around the beginning of November. This is traditionally called the *brassage* in France. The apples are sorted, washed, and milled, usually in a centrifugal mill. There is a very popular piece of equipment in France that combines the washing with an elevator and a mill on top (see a typical traditional French pressing line at Écomusée de la pomme et du cidre in figure 1.3 on page 23). The pulp is then left for maceration in a *conquet* (which is a large buffer container) for a period of a few hours to a full day—this varies with the producer and with the temperature: At higher temperatures, the maceration time should be kept shorter. The press is either a hydraulic rack and cloth or, in larger operations, a horizontal pneumatic model. There are only a few producers that use a belt press, but some have told me they don't like them as they think the quality of the juice is not as good and it will not keeve as readily.

The pre-fermentation processing is important to obtain the typical French cider that retains a good amount of residual sugar. The producers want a good clarification and a reduction of the natural nutrients, as these are the conditions that permit an adequate control on the speed of fermentation. The traditional way to achieve this is by keeving (described

Figure 3.11. Medium-size craft producers often use horizontal pneumatic presses, as these permit a good reduction of labor costs. This one is at Vergers de Kermao in Brittany.

in chapter 1). However, in recent years, keeves have failed more often than they used to. This is attributed to a combination of reasons that are explained in a paper by Bauduin and Le Quéré.* When such failures are only occasional, it is no big problem because the *cuvée* (the whole batch) may then be fermented to dryness and distilled for calvados or lambig. Some producers have, however, developed alternative methods to maximize the chances of success. At the Domaine Duclos-Fougeray, Hervé Duclos uses a flotation technique where he injects gas in the bottom of the tank, which provokes a more rapid rise (in one day) and a better compaction of the chapeau brun (brown cap). And some producers have completely abandoned the keeving process. For example, at Ferme de la Sapinière, Michel Legallois simply does a débourbage (pre-fermentation clarification) with complete enzymatic depectinization and clarification. This procedure is not as efficient in reducing the natural nutrients in the must, but he compensates by racking sooner and more often, and by filtering the yeast while racking.

Most French producers rely on the natural wild yeast for their fermentations. A small dosage of sulfite, about 50 ppm SO_2, is used by some before the fermentation. The tanks are most often fiberglass, either fixed or variable volume. We see stainless steel tanks, but more rarely. A number of producers still ferment in wood barrels. The fermentations are managed to maintain a slow and regular pace. The fermentation speed control is accomplished by racking, often complemented by filtering or centrifugation to reduce the yeast biomass if judged necessary. The technically oriented producers use a microscope to make a yeast count for a more precise management of the fermentation speed. Most cuvées are ready for bottling during spring.

French *cidre* is always sparkling, and most producers use the ancestral method. The most widely used bottle type is a lightweight, green-colored, champagne-type bottle, closed with a mushroom cork and wire cage. The preferred sweetness category is the demi-sec (medium), which contains between 28 and 42 g/L of residual sugar.

* Rémi Bauduin and Jean-Michel Quéré, "*Enquête sur la réussite de la clarification haute auprès des transformateurs,*" IFPC, December 2014. May be downloaded from the IFPC website: http://www.ifpc.eu/fileadmin/users/ifpc/infos_techniques/Art_clarification_haute_RPAC_37.pdf.

Figure 3.12. A display of Breton cider bottles for tasting at the CiderDays festival in 2015. Note the only clear bottle is the leftmost, which is a Guillevic single variety. All others are Cornouaille PDO.

To obtain this, they bottle the cider at a specific gravity (SG) between 1.017 and 1.024, and aim for a drop of approximately 4 points in the bottle. If the cider is bottled at a higher or lower gravity, it would then become a *doux* (sweet) or a *brut* (dry). Naturally, the speed of fermentation also needs to be just right at the moment the cider hits the target SG for bottling, and the cider has to be well clarified. Typically, neither sulfite nor anything else is added at bottling. To improve the reliability of the method, some producers do a yeast count before bottling and either filter part of the cider to reduce the yeast biomass or add dried yeast if the count is too low.

French ciders produced this way are great and may be sublime when kept in a cool cave, and ideally are drunk on the spot. However, these ciders often lack good stability: Too many times I have tasted undrinkable bottles (with an aroma about just as pleasant as that of old dirty socks) when they had traveled across an ocean and were kept in bad conditions. To overcome this problem, producers who are in the export market now often use some other method of bottling—for example, the Charmat, the transfer or the traditional method, often complemented by chemical stabilization. Another technique I have seen is to do a partial carbonation to about 2 bars (29 psi) as a complement to natural prise de mousse. Charmat and injection methods are not permitted by the PDO specifications, and producers who decide to go that route won't have the PDO label, but they still may use the PGI label.

CHAPTER FOUR

Spain
Sidra and *Sagardoa*

Spanish cider is produced in the north of the country—the main centers of production being in the Principality of Asturias where it is called *sidra*, and in the Basque Country where it is called *sagardo* or *sagardoa**—in cideries that are identified as *sidrería* or *sagardotegi* respectively. Sometimes also the word *llagar* is used, which really means the "press house." Most of the time, these cider houses serve some traditional food that pairs well with the cider. In addition, some cider is produced in Galicia, which is just west of Asturias, but the volumes are much smaller. In fact, Galicia does produce a lot of cider apples but exports most of them to Asturias and the Basque Country. Some Basque cider is also produced in France, in the

---

* When the "a" is added at the end of the word, it acts as an article meaning "the"—hence either form may be used depending on the context.

Figure 4.1. An advertisement in Cuba for Asturian *Sidra Champagne* in the mid-1950s. Illustration by Valle, Ballina y Fernandez, S.A. (Sidra El Gaitero).

French Basque Country, a region adjacent to the border with Spain, and where it is called *sagarno*. And let's not forget the word *apple*, which in Spanish is *manzana*, while in the Basque language it is *sagar* or *sagarra* according to the context.

Northern Spain is certainly one of the oldest poles of cider making tradition in Europe. Some ancient documents that refer to cider making in the region date back to the eighth century, and it is very plausible that cider was made earlier than that. I need to mention here that there is quite a bit of old historical literature, mostly originating from French authors, who claimed the Basque Country was the cradle of the cider making tradition in Europe. However, the oldest documents were found in Asturias and the evidence is that the true origin of Spanish cider culture would be Asturian rather than Basque. For my part, I am not a historian, and this book doesn't pretend to contribute to this historical debate. I will simply quote here my collaborator and friend Edu Coto, who studied the matter quite extensively. He wrote to me:

The Asturian cider culture has been widely neglected by cider historians, probably because they didn't have access to the proper historical references. I hope my great friends from Basque Country don't get offended, but maybe it's time to admit that the oldest cider-related documents discovered in Spain come from the region we know nowadays as Asturias, from the time there was an Asturian Kingdom that covered the whole of northern Spain and had its capital city in Oviedo. The Kingdom also included a big portion of what we now know as the Basque Country. Such documents mentioning orchards and vineyards meant to produce cider and wine first appeared around the year 800 in and around Oviedo, the heart of modern Asturias. And as the Kingdom expanded, its influence grew on the new territories. Also at that time, the Camino de Santiago de Compostela (The Way of Saint James) was created by the Asturian King, and had a huge influence due to the sharing of knowledge, information and culture between pilgrims from all of Europe. All this to say that it is only 200 to 300 years later that similar cider-related documents began to be more common in the Basque Country.

As in other European cider making regions, the heyday of cider production in Spain occurred by the end of the 1800s and first part of the 1900s, until the Spanish Civil War, which started in 1936. By the end of the nineteenth century, the annual cider production in Asturias was on the order of 25 million liters. During that period, in Asturias a cider style called *sidra champagne* was developed,* and it was produced in large quantities for domestic and export markets. Most countries of Spanish heritage in the Caribbean and in Central and South America, such as Cuba, Argentina, Chile, and Uruguay, were avid consumers of the Asturian sidra champagne. This cider is still produced and exported, but it cannot carry the name anymore, as the word *champagne* is now strictly reserved for the sparkling wine production of the Champagne region of France. We can easily see in

---

* Sidra champagne was first produced in 1857 by Tomás Zarracina in Gijón. It is interesting to note this is earlier than the development of cava sparkling wines, which started being produced in 1872 in Catalonia.

figure 4.1 that the packaging was designed as an almost perfect imitation of the true champagne.

In parallel, the cideries in Asturias make *sidra natural*. It is mostly for the local market, as this has always been a favorite drink of the people. The main centers of cider production in Asturias are around the towns of Villaviciosa, Nava, Siero, Sariego, Oviedo, and Gijón. Nowadays, Asturias has about 100 registered commercial-scale producers, plus an unknown number (some estimates run at about 1,000) of very small producers that may make a few thousand liters apiece and only distribute their cider locally or among their family and friends. Thus the total cider production is very difficult to evaluate precisely, as the small producers are not included in the statistics. The local Asturian market is unofficially estimated at around 40 million liters of sidra natural (and this is a pretty old number), but the total cider production is probably over 80 million liters if we take all forms of cider into account: the sparkling cider (nearly 40 million liters, the greater part of which is exported internationally or to other regions of Spain); the exports of sidra natural, which is becoming very popular in United States; the production from the small producers; and the other types of cider produced, such as ice cider. In fact, Asturias is considered the region of the world where people drink the most cider: With a population of 1 million and a local market of over 40 million liters, this amounts to more than 40 liters as the yearly average per person (and it could be more than that).

In the Basque Country, the main center of production is around the towns of Astigarraga and Hernani, near San Sebastian in the province of Gipuzkoa. Most of the cider is produced in that province, but smaller quantities are also produced in the other provinces of both the Spanish and the French Basque Countries. The cider production was estimated to be about 8 million liters before the Spanish Civil War (1930s), but it decreased during and after the war, down to a low of around 1 to 2 million liters annually during the 1970s. A renaissance began in the late 1970s and '80s, and since then cider production has picked up tremendously to reach a volume (in 2018) of about 12 million liters. Currently, some 60 cideries are registered with the Sagardoa Route organization. To this, we may add a number of smaller and very local cideries and a handful in the French Basque Country to bring the total of Basque cider producers to nearly 100. Many cideries were built during the 1980s and used some secondhand material (presses and large chestnut barrels) bought from Asturian cideries that, at that time, were going through a modernization and consolidation cycle.

I visited the cider making regions of Spain with my wife in the late summer of 2014. We were part of a delegation of 14 people interested in cider: cider makers, traders, authors, and bloggers from the US, Canada, and U.K. Among the better-known participants, we may note: Steve Wood and Nicole Leibon of Farnum Hill Ciders in New Hampshire; Mike Beck of Uncle John's Cider Mill in Michigan and former president of the American Cider Association (ACA); Ben Watson, who is a book author and my editor at Chelsea Green Publishing; Bill Bradshaw, the photographer and author from U.K.; and Brian Rutzen of The Northman in Chicago. The tour was organized by Eduardo Vázquez Coto (better known as "Edu" Coto) and Begoña Medio. Edu is a cider taster and blogger who has been a judge at many international competitions, and whom I met when we were both at the 2014 GLINTCAP (Great Lakes International Cider and Perry Competition) in Michigan. He now runs, since 2015, a cider trade business, Guerrilla Imports. He is also deeply involved in important cider-related events in both the Basque Country and Asturias (as well as in Germany where he lived and worked 11 years), and he participates in the promotion of the cider culture. Edu knows everybody in the Spanish and German ciderlands, and he helped me in the writing of this chapter. For her part, Begoña is in the travel and tourism business, and she organizes cider tours.

It is important to understand that the cider culture is a very serious thing in northern Spain and is truly unique. Nowhere else in the world is cider present everywhere, and nowhere does it draw so much attention from the general public via many festivals and events in towns and villages, such as cider competitions, parades, music, and fiestas, the peak of which is the Fiesta de la Sidra Natural in Gijón at the end of August. When walking around in any city, we can see sidrerías on almost every block, where people eat traditional food and drink cider. In the Basque Country, there is an important event every second year in November, the Sagardo Forum in Hernani, which offers conferences and a cider competition. This event draws many cider specialists from all parts of the Cider Planet. In Asturias, we have the SISGA (Salón Internacional de les Sidres de Gala) in September, which is a fair coupled with a cider competition.

A remarkable feature of the Spanish cider culture is the way cider is poured, from overhead while holding the glass low—this is called *escanciar* in Spanish, while the person making the pour is the *escanciador*. The following description was written by Edu Coto:

Figure 4.2. *El Arbol de la Sidra* (The cider tree) in Gijón is a sculpture made with 3,200 empty bottles of cider. According to the artist, this cider tree is a metaphor for the tree of life. It is the visual representation of how it is possible to conserve nature's resources by reusing everyday objects.

Figure 4.3. A parade with musicians in traditional costumes during the Fiesta de la Sidra Natural in Gijón.

The traditional skill of pouring of Asturian cider is unique. The bottle is held in one hand with the arm reaching as high as possible. The glass is held, at an angle, in the other hand with the arm stretched down as low as possible. The cider is carefully poured so that a thin stream of liquid drops from a height into the tip of the glass. Only a small amount of cider is poured, just enough to be consumed in one or two mouthfuls. The aim is to release the endogenous carbon dioxide in the cider, and to volatilize part of the acetic acid.

I can testify that pouring cider this way without spilling most of it on the floor does require a lot of skill—and there are even competitions for the best escanciadores. To make the pouring easier, one can use a small gadget that is fitted on the bottle neck to help the pouring, called a *tapón escanciador*. Alternatively, there also exist some electric pourers.

Figure 4.5. These escanciadores are pouring for the cider competition during the Fiesta de la Sidra Natural. Note the bottles are wrapped in aluminum foil so the judges can't see the name of the cider they are going to taste.

Figure 4.4. Pouring at a cider booth during the Fiesta de la Sidra Natural in Gijón.

Another spectacular way of serving the cider is by tapping a cask, from which a stream of cider gushes out and is caught with the glass. In fact, this is the original way to serve the cider, as the bottling of cider is a relatively modern invention. This ritual is called *txotx* in Basque Country and *espicha* in Asturias. The txotx (pronounced "choch") season in the Basque Country runs from midwinter when the first barrels complete their fermentation up until the end of spring. Originally the idea was to let traders taste the cider so they could decide which barrel they wanted to buy, but nowadays this has become an event where people come to eat traditional food while tasting the fresh cider. The word *txotx* itself originally meant the small stick of wood that is used for sealing the hole by which cider pours from the barrel. These peculiar ways of serving the cider do have good reasons for their use. As mentioned by Edu, it permits aeration of the cider, and as the cider hits the side of the glass, the impact liberates the dissolved carbon dioxide (CO_2) gas. This is amplified by the design of the glass itself, which is very thin and vibrates as the cider hits it.

Figure 4.6. The txotx at Petritegi in Astigarraga. We see here Bill Bradshaw, a well-known professional photographer of the Cider Planet, trying to keep his camera away from the gush of cider. Most cider afficionados have seen some photos from Bill, and this book does include a few.

Figure 4.7. The tap on a barrel, at Trabanco.

Figure 4.8. During the txotx or espicha, the cider violently hits the side of the glass, thus aerating it and liberating the dissolved carbon dioxide gas.

Figure 4.9. Members of the Buena Cofradía de los Siceratores de Asturias, with the author and his wife at the Sidra El Gaitero.

We can't conclude this section about the cider traditions without a mention of the Buena Cofradía de los Siceratores de Asturias, a merry association that was founded in the town of Nava and has as its main objective the promotion of Asturian cider. Members of this *confrerie*, with their easily recognizable clothing, are often present at cider events all around Asturias. They have songs and rituals that make any event a memorable one.

Certification of Origin Labels

Both the Basque Country and Asturias have their own PDO labels for cider (in Spanish they are known as DOP, for Denominación de Origen Protegida). The most recent is the Basque label, Euskal Sagardoa (meaning Natural Cider from the Basque Country), which started being used with the 2016 crop but is still not yet officially approved by the European Union. Nonetheless, most producers do adhere to the

(continued on page 135)

Collaborators and Cideries Visited

A number of people have contributed to the writing of this chapter. I already introduced Edu Coto, the organizer of our tour in Spanish ciderland. In addition to Edu, I wish to mention and thank:

Miguel Ángel Pereda Rodríguez is a small-scale cider maker and the author of a book on cider making, *Elaboración de sidra natural ecológica*, published in 2011. This is a very good book on cider making in general, and it's well anchored on good science. It mostly addresses the making of purely natural traditional Spanish cider, without yeast or sulfite addition. Miguel Ángel is a long-time correspondent, and I finally had the pleasure to meet him and his wife during our tour. His main contribution is on Asturian cider.

Mikel Baleztena is my main collaborator for Basque cider. He works with the Bereziartua Sagardotegia in Astigarraga. I met him first during our Spanish tour, and again at the 2018 Cider-World fair in Frankfurt. He is not himself a cider maker, but he is the sort of person who always knows someone who will have the answer to my questions.

During our 2014 tour we visited a number of cideries that were all of a good size, the smaller ones having a production capacity of just under a million liters annually. These were chosen to give us a good sampling of the high-quality producers of the region. It should be understood, however, that there are many small and very small producers who also make high-quality ciders.

In the Basque Country we stayed around the town of Astigarraga, which is an important center of cider making for the region. We were first welcomed at the Museo de la Sidra Vasca (Basque Cider Museum) for an introduction to Basque cider. There was a demonstration orchard and some old traditional cider making equipment. The cideries we visited:

Figure 4.10. Steve Wood contemplating a 20,000 liter chestnut barrel at Petritegi. The size of these barrels (and the number of them in a typical sagardotegi or sidrería) is quite striking.

Zapiain is the second largest Basque producer, with a production at the time of our visit of around one and a half million liters annually. This is also a very ancient cidery, with historical mentions dating back to the year 1695.

Petritegi is an important producer with about three-quarters of a million liters.

Bereziartua was established in Astigarraga in 1870. Their production runs at a bit over a million liters.

These three cideries were very impressive. We saw our first specimens of the traditional wooden vats made of chestnut or oak, which are really huge: Each one can contain up to 20,000 liters. They are

Figure 4.11. This beautiful house in the town of Nava clearly states this is *the* place for cider!

often stacked in two rows face to face in very large cellars. And in addition to these cideries, I visited on my own the Txopinondo cidery in Ascain, France, which is much smaller than those just noted and is owned by Jon and Dominic Lagadec.

The second part of the tour was in Asturias, where we visited cideries around the towns of Villaviciosa, Nava, and Gijón. In Nava there is also a very nice museum (El Museo de la Sidra de Asturias) which is definitely worth a visit. We visited:

Trabanco is an important cidery founded in 1925, and it is the largest producer of sidra natural in Spain. Their traditional production site is in Lavandera near Gijón, and they have a second production site in Sariego that mostly produces more modern-style ciders. We had the chance to meet Samuel Trabanco, a man with a great sense of humor who toured us through the most unusual cellar in an ancient mine tunnel and invited us for a truly gastronomic dinner.

Llagar Castañón in Villaviciosa was founded in 1938 by Alfredo Garcia Menendez. The present owners are Julián Garcia Castañón and his charming wife, with whom I had a very pleasant conversation with my rudimentary knowledge of Spanish. They produce the Val de Boides, a highly regarded sidra natural DOP.

Mayador in Villaviciosa is a large and industrial-type cidery. It isn't organized for touristic visits, hence it doesn't have the charm of the other sites we saw. They produce traditional sidra natural as well as some industrial ciders.

Valle, Ballina y Fernandez (Sidra El Gaitero), established in 1890 in Villaviciosa, is the largest producer in Spain, with a current capacity on the order of 25 million liters, of which a large part is sparkling cider. Just imagine: In one cellar, there were 93 tanks, each with a capacity of 56,000 liters. A quick calculation tells us this is a capacity slightly more than 5 million liters in just one room—and there was another (slightly smaller) cellar in the next building. This producer was already famous at the beginning of the twentieth century, as they produced and exported large quantities of El Gaitero Sidra Champagne. There is a rich history about this cidery that is told in a beautiful book: *Valle, Ballina y Fernández S.A.: Historia de una empresa*, by Francisco Crabiffosse Cuesta, published in 2010, and from which I extracted this image of "El Gaitero."

Viuda de Angelón in Nava is one of the smaller producers we visited in Asturias, with "only" a million liters annually. It has been active since 1947. To our surprise, we tasted there a very nice ice cider that was on par with most ice ciders from the cold regions of North America.

Figure 4.12. El Gaitero (the piper) became the iconic representation for the cider produced by Valle, Ballina y Fernandez. Illustration by Valle, Ballina y Fernandez, S.A. (Sidra El Gaitero).

specification, and while they still aren't allowed to use the official EU label, they have designed one that is recognized in Spain. In Asturias, the PDO label Sidra de Asturias has been in existence since 2005 and was modified in 2018. The specifications of both these labels define a list of approved cider apple varieties that should be grown locally in their respective region, some norms on orcharding practices, and how the cider should be produced. They also dictate ranges of values for properties such as sugar, alcohol, volatile acidity, and the testing required for the cider to be approved and allowed to bear the label. At this moment, the number of bottles produced under the PDO labels in both regions is still quite small (on the order of 10 percent in Asturias, for example) for a number of reasons that are discussed later in this chapter. Some work is being done to increase this proportion.

The Orchard

The first thing that struck me during our visit to Spanish ciderland is the landscape of these regions. The word that comes to mind is *bumpy*. There are hills everywhere, and it seems to be very difficult to find even a small piece of land that is flat. When driving, you are always either turning as

Figure 4.13. Typical hilly landscape in Asturias, as seen from the Trabanco cidery near Gijón.

you go around a bump, or you are going up or down, or you are going through the bump in a tunnel. . . . Hence for orcharding there are essentially two options: slopy or very slopy. This makes it extremely difficult to use large-scale intensive orcharding practices such as seen in other apple growing regions. And in effect, most orchards we saw were rather small (less than one acre, or half a hectare), mostly of high-stem standard trees on relatively large spacing. Traditionally, such orchards had mixed use, as the land was also used for livestock pasture. I was actually laughing with Steve Wood one day, pretending that for harvesting you would simply have to shake the trees and all the apples would roll down the slope to be picked at the bottom! But it doesn't quite work that way. . . . And simply going through the orchard with a tractor for spraying appears like an almost impossible task in many locations.

There are a number of reasons that explain the scattering of the orchard into dispersed small plots. First, appropriate flat areas of a decent size are extremely scarce and very valuable. A second reason, which Edu Coto told me about, is that through recent history a lot of subdividing of the land into smaller lots has occurred, thus making it increasingly difficult to have an orchard large enough to justify the higher equipment costs associated with more intensive culture.

Both the Basque Country and Asturias are in deficit of apples for the cider produced. For example, Asturias has approximately 6,500 hectares of cider apple orchards, with most being the traditional type with standard trees—sometimes aging, neglected, and giving poor crops. These orchards may yield some 25,000 to 35,000 tons of apples on average (although there are no official statistics for this), with important variations from year to year. This yield is largely insufficient for the quantity of cider produced. (One would need some 60,000 to 70,000 tons of apples to produce 40 million liters of cider.) Thus, for large cideries, apples need to be imported: The percentage of imported apples needed may range from 35 to 85 percent depending on the crop in a particular year. The situation is quite similar in the Basque Country, and from what I was told, the apple deficit is of the same order of magnitude. One apple grower with whom I spoke mentioned that the neighboring province of Galicia is an important provider of apples for both Asturian and Basque cideries, and apples are also imported from many other countries of Europe. France (mostly Normandy) and Poland are important sources. It is pertinent to mention, however, that local administrations now encourage the rejuvenation of old orchards and the planting of apple trees, and hopefully in a not-too-distant future, the importation of cider apples would become the exception rather than the norm. In the meantime, however, this deficit in locally grown cider apples limits the amount of cider that may be produced and sold under the respective PDO labels, as the cider produced with imported apples can't bear the label.

We note that in the Basque Country the Euskal Sagardoa PDO specification permits the culture of dwarf apple trees with densities of up to 2,200 trees per hectare (900 per acre) for intensive orchards. However this is not permitted in Asturias, where the maximum tree density permitted by the Sidra de Asturia PDO is 921 trees per hectare (370 per acre), with trees on semidwarf rootstocks such as MM 106 or M 7. This corresponds to the bush type orchards we see a lot in France and in England. Naturally, ciders that do not bear the PDO label are not subjected to those limits.

Apple Varieties

Although the Basque Country and Asturias are neighbors, we don't find the same cider apple varieties in the two regions. The Basques and the Asturians each have their own specific pommages. And even the French Basque Country has varieties that are different from those grown on the Spanish side. The approved pommages for the PDO labels are somewhat restrictive and contain only a very small subset of the very rich pomona of the region, which may contain thousands of distinct varieties, most being local and grown only at a very small scale. The lists of authorized varieties are an effort to select the best ones to achieve a high standard of quality for the PDO ciders. This limitation has two effects: The first is that cider makers who have unauthorized varieties in their orchards will not be allowed to make ciders that will bear the PDO label; and the second is that new plantings are almost exclusively of the approved varieties, which in turn risks the loss of some valuable, unapproved varieties in the long term and reduces genetic diversity.

Many varieties of both regions ripen very late, sometimes as late as the end of November or even December. This is a natural result of the selections that were made to account for the mildness of the climate in September and October in Spain, which is too warm to initiate the cider making process. Hence there is great advantage to having apples that ripen very late so they can be processed when the temperatures get colder. It may be pertinent to mention that I have seen citrus fruit trees and palm trees growing on the same locations as apple orchards, thus giving a clear indication that the temperatures never get really cold in those districts.

Basque Country

The Euskal Sagardoa PDO specification indicates a list of 115 authorized cider apple varieties, of which 24 are considered the most important. These 24 varieties currently represent about 75 percent of the cider apple production, but the aim is to concentrate new plantings with them in order to eventually reach 85 percent of the production. They are listed here with their respective flavor classification:

- **Ácida** class (higher in acid and lower in tannins, equivalent to *sharp*): Errezila, Goikoetxe, Txalaka, Urtebi Haundi, Verde Agria, Bostkantoi, Haritza, Azpeiti Sagarra, Manttoni, Ibarra.
- **Amarga** class (lower in acid and higher in tannins, equivalent to *bittersweet*): Gezamiña, Urdin, Mozoloa, Patzuloa, Mikatza, Udare Marroi, Txori Sagarra.
- **Ácida-amarga** class (higher in both acid and tannins, equivalent to *bittersharp*): Moko, Limoi, Merabi, Mokote, Urtebete, Urtebi Txiki, Saltxipi.

As previously, we will use the English equivalent class names to make the following text easier to read.

There isn't much documentation on the Basque cider apple varieties. To the best of my knowledge, an extensive reference has not yet been published. I was able to find some bits of information from my contacts and from the internet for a few of the most popular varieties. Some of the photos were taken by my friend Mark Gleonec from a display at the Sagardo Forum in 2017. Here we will list some of the better-known varieties.

Anisha (sharp) is a variety that is grown in the French Basque Country, where it is one of the best known of the traditional varieties. It is used for cider and as a table fruit. This is a small russeted apple that ripens relatively early but keeps well for use in cider. The juice is high in acid and sugar, with a hint of aniseed flavor.

Errezila (sharp), also called Reineta, is a medium-size russet apple of green-brown or greyish color with rough skin.

Figure 4.14. Anisha apples.

Figure 4.15. Mamula apples in a French Basque orchard. This variety is closely related and quite similar to the Gezamiña.

Figure 4.16. Mozolua apples. Photo by Mark Gleonec.

It is one of the most widely grown varieties, and also one of the few to be known outside of the Basque Country. It ripens late, by the beginning of December. The sugar content is very high, and so is the acidity (which ranges from 10 to 12 g/L as malic acid), while the tannin content, although relatively low, is still enough to provide light bitterness. The Errezila is also used for eating and cooking.

Gezamiña (bittersweet) is a large green apple with skin that becomes greasy. It is a heavy annual producer; its fruit ripens in the second half of October. The acidity is very low, and the tannin content is medium to high. My friend Alain Borda, who is Basque from France, explained to me once that the Geza apples are in fact a family of very similar varieties that also include the Mamula apples, popular in the French Basque Country. In general these are lightly colored (white or light yellow-green), large apples with a sweet flesh, little acidity, and some tannic bite.

Goikoetxe (sharp) is a large apple, red-striped on a green background. The tree is productive, with alternating production years, and needs thinning. The apples ripen in the second half of October. The juice is well balanced, colored, with good sugar, medium acidity, and low to medium tannins.

Moko (bittersharp) is a medium-large, green and red apple. The production is quite regular, with the fruit ripening in the first half of October. Both the acidity and the tannins are very high, and the variety is mostly used for making adjustments to the musts.

Mozolua (bittersweet) is a very large, green-yellow apple with rough skin. An alternate-bearing variety (produces fruit in alternate years), it ripens end of October. This variety gives sweet juice with low acidity and a medium tannin content.

Txalaka (sharp) is a medium to large green apple, very juicy with relatively little aroma. It is productive and bears annually, and the fruit ripens during the first half of October. Its juice is quite acidic, high in sugar, low in tannin, and lightly colored.

Figure 4.17. Txalaka apples. Photo by Mark Gleonec.

Urtebi Haundi (sharp) is a green-yellow, juicy apple of large size. The trees are big, productive every year, and the apples ripen by end of October. The juice is lightly colored, has medium to high acidity, and is low in tannins.

Urtebi Txiki (bittersharp) is a medium to large green-yellow apple. It is a good producer but only bears every other year. The fruit ripens in early November. The acidity and tannin content are medium, making it a well-balanced apple.

Asturias

The specification for the PDO Sidra de Asturias gives a list of 76 authorized cider apple varieties that are grown in Asturias. It should be noted that in the original specification from 2005, only 22 varieties were permitted in the making of ciders with the PDO label. This was, however, considered too restrictive by many producers, and in 2018 an amendment to the specification added 54 varieties to the list. Some of these newly approved varieties are traditional, often local, varieties that had not been included in the original specification for different reasons, while others are recently introduced cultivars from breeding programs.

Table 4.1. Cider Apple Classification in Asturias

	Acid < 4.9 g/L (low)	4.9 g/L < Acid < 6.6 g/L (medium)	Acid > 6.6 g/L (high)
Tannin > 2 g/L (high)	Amarga (full bittersweet) 3 varieties	Amarga-semiácida (bitter mildly sharp) 2 varieties	Amarga-ácida (full bittersharp) 4 varieties
1.45 g/L < Tannin < 2 g/L (medium)	Dulce-amarga (mild bittersweet) 3 varieties	Semiácida-amarga (mild bittersharp) 2 varieties	Ácida-amarga (sharp mildly bitter) 5 varieties
Tannin < 1.45 g/L (low)	Dulce (sweet) 11 varieties	Semiácida (mild sharp) 17 varieties	Ácida (full sharp) 29 varieties

The Asturians have a very complete classification system for their varieties, which contains nine categories defined in function of the acidity and tannin concentration of the juices. They are shown in table 4.1 with the number of corresponding varieties in the PDO specification list, where the tannins are expressed in g/L of tannic acid, and the acidities are in g/L as malic acid equivalent.

It is interesting to note that three-quarters of the varieties are in the *dulce* (sweet), *semiácida* (mild sharp), or *ácida* (full sharp) classes, thus indicating a low value for tannin content.

There is some excellent documentation on the 22 varieties that were listed in the original specification of the PDO, as these have been extensively studied and characterized by the SERIDA.* The publication *Descripción de las variedades de manzana de la D.O.P. Sidra de Asturias* by Enrique Dapena de la Fuente and María Dolores Blázquez Noguero, published by SERIDA in 2009, gives complete descriptions, technical data, and pictures for each of these varieties. Such work hasn't been completed yet for the 54 newly added varieties, but I would think this will probably be done in the near future.

Following are short descriptions of a few important varieties chosen among the most popular and most recommended by my collaborator Miguel Ángel Pereda Rodríguez.

Carrió (mild sharp) is a medium-size apple, mostly red over a green-yellow background, with some russeting. The tree, vigorous and productive, ripens its fruit late, by the middle of November. The juice has high to very high concentration in sugar, low to medium acidity, and low to medium tannin content.

Collaos (mild sharp) is small to medium size and has a conical shape. Its color is green with some russet in the stem cavity. It ripens late, by the end of November. The tree has medium vigor, good

---

* SERIDA (Servicio Regional de Investigación y Desarrollo Agroalimentario) is a public organization for research and development in agriculture (and they do a lot on cider apple culture) for Asturias. Their website (www.serida.org) contains many valuable documents that may be downloaded.

Figure 4.18. Fuentes apples.

productivity, and average alternant bearing tendencies. The juice has low concentrations of sugar and tannins, with medium to high acidity.

Durona de Tresali (full sharp to sharp mildly bitter) is a medium-size greenish-yellow apple that ripens by the end of November. The tree has very little sensitivity to major sicknesses and is vigorous and productive. The juice has fairly low sugar, good acidity, and slight bitterness.

Fuentes (full sharp) is a mostly brownish-red apple of small to medium size that ripens late, by mid-November. The tree is very vigorous and has a good productivity. It is moderately prone to alternant bearing. The juice has low sugar and tannin contents, and high to very high acidity.

Limón Montés (full sharp) is a medium-size apple of greenish-yellow color. The tree has medium vigor, average productivity, good resistance to sicknesses, and ripens its fruits by mid-November. The juice is relatively low in sugar and in tannins, and high in acidity.

Raxao (full sharp) is medium-size apple with a flat to conical shape. The color is red-striped with some russet in the stem cavity. The tree is vigorous, has good productivity, but is alternate bearing. The apples ripen in the first half of November. The juice is relatively low in sugar and in tannins, and high in acid.

Regona (sharp mildly bitter) is a green apple of medium to small size that ripens by mid-November. The tree has medium vigor, good productivity, but is subject to alternate bearing. The juice has relatively low sugar, high to very high acidity, and a medium concentration of tannins.

Verdialona (sweet) is an apple of small to medium size, green-yellow in color with some russet in the eye cavity. It ripens by mid-November. The tree has good and regular productivity. The juice has medium richness in sugar and is low in acid and tannins.

Cider Styles

The cider styles we find in Spain are fairly well defined by the specifications of the two PDO labels we mentioned earlier.

In Asturias, distinct types of cider are defined by the PDO Sidra de Asturias: Sidra, which is sparkling (*sidra espumosa*) and is actually a modern interpretation of sidra champagne we saw in the beginning of this chapter, and sidra natural, which may be of the traditional style or of the *nueva expresión* (more modern) style. Hence we have:

Sidra natural tradicional is the ubiquitous traditional cider that is normally poured from overhead. This cider is still or perlant (very slightly pétillant); it is not filtered and thus some cloudiness and sediment is normal. In fact, the escandiador will shake the bottle before opening and pouring it. Sidra natural tradicional is produced without addition of sugar, CO_2, or other additives, and is dry because the fermentation is complete. The color is pale with some straw-yellow, and the flavor is sharp and fresh, often with citric and floral aromas, in balance with some slight bitterness and astringency. This cider is presented in a distinctive green glass bottle closed with a cork.

Sidra natural nueva expresión is a more recent development where the cider is to be served and consumed as a fine wine (hence it is not poured by an escanciador). It is similar to the traditional style except for the final processing, where it is filtered and stabilized to ensure perfect clarity and a longer shelf life. The bottles used are also more wine-like, altogether making this a premium product.

Sidra [espumosa], the sparkling cider, which may be *seca*, *semiseca*, or *dulce*—corresponding respectively to dry with less than 30 g/L of residual sugar, medium with 30 to 50 g/L of sugar, and sweet with 50 to 80 g/L of sugar. For this style, it is permitted to back-sweeten the cider prior to bottling. The carbonation may be obtained by in-bottle fermentation (the same process as for cava sparkling wines, which is the traditional method), by the Char-mat method, or by the injection method. The CO_2 pressure in bottle at 20°C (68°F) should be higher than 3 bars (44 psi). Champenoise bottles with a mushroom cork are normally used for this cider style.

In all cases, if the cider is to have the Sidra de Asturias PDO label, it should have the following properties: alcoholic strength at 5 percent ABV minimum (they usually run at around 6 percent), volatile acidity lower than 2.0 g/L (expressed as acetic acid), and total SO_2 lower than 150 ppm for sidra natural, and lower than 200 ppm for sidra.

In the Basque Country, the only defined cider style is the sagar-doa, which is a traditional sidra natural that shares many common points with the one from Asturias but with its own distinct personality and flavor. From the specification of the Euskal Sagardoa PDO, this cider is made using traditional Basque cider making methods, is unfiltered and may be slightly cloudy, has a yellowish to yellowish-golden color, and has some integrated CO_2 (although it remains still or only slightly perlant). Its characteristic aroma and flavor profile should feature a balance between the sharpness from the acidity of the apples and some bitterness from the phenolic compounds. The cider is dry, with less than 4 g/L of residual sugar. The volatile acidity should be lower than 2.2 g/L (expressed as acetic acid), the total SO_2 lower than 100 ppm, and the alcoholic strength higher than 5 percent ABV. All producers use a green glass bottle model, which is more elongated than the one used in Asturias.

It is worthwhile to elaborate on the question of the permitted levels of volatile acidity. As we just saw, these levels are limited to 2.0

and 2.2 g/L respectively for Asturian and Basque ciders, levels that are much higher than what is permitted, for example, in France for their cidre, where the limit is set at 1.0 g/L. True, most Spanish ciders will have lower levels than the maximum permitted, but they often run somewhere between 1.0 and 1.5 g/L, and as such would almost inevitably exceed the maximum permissible in France.

This volatile acidity we find in Spanish ciders is a result of the traditional cider making practices, which we will see next. These

Figure 4.19. This is the standard bottle used by all cideries in Asturias for the traditional cider, and it is returnable for reuse. (The photo shows the Val de Boides traditional sidra natural produced by Llagar Castañón. Note the DOP label, the lower label of the left bottle.)

Figure 4.20. Pomarina is a trademark of Valle, Ballina y Fernandez for their more modern-style ciders. *On the left*, a sidra natural *nueva expresión* that uses a bottle of proprietary design, and *on the right* a *Sidra espumosa* that uses a champenoise bottle.

Figure 4.21. A lineup of sagardoa bottles at the Astigarraga museum. Note the one bottle with a screw cap while all others have corks. That one is the Txopinondo from France.

practices give the cider its characteristic sharp and slightly acetic flavor. It is, however, important to understand this flavor is very different from that of vinegar, although excessive concentrations may effectively give a quite harsh flavor and throat-burning sensation reminiscent of vinegar. I have heard of cider makers who thought one simply had to mix a bit of vinegar into normal cider in order to imitate the Spanish cider style. May I dare say this is wrong? Hopefully the description that follows will be sufficient to convince readers that there is a lot more to it.

Cider Making

Cider making in northern Spain has some interesting particularities that we will try to highlight here. As mentioned previously, the production is split between some important producers who use more modern technologies in their practices, and a large number of small producers who mostly adhere to more ancient and traditional practices. It should also be said that, in my opinion, the sidra natural and sagardoa styles of cider are probably the most difficult to imitate outside of their respective regions of origin. This is a consequence of many factors: the pommages used in the two regions, with apple varieties (and flavors) that are not found anywhere else; the traditional pressing, where the pomace remains under the press for days; the extremely rich natural flora of microorganisms that interact with the cider; and the climate in fall, which is milder than in other cider-producing regions, thus promoting a malolactic transformation during the early stages of the fermentation process.

Fruit Handling

The apples are generally collected on the ground. The trees are shaken and long sticks are used to make the apples fall from higher branches. As most of the orchards are small and on slopy ground, mechanical harvesting is not in general use, and most apples are collected manually. In the Basque Country they use a traditional tool called a *kizkia* to collect the apples on the ground. It consists of a wooden handle with a steel spike on the end. We had a demonstration at the museum in Astigarraga, and the speed at which one can collect apples this way is quite amazing. However, this does make a hole in the apple and thus the crop needs to be processed rapidly to avoid decay.

Some cideries are large multimillion-liter capacity operations. The implication of this is that only the smallest producers may have their own orchards and be self-sufficient in apples. The more important producers need to secure their apple supply from many growers. Some of them additionally need to complement the local supply with imported apples. In the larger cideries, the apple reception area is an important sector and must be well organized so that the trucks can easily unload their cargoes of apples. Managing the shipments from different orchards, ensuring the proper ripeness, and mixing different categories of apples to create correctly balanced blends is quite a challenge. Most cideries use boxes for this, called *manzaneros*, where each box contains a certain category of apple of a given ripeness. Then when time comes, the apples from such and such boxes are sent to the mill and pressed. Water is used as a medium to transport the apples through troughs, thus simultaneously washing them.

The apples are normally blended before milling. According to my collaborator Miguel Ángel Pereda Rodríguez, the apples are mixed in the following proportions to yield the typical Asturian flavor:

40 percent ácidas (full sharp)
25 percent semiácidas (mild sharp)
15 percent dulces (sweet)
15 percent dulce-amargas (mild bittersweet)
5 percent amargas (full bittersweet)

In the Basque country, although the apple categories are not as well defined, the proportions are pretty much the same: A standard blend would normally be made with about two parts of apples that are rich in acid for one part of apples that are rich in tannins.

Milling and Pressing

The Basques were possibly the first to develop presses that can handle large quantities of apples. In fact, old Basque farmhouses most often incorporated a press within their structure. I visited and took pictures at one such farmhouse near Ustaritz in France that dated back to the seventeenth century (this farmhouse is now transformed into a bed-and-breakfast, where we stayed, and the owners even had a cider orchard in the backyard to add to my pleasure . . .). As we can see in figure 4.22, the box that holds the pomace is built of stone and is an integral part of the foundation of the building. It had quite large dimensions: approximately 3 to 4 meters square by a little less than 1 meter high (about 12 feet × 12 feet × 3 feet), thus having the capacity to hold some 5 to 6 tons of apples in one pressing. Over this box was a huge beam with three wooden screws to apply the pressure (only one is visible in figure 4.22). One can only imagine the work needed to crush by hand the amount of apples required to fill this press, with a wooden mass such as seen in figure 2 on page 54. Once filled, planks were layered over the pulp, and beams were positioned under the three screws. The pressure was essentially provided by the weight of the large beam, and considering the dimensions of the box, this pressure was very small compared to modern pressing systems. Total time required

Figure 4.22. This ancient press near Ustaritz in the French Basque Country is an integral part of the farmhouse structure.

for a press cycle, including filling, crushing, pressing, and emptying, was well over a week.

Nowadays, such presses aren't in use anymore. They require too much work and are very inefficient. However, the heritage from these is still alive, and box presses are in use with many producers. It is worth describing in detail the traditional pressing sequence at a very small operation in Asturias, as it is quite specific to the region, and also has an influence on the final product's flavor. This particular example has been filmed by Miguel Ángel Pereda Rodríguez, who also provided a photo of the press (figure 4.23). It is an old wooden press equipped with two ratcheted screws to apply the pressure.* The press box is approximately 1.5 m × 1.35 m × 1 m high (5 × 4.5 × 3.25 in feet), for a capacity of 2 cubic meters (70 cubic feet) of pomace, or 1.2 tons of apples. The filling of the press takes about an hour and a half, thanks to the use of a motorized mill that

---

* This video may be seen on YouTube at https://m.youtube.com/watch?v=7hQyORX9AcQ&t=11s.

Figure 4.23. The traditional wooden press is being filled with pomace. Photo by Miguel Ángel Pereda Rodríguez.

replaces the manual crushing. This is done by late afternoon or at dusk, as the temperature falls. Once filled, the press is left overnight for maceration of the pulp before any pressure is applied. The next morning, planks are layered on top of the pomace, then beams are placed over the planks, and the operators start to apply the pressure with two screws. The juice flows all day, but by the end of the afternoon, the *magaya* (pomace cake) becomes too compressed and clogged, and the juice flow stops even if more pressure is applied. It is then time to make a *corte*. This operation consists of removing the beams and planks, and then breaking up the magaya with a shovel. Once done, the planks and beams are reinstalled, pressure is reapplied, and the juice starts flowing freely again. It will be left the whole night under pressure, and the next morning it will be time to make a second corte in the same manner. A third corte is usually done later in the day, but as juice is extracted, it becomes less and less worth the effort to make additional cortes. Miguel Ángel mentioned they have been able to make four cortes in a three-day press, to obtain a total yield of 70 percent in juice. He also pointed out that, formerly, the process could last up to six days, but now, with climate change, it is not advisable

Figure 4.24. A large box press displayed at Mayador in Villaviciosa. Not that long ago, most larger cideries used this model of press, but many have now replaced them. This unit is not in use anymore, but we can appreciate its dimensions. Photo by Bill Bradshaw.

to exceed three days because there are more risks with higher temperatures, in particular from spoiling yeasts of the genus *Hanseniaspora*, which may cause off-flavors in the cider.

Larger cideries have mostly abandoned the traditional box presses and have replaced them with more modern equipment. I have seen some hydraulic basket presses and a number of horizontal pneumatic presses, which can be of impressive capacity. I have also seen a few belt presses. But for the production of the traditional sidra natural or sagardoa, either basket or box presses or horizontal pneumatic presses are preferred. My understanding is that the extraction in a belt press is too fast to permit the transformations required to obtain the typical flavor of sidra natural. At Trabanco's Gijón production site, they still use a battery of traditional box presses to make their sidra natural.

Regarding mills, most of the modern types may be seen. Interestingly, Spain is the only place where gear crusher mills are in general use, mainly in large operations. These consist of two wheels with large rounded teeth in counter-rotation. The apples are trapped by the gears and crushed between the wheels. This mill design was fairly popular in Europe by the end of the nineteenth century, but in other countries it was abandoned in favor of centrifugal mills, which produce a finer pulp. Some of the mills we saw were very powerful, capable of processing up to 15 tons of apples per hour.

Fermentation

It is now fairly well understood that the long pressing times seen in Spain combined with relatively mild temperatures have a profound impact on the cider flavor. Studies have shown that bacterial and yeast growth do start during the pressing and that malolactic transformation happens spontaneously before or simultaneously with the alcoholic fermentation.* This indicates that the characteristic sharp

---

* See, for example, Monica Herrero, Luis A. Garcia, and Marion Diaz, "Organic Acids in Cider with Simultaneous Inoculation of Yeast and Malolactic Bacteria: Effect of Fermentation Temperature," *Journal of The Institute of Brewing*, 105, no. 4 (1999): 229–32, https://onlinelibrary.wiley.com/doi/pdf/10.1002/j.2050 -0416.1999.tb00023.x.

and slightly acetic flavor of sidra natural and sagardoa is due to the action of lactic acid bacteria rather than acetobacter. We also can't overemphasize the influence of the very rich flora of microorganisms present in Spanish cideries, which may interact with the cider and impart specific flavors: A study has identified no less than 560 species and strains of yeast in Asturian cideries.* Additionally, these long pressing times induce chemical reactions involving oxidation and enzymatic transformations on numerous compounds that may impact the flavor of the cider.

The fermentation process in itself is pretty straightforward, naturally with variations from producer to producer. In small traditional operations, the freshly pressed juice may simply be put in barrels without any yeast or sulfite addition and left until the fermentation is completed. Racking during fermentation is not frequent, and often no other form of treatment is done. By the end of winter or spring, the cider is dry and it is then bottled or served directly from the cask. Larger cideries have implemented more testing and operations, with strict sanitary control. Usually, the juice will be sulfited and left for decantation before it is pumped to the fermentation tanks. Most of these are stainless steel and temperature-controlled. Lots of testing is done to monitor the evolution of the fermentation and of different compounds. Particular attention is given to the amount of volatile acidity. While some older drinkers like the cider to burn a bit in the throat, modern tastes prefer a smoother flavor. Hence nowadays cideries are much more careful about sanitation and succeed in controlling the volatile acidity to lower levels than historically seen.

Once the fermentation is completed, some post-fermentation treatment may be done, for example, by fining or filtration, but these would mainly be for the nueva expresión style or for the sidra espumosa cider. The sidra natural is traditionally left unfiltered.

It may be noted that for all ciders that are to bear the PDO label, the following is forbidden: chaptalization (or all operations intended

---

* In: Carmen Cabranes, Javier Moreno, and Juan Mangas, "Dynamics of Yeast Populations during Cider Fermentation in the Asturian Region of Spain," *Applied and Environmental Microbiology*, 56, no. 12 (December 1990): 3881–84, http://doi.org/10.1128/aem.56.12.3881-3884.1990.

to modify the natural richness of sugar in the must); the use of concentrates, additives, or artificial sweeteners; dilution with water; and pasteurization. Back-sweetening and CO_2 injection are only permitted in Asturias for the production of sidra (espumosa). However, the CO_2 used for carbonation has to be obtained from the main fermentation, as the addition of CO_2 from an external source is forbidden by the PDO specification. Such a process requires quite a bit of special equipment to collect the CO_2 produced in the fermentation tanks. It then needs to be purified and compressed at a low temperature to liquefy it, and then pumped into storage tanks from which it will later be reinjected into the cider at bottling time. Smaller operations do not have the equipment to do this, and those that make sidra espumosa will rather opt for a method that involves a prise de mousse.

CHAPTER FIVE

Germany
Apfelwein

In this chapter we will look at the cider produced in Germany, with also some regards to Austria, Switzerland, and Luxembourg, which all share quite similar and rich cider traditions. In Germany, cider is called *Apfelwein*, which literally means "apple wine," a name that can be used for all types of ciders, whether industrial, farm, or craft; cloudy or clarified; single or mixed varieties; sparkling or still. A cidery is often called a *Kelterei*, which could be translated as "press house." The main center of production is the German state of Hesse (Hessen in German), and particularly the area surrounding the city of Frankfurt am Main, the heart of German ciderland.

This region has a long history of cider making. Already under Charlemagne in the ninth century, there are references to cider produced in the Carolingian Empire. This empire covered most of central Europe, and while the documents in question (which mostly related to taxes) do not specify where cider was produced within the empire, it is quite plausible that cider was made in Germany at that period. Whatever the case, most probably the Romans introduced the first *Malus domestica* apple varieties and the technologies permitting the extraction of the juice and the making of alcoholic beverages (wine or cider). And while some migration of cider apples occurred from northern Spain to France and England, there is no evidence that these migration movements touched Germany. As for Hesse and the Frankfurt region, it would have been mostly a wine making region up to the Little Ice Age era, during which the grapevine crops failed and hardier apple trees were planted in replacement. Some of the oldest known documents pertaining to how Apfelwein was made in Hesse date back to 1638. And as in other regions of Europe, the cider industry grew a lot during the phylloxera epidemic that affected the grape culture during the latter part of the nineteenth century.

The annual production in Hesse is on the order of 40 million liters. Of this, about one-third is made by one large industrial cidery, Possmann, and the rest of the production is spread among more or less 60 smaller producers. The majority of them (40 in 2019) are members of the association Verband der Hessischen Apfelwein- und Fruchtsaft-Keltereien (Association of Apple Wine and Fruit Juice Press Houses in Hesse), which was founded in 1948. A certification of origin label is assigned for the cider produced in Hesse, Hessischer Apfelwein PGI, which was registered with the European Union in 2010. This PGI requires the apples to come mostly from traditional orchards in Hesse, and these apples should contain at least 6 g/L of acidity. The specification also forbids adding water or sugar in the production process. A Hessischer Apfelwein should have a minimum alcohol content of 5 percent, be dry, and may be slightly pétillant. What I found surprising is that this PGI label is not used much by the smaller producers—at least those I talked to. I was told that Possmann (the large industrial cidery) does make a cider with the PGI label. I haven't been able to get an answer as to why this PGI label wasn't in general use with the craft producers.

Other regions of Germany where cider is produced are the Trier and Saarburg area (Saarland), east of Frankfurt near Luxembourg; the

Baden-Württemberg in the southwest, and in particular the Swabia region between Stuttgart and Ulm; plus small productions in Bavaria in the southeast; and a few others regions in more northern locations. These bring the total annual production of Germany to about 60 to 70 million liters.

In Austria, we find old cider traditions in Mostviertel and in Styria. Mostviertel is, however, better known for its perries, and we will devote a chapter to this production later on. In Switzerland, I have seen reports mentioning that there were some 800 cideries at the beginning of the twentieth century, with cider and perry being very common drinks in the countryside. However this number has nowadays

Figure 5.1. The Zu den drei Steubern is one of the oldest and most typical Kelterei in Sachsenhausen. Note the evergreen wreath over the door. Photo by author with processing by Bruno Roy.

tremendously decreased. Many of the traditional cideries have merged into a few very large industrial plants that mostly produce fruit juices and, sometimes, a little bit of cider. The small craft cideries had almost completely disappeared, but in recent years we have seen a number that have started operation. An even more extreme situation has occurred in Luxembourg, where there was no more cider production by the end of the twentieth century, until recently from Carlo Hein, who founded the Ramborn Cider Company, which remains the only cidery in the country.

The city of Frankfurt is famous for its historic cider quarter (called Sachsenhausen), just south of the Main River, which fortunately escaped from war destruction. Many cider bars are in this quarter and were originally small cideries. These mostly proliferated during the end of the nineteenth century, as cider became the main drink of the people in replacement of wine, which was then becoming very scarce because of the phylloxera outbreak that damaged vineyards. According to tradition, when the cider was ready to drink, the owner or cider maker would hang an evergreen wreath outside the door to let people know. We still often see these wreaths in Sachsenhausen.

Frankfurt hosts an annual fair in spring, which is a major international cider event. This fair was initiated in 2009 under the name Apfelwein im Römer, and directed by Andreas Schneider and Michael Stöckl. The name was later changed to Apfelwein International and more recently to CiderWorld and the direction passed to Michael Stöckl and Christine Isensee-Kiesau. A cider competition, the CiderWorld Award, is held simultaneously. I had the pleasure to attend this fair in April 2018 with my friend Mark Gleonec, and we were both invited to be part of the jury for the cider competition. This was an excellent opportunity to discuss German cider traditions with many cider makers and other actors of the cider scene. The city is also host of the Global Cider Forum, an international conference on the cider market, its products, and its trends, which takes place annually in October.

Figure 5.2. A view on the main floor of the fair CiderWorld'18 in the beautiful Gesellschaftshaus Palmengarten, Frankfurt am Main.

My first encounter with ciders from the Germanic countries was, however, a few years before that, in Austria, where I attended the Salon des Mostes in 2015. Although the emphasis of this event was more on perry, there were quite a few stands for German ciders and, naturally, plenty from Austrian producers. One of the ciders that struck me most there was a *Schoppen* from Jörg Stier—before that time, I had no idea German ciders could have such intense flavor.

Figure 5.3. In Austria at the Salon des Mostes in 2015, this charming young lady was offering a tasting of the sparkling ciders by Rosstrieb-kellerei, a producer in Baden-Württemberg.

The Orchard

As in other European countries, the traditional cider orchards in Germany, such as the one we see in figure 5.4, page 163, with Andreas Schneider, had their heydays during the nineteenth and first part of twentieth centuries. Since the 1950s, the number of them has decreased dramatically and they have mostly been replaced by high-density intensive orchards of popular market varieties, which for their part have seen important growth. This had an impact on the availability of many cider apple varieties that were grown in the traditional orchards, but do not find a place in the modern orchards. This problem is particularly acute in the region of Frankfurt because urbanization has also taken its toll on the traditional orchards. It is estimated that in the last 50 years, about 70 percent of the traditional orchards have disappeared. In more rural areas, for example in Baden-Württemberg, we see more of the large, old traditional orchards.

(*continued on page 166*)

Collaborators

I have had the chance of being helped in the writing of this chapter by some great people who are very knowledgeable on German cider and tradition:

Andreas Schneider is the owner of the fruit farm Obsthof am Steinberg near Frankfurt, which was founded by his parents in 1965. He inherited the farm in 1993, which then was mostly producing table apples, and started making cider that same year. He soon converted the farm to organic management and expanded the orchards. Nowadays, the farm has 8,500 fruit trees on 15 hectares (37 acres), and includes 250 different varieties, of which 125 are apples. Andreas is certainly one of the better known and emblematic cider makers of Germany. His ciders are of the highest quality, and this is no doubt due in good part to his orchards. In effect he grows all his apples organically in low- to medium-density orchards. When walking through the rows of trees, it becomes so easy to appreciate the amount of loving care that goes into those trees. There are two more things I would like to mention about Andreas. First, one of his orchards is probably the most beautiful orchard I have seen in my life. This is a century-old orchard with huge high-stem trees of traditional varieties that we see in figure 5.4. And second is his way to walk with visitors in his orchards with a basket containing bottles. He then stops, opens a bottle, fills glasses, and explains that this particular cider comes from the tree or group of trees surrounding us. The stories make it magical.

Norman Groh operates Weidmann & Groh with his father-in-law, Reiner Weidmann. I met Norman Groh in 2014 at the GLINTCAP cider competition in Michigan where both of us were judging. And naturally when I visited the region in 2018,

Figure 5.4. Andreas Schneider (*right*) and Mark Gleonec near a magnificent century-old Kaiser Wilhelm tree, tasting a cider produced from this particular tree.

Norman was on the list of visits I planned to make. Weidmann & Groh is a fruit farm, cidery, brewery, and distillery. The farm has a total of 10 hectares (25 acres) of orchards, of which three are apples. The production is on the order of 40,000 liters of cider, in addition to fruit spirits, beer, and whiskey. The cider production is obtained from the harvest of their farm, which is supplemented with fruit bought from other producers. Their ciders are of the modern style (see further on a discussion on German cider styles) and of the highest quality, having won numerous awards in international cider competitions.

Konstantin Kalveram is coauthor with Michael Rühl of two books on Apfelwein and its producers: *Hessens Apfelweine*, published in 2008, and *Frankfurts Apfelweinführer*, published in 2011. He was

Figure 5.5. Konstantin Kalveram (*left*), Mark Gleonec, and the author beside an old traditional press at the Possmann cidery.

Figure 5.6. Jens Becker (*left*), owner of the Apfelweinhandlung cider store, and Frank Winkler (*right*), owner of the restaurant Daheim im Lorsbacher Thal, with Mark Gleonec, as we spent some pleasant time at the Zu den drei Steubern.

also co-owner of a cider store, the Apfelweinkontor in Frankfurt, and now works at the Possmann cidery. Konstantin is the person who knows everyone on the Frankfurt cider scene, plus all about cider history, and he was a great help for the organization of our tour of cideries.

Hans-Joachim Bannier is a pomologist and author who cofounded Pomologen-Verein, a German pomological organization that is involved in the conservation of traditional fruit varieties. He also maintains a private conservation orchard of about 350 fruit varieties, mainly apples but also cherries, plums, and apricots, which he considers a "Noah's Ark" for endangered varieties. This orchard, Obst-Arboretum Olderdissen, is in Bielefeld, about 300 kilometers north of Frankfurt. Bannier reviewed the descriptions here of the German cider apples.

Additionally, I wish to acknowledge the contributions from persons whom I have visited or with whom I have been in communication and who all have had some influence on the writing of this text: Jörg Stier and his son Marco of Kelterei Stier; Frank Winkler, owner of the restaurant Daheim im Lorsbacher Thal, where I ate numerous times and where there is the largest selection of ciders from all over the world (Frank says he has over 250 different ciders in his cellar); Jens Becker, cider producer and owner of the Apfelwein-handlung cider store; and Hendrick Docken, artist and hobbyist cider maker. All those listed here are in Frankfurt or in the vicinity. On our way back, we stopped in Luxembourg to meet Carlo Hein and Adie Kaye of Ramborn Cider Company. I will also mention the contributions from Toni Distelberger in Austria, whom I will present in an upcoming chapter on perry, and Alexandre Maillefer of Cidrerie de Grosse Pierre in Switzerland. And special thanks to Darlene Hayes, who had some great suggestions to make this chapter more complete.

It is interesting to note that in Germany, a lot of the cider producers don't have their own orchards and buy their apples from fruit growers. Many of these growers have part of their orchards for market fruits and part for cider apples. What I find paradoxical is that even if the cider apples are in shortage, their price remains very low, at €120 to €150 per ton. These sorts of prices don't create a sufficient incentive for a farmer to start planting new cider orchards—or even to maintain the existing ones. The price of cider apples would have to be much higher to permit a reversal of the decline in cider orchards. Parallel to that, the price of cider in Germany is the lowest I have seen, and we can find pretty good cider for less than €2 for a one-liter bottle. We can then understand that the producers aren't willing to spend much for the apples they buy. When they can't get proper locally grown cider varieties, they will use downgraded market apples, apples from other regions of Germany or other European countries, or concentrate. The exception to this is with organic cider, where the cider maker generally has a contract with an organic apple grower at a much higher price—I have heard of prices up to €750 per ton for top-quality, perfectly ripened organic apples of a proper cider variety. Another point worth mentioning is that we don't see many modern bush-type medium-density cider orchards as are found in France or the United Kingdom, for example. No doubt this is a direct consequence of the low value of cider apples, as growers will get a better return on their investments if they rather choose to invest in an intensive orchard of standard market varieties. Again, the exception to this would be with organic orchards.

All this is to say that the bulk of the locally grown cider apples come from the old traditional orchards that remain. The management of such orchards is minimal, and they are mostly unsprayed. The harvest is usually done by hand, collecting the apples on the ground. In most orchards, the trees' branches are shaken to provoke the fall of the apples. Mechanical harvesting machines are not common, but a few larger operations have started using them and their use is increasing.

On the subject of cider apple orchards, I wish to highlight here the work done in Luxembourg by Carlo Hein of the Ramborn Cider Company. At the time he founded his cidery, pretty much all cider orchards had been left abandoned for decades, as there was no more cider production in the country. The trees were in quite bad shape from not

Figure 5.7. An old orchard in Luxembourg, where we also see newly planted young apple trees with protection from grazing animals.

having been pruned, and were infested with mistletoe. These were small traditional orchards of standard trees that were spread all over the region. Carlo had the objective of restoring these old orchards to use the fruit for a rebirth of cider production. He started working with the many farmers who owned the orchards, helping them rejuvenate their trees by severely pruning to clear the mistletoe, and also by planting new trees where old ones had died. He now buys their apples for a good price, thus ensuring the long-term viability of cider apple production.

Apple Varieties

Most apple varieties grown for cider in Germanic countries are of the sharp and bittersharp classes. Sweets and bittersweets are virtually unseen. Although a number of varieties are grown for the sole purpose of cider making, many of the sharp varieties are in fact old traditional varieties of dessert apples that are now mainly used for cider.

There are many great pomological reference books that describe German apple varieties. One that I like for the quality of the illustrations is by Rudolph Goethe, *Aepfel und Birnen, die wichtigsten deutschen Kernobstsorten*, published in 1894; and for Swiss varieties there is the work of Gustav Pfau-Schellenberg, *Schweizerische Obstsorten*, published between 1863 and 1872. Two very nice and recent references are, first, a book from Luxembourg, *Äpfel und Birnen aus Luxemburg* by Raymond Aendekerk, Hans-Joachim Bannier, Doris Bauer, Hans-Thomas Bosch, Richard Dahlem, and Marc Thiel, published in 2016. The second is an Austrian book, *Äpfel & Birnen, Schätze der Streuobstwiensen*, by Gerlinde Handlechner and Martina Schmidthaler, published in 2019 by the Moststraße organization. This book is also presented further in the chapter on Austrian perry. Following are some of the more important apple varieties for cider.

Bittenfelder Sämling (bittersharp) is a chance seedling discovered near Stuttgart in southern Germany, where it was already known in 1900. The apples are small to medium size, yellowish, and rarely partly covered with some red. They ripen late, by the end of October or November. A bittersharp cider-only variety, the juice has high concentrations of sugar and acid, and is highly valued for cider making. The tree is robust, resistant, and hardy. Seeds from this variety are used to produce standard seedling rootstocks.

Bohnapfel (sharp to mild bittersharp), whose full name is Grosser Rheinischer Bohnapfel, is the emblematic cider apple variety, the best known and most widely used in all of the Germanic ciderland. It is also known in the French part of Switzerland, where cider maker Jacques Perritaz (Cidrerie du Vulcain) calls it Pomme de fer. It originated in Germany and was already known by the end of the eighteenth century. The tree is hardy and resistant, although slight sensitivity to scab and canker is noted. The variety is triploid, the bloom is mid-season to late, and the fruit is harvested by mid- to end of October. The productivity is good although somewhat biennial. Analysis results indicate good sugar content, an acidity in the medium to high range, and a low to medium tannin concentration, which would classify it as a sharp to mild bittersharp. This apple is

Figure 5.8. Very realistic wax models of the variety Bohnapfel.

naturally well balanced and used by most cider makers for single-variety, full-bodied, and full-flavored ciders as well as in blends.

Boskoop (sharp), whose full name is Schöner aus Boskoop and is also known as Belle de Boskoop, is of Dutch origin and was discovered by the mid-1800s. It is a popular table and cooking variety through all of northern Europe. This big fruit is beautiful and russeted, highly flavored with a characteristic acidulous flavor reminiscent of lemon. The juice is high in sugar and very high in acid content. The tree is large, vigorous, and very hardy, although it is slightly susceptible to scab. For cider making, Boskoop is mostly used in Germany, where we may see it in single-variety Apfelwein.

Erbachhofer Mostapfel (mild sharp to bittersharp) is a cider-only apple introduced around 1925. It originally was spread in south and southwest Germany. Nowadays the Erbachhofer is also grown in Austria and in Luxembourg, where cider maker Carlo Hein (Ramborn Cider Company) makes an excellent single-variety cider from it. The tree is hardy and requires little care, being naturally pest-resistant. The apples are harvested in October, are small

Figure 5.9. Erbachhofer single-variety cider at Ramborn in Luxembourg, with the book *Äpfel und Birnen aus Luxemburg.*

to medium size, bright red, and the skin may be greasy. The flavor is slightly acidic, spicy with good sweetness.

Goldparmäne (sharp), also known as Wintergoldparmäne, may be Dutch, French, or from another country in northern Europe; the origin of this variety is not known. Different stories have been written by pomologists, and one is that the variety could have appeared in the Netherlands early in the eighteenth century bearing the name Kroon Renet. By the beginning of the 1800s, it was well known in France as the Reine de reinettes, and in England either as the King of the Pippins or as the Golden Winter Pearmain, this last name being the English version of the current German name. This is a great apple for many purposes, being extremely flavorful, full of sugar and acid, and nicely balanced. This is also a very beautiful fruit, of medium size, and deep golden color with darker orange-red stripes or blush. The tree is of medium vigor, quite productive, but some susceptibility to scab and canker is noted. In Germany, it is one of the most highly praised for single-variety Apfelwein.

Kaiser Wilhelm (sharp) is a German variety that originated near Solingen by the 1860s. The variety makes beautiful, large, and vigorous trees, a specimen of which we saw in a previous photo with Andreas Schneider (figure 5.4, page 163). Susceptibility to canker is noted in some locations. The apples are large and juicy, sweet with some acid, ripe by end of September to October, and keep well. This is mainly a table and kitchen variety, but it is also often used for cider making in Germany.

Roter Trierscher Weinapfel (sharp to bittersharp), also known as Red Trierer, was in former times an important cider variety and originated around 1825 near the city of Trier in Germany, by the border with Luxembourg. It was also grown in France where it is known as Rouge de Trèves, and in fact the French used to export large quantities to Germany before the First World War.

Figure 5.10. These Reine de reinettes apples from the author's orchard are the same variety as Goldparmäne.

Nowadays the variety is not grown as much because its fruits are a bit small and it is susceptible to scab. The tree is of medium vigor and hardy; it blooms late and ripens its crop by the end of October. The fruits are striped red, often undersized, and have a conical shape. The juice has a medium sugar content, high acidity, and low to medium tannin concentration. There exists as well a Weisser (White) Trierer, which also has good properties for cider making, but it is not as widely spread.

Sauergrauech (bittersharp), also known as Pomme Raisin, is a cider apple from the canton of Bern in Switzerland. It is mainly grown in that country. This apple is praised for its very juicy flesh, which has good balance of acidity, tannin, and sugar. The tree is adaptable to many conditions and is of moderate vigor. Some scab sensitivity is reported. The apples are striped red, small to medium size, and of conical shape. Blooming is early to mid-season, and the apples ripen in October. Swiss cider maker Alexandre Maillefer (Cidrerie de Grosse Pierre) says it produces a cider with excellent organoleptic qualities. A red variant called Roter Sauergrauech also exists, which has similar qualities.

Schafsnase (sharp), is also known as Rheinische Schafsnase. There are a number of apple varieties by the name Schafsnase. But the one better known and most often used for cider making is the Rheinische Schafsnase, a cider apple that originated from the Taunus mountains north of Frankfurt before 1800. It is now mainly spread in the state of Hesse around Frankfurt. The name means "sheep nose," and it has that characteristic shape. It is a rather sharp apple with medium sugar content that ripens in late September and may be used until December. The fruit is midsize, yellowish with red stripes, and very juicy. The tree is undemanding and productive.

Waldhöfler (bittersharp) is sometimes called Waldhöfler Holzapfel, where the word *Holzapfel* in German means a "wild or crab apple." It was discovered around 1850 in Thurgovia (Switzerland) and is mostly grown in that country. The Waldhöfler is a full bittersharp cider apple, with high concentrations of sugar, acid, and tannins. It blooms late and the fruit is harvested by the end of October.

Weihrouge (sharp to bittersharp), also written Weirouge by some authors, is a redflesh apple that is used by some producers to give a rosé color to the cider. It was named and released by the Weihenstephan University, near Munich in Bavaria, in 1980, but in fact it could be older, as some pomologists think it is identical with the variety Roter Mond (Red Moon) that was obtained in 1915 by the renowned Russian breeder Michurin and introduced in Germany by the 1930s or 1940s.

In addition to these varieties, a number of other apples are used for cider. Most of these are older traditional dessert varieties, which have stronger flavor and usually more tannins than modern commercial apples, and would be classified as sharps. Many are of the russet or reinette types. Among the most often seen, we may note: Ananas Renette, Carpentin (also spelled Karpentin, and one of Andreas Schneider's favorites), Champagner Reinette, Eifeler Rambur, Goldrenette von Blenheim (Blenheim Orange), Gravensteiner, Königlicher Kurzstiel (Court Pendu Plat or Wise Apple), Landsberger Renette, Orleans Renette, Rheinischer Winterrambur (Rambo), Weisser Winterkalvill (Calville blanc d'hiver), and Zabergäu Renette. Two others that are more specific to Luxembourg are Luxemburger Renette and Triumph aus Luxemburg. And to Switzerland: Tobiäsler. In Austria, the most important cider apple variety is the Bohnapfel, which may be blended with modern commercial dessert varieties such as Jonagold or Gala.

Speierling and Other Fruits Traditionally Added to the Cider

One special tradition with the *Frankfurter Apfelwein* is to add a small quantity of speierling fruit in the cider. The speierling tree is in fact the service tree (*Sorbus domestica*). It appears that the culture of this tree dates from the Romans, who brought seeds when they occupied the territory. Its main use at the time was in wine making, as it improved the stability and quality by increasing the tannin content of the must.

And later, when the people of the region got to making cider, the habit of using speierling passed from wine to cider.

Old specimens of speierling trees may become huge and certainly are majestic. According to Norman Groh, whom we see beside the tree in figure 5.12, that particular tree would be one of the largest known specimens in Germany, and it easily provides all the fruit required by the operation of Weidmann & Groh. The fruit has a shape similar to that of a small apple or pear, and has a size of about 2 to 3 cm (1 inch); its color is green when unripe, yellowish to brown when ripe. It is quite bitter and astringent, in particular when unripe. Thus, the addition of unripe fruit or juice increases the tannin content of the must when the blend consists mostly of varieties that are low in tannin. I was also told that this addition improves the clarification of the cider. Interestingly, all the producers I talked to had different methods to use speierling in their ciders. Some even keep their procedure secret! Here is a summary of what I was able to gather:

- Speierling is normally used in a proportion of 1 to 3 percent of the total volume.

Figure 5.11. Speierling leaves and fruits. Photo by Obsthof am Steinberg, photographed by Jochen Kratschmer.

- At the Possmann cidery, they mix the speierling fruits with the apples at milling time, in a proportion of 2 percent.
- At Weidmann & Groh, the speierling fruit is harvested three weeks before maturity and the juice is extracted on a small press. This juice is kept in the cold for three weeks to a month and added to the cider as it reaches the end of fermentation.
- Cider maker Hendrick Docken harvests the fruit in August, about two months before maturity, and much earlier than other producers. He then

Figure 5.12. Norman Groh standing by a large speierling tree.

presses it and keeps the juice three months in the cold before adding it in November to the cider, after the turbulent phase of the fermentation. He adds 1 liter of speierling juice to 100 liters of cider.
- At Obsthof am Steinberg, Andreas Schneider harvests the fruit late, by the end of October. He likes the fruit to be fully ripe but still firm. He adds up to 2 percent of speierling juice to the fermenting must.

Apart from speierling, other bitter or astringent fruits may be added to the cider for the same purpose of increasing the tannin content. Quince (*Cydonia oblonga*) and medlar (*Mespilus germanica*), locally called Mispel, are most often seen. Cider with quince is usually called *Apfel-Quittenwein*, and is produced by adding about 10 percent of juice pressed from well-ripened quince fruit. Cider with medlar may be called *Mispel-Apfelwein* or *Apfelwein mit Mispel*. It is usually made by adding about 5 percent medlar juice to the must.

Apfelwein Styles

We find two quite distinct styles of Apfelwein in the Frankfurt area. One is the traditional Apfelwein while the second is of a more modern style. In all cases, these ciders are relatively high in acid and low in tannins. Their color is usually rather light, ranging from light straw to gold. And their alcoholic strength may be between 5 and 7 percent ABV. The flavor is rich, slightly sharp, with some astringency but no bitterness. The traditional Apfelwein is a simple, unsophisticated

Figure 5.13. The modern-style Apfelwein comes in clear glass bottles and is usually served in a wine glass, while the traditional style is served in a Gerippte from a Bembel or a brown glass bottle. Photo by Konstantin Kalveram.

farm-style cider that would not be clarified or filtered, generally dry and still, traditionally fermented in a wooden barrel. Nowadays, it is fermented in standard tanks, except maybe for a few old-style makers who still use barrels. This is the kind of cider that will usually be served in any cider bar in Frankfurt. For service, a *Bembel* is used, a traditional stoneware pitcher (many different sizes are available), which is filled from the barrel and brought to the table. The cider is served in a ribbed glass called a *Gerippte*—I was told the reason for the ribs on the glasses is that, after eating good Frankfurt sausages, the fingers could get a bit greasy, and the ribs help prevent the glass from accidentally slipping when holding it. This style of cider is also often called *Stöffsche* or *Schoppen*, a word that really means the standard serving glass size, which may be 250 or 300 mL. But the word is also used by extension to name the cider itself.

The modern-style cider doesn't have a special name other than Apfelwein. It is, however, easily recognizable in that it is bottled in clear glass bottles, which let the customer appreciate the perfect clarity of the product. The price tag is also higher than for traditional

Figure 5.14. A display at the Possmann cidery showing a Bembel, Geripptes, and a bottle of traditional *Frankfurter Apfelwein*.

Apfelwein. This cider is still and usually relatively dry (*Trocken*), although some producers do make semidry (*Halbtrocken*) and medium-sweet (*Lieblich*) cuvées. It should be served in white-wine glasses. These ciders may be produced either from a blend or from a single variety of apple, with or without addition of speierling, quince, or medlar. Usually the most sophisticated (and expensive) products are of a single variety such as Bohnapfel, Boskoop, or Goldparmäne, which are among the most highly praised. Apfelwein is also available as pétillant and sparkling. The traditional method sparkling ciders are presented in standard champagne-type bottles and called *Apfelschaumwein*, while the pétillant ciders are called *Apfelperlwein*.

Other regional styles or names also exist. In Luxembourg and in the Trier region (Saarland), the traditional cider is sometimes called *Viez*. This word comes from Latin and means second category, as the grape wine was considered first category, and the cider was seen as a lower-class drink. In Austria, the apple cider is called *Apfelmost*. This cider is very close to the modern style in Germany. The same name is

Figure 5.15. A view of the bar at the restaurant Daheim im Lorsbacher Thal in Frankfurt, showing a large Bembel mounted on a stand to make it easier to pour, as well as smaller Bembels on the shelves in the back. In the front we can notice modern-style Apfelwein bottles.

also used in Swabia (Baden-Württemberg, in the south of Germany), but in this region it is rather used for the traditional style of cider. And the name *most* by itself usually indicates a cider that may be made from a mixture of apples and pears.

Cider Making

This presentation of Apfelwein making in Germany is largely inspired by the methods used at Obsthof am Steinberg by Andreas Schneider, and at Weidmann & Groh by Norman Groh. Both had the patience to answer my technical questions. We will first visit Andreas Schneider, who has quite an unconventional approach to cider making. In an interview that he gave to Pete Brown and Bill Bradshaw for the writing of their book *World's Best Ciders*, he said his secret for making good cider is that he waits: He waits for his large trees to start producing high-quality fruits; he waits for the right moment to harvest the

Figure 5.16. Hans-Jörg Wilhelm (Hohenloher Schaumweine in Baden-Württemberg) is a specialist in the production of sparkling cider using the traditional method. This was his display at CiderWorld'18, and he had in addition to *Apfelschaumwein* some *Birnenshaumwein* (perry) and some *Apfel-Quittenschaumwein* (apple-quince).

apples; he waits during the slow wild yeast fermentations; and he waits again during a long maturation before drinking or selling the cider. I had written in my previous book that "patience is the mother of all virtues for a cider maker," and obviously Andreas Schneider is a patient man. He is also an adept of a minimum intervention approach—as he told me, he practices a "controlled do-nothing" . . .

The Obsthof am Steinberg cidery is medium size, and the production may vary between 40,000 and 85,000 liters depending on the apple crop. This production is divided between the traditional-style house cider, the *Hausschoppen*, and high-end bottled ciders, which may be single variety, a blend of two or three varieties, or orchard-based, meaning the cider is from a group of trees that are close together. They may produce up to 50 different ciders in a year, with most of them being made in small batches for the higher-end products. Yes, up to 50 different ciders. And this is not unique to this cidery, as I have seen others (Kelterei Steir, for example) that also make similar numbers, and it seems to me this would be characteristic to the region. This is because they pretty much all have many single-variety ciders, then numerous *Apfelwein mit Speierling*, and *mit Mispel*, and so on.

Let us now look at how Andreas Schneider makes his high-end bottled ciders. For these, all that concerns fruit collecting, handling, and ripening is of utmost importance. All the apples are manually collected on the ground after they fall naturally, without shaking the trees. This ensures maximum tree-ripening. Up to 10 harvesting passes may be done, and all the varieties are collected and kept separately. Whether additional maturation is required before pressing is judged from experience, and only perfectly ripened apples will be milled. Juice extraction at Obsthof am Steinberg is done on a belt press of the single belt type, which are very popular among medium-size producers. Other types are also found at this production level, such as hydraulic rack and cloth and horizontal pneumatic. Pulp maceration between milling and pressing is not general practice in Germany, but there are exceptions, as producer Jörg Stier does for some of his ciders.

Pressing is done one variety at a time except for the orchard-based ciders, where all the apples from a group of trees are pressed together. After pressing, Andreas Schneider will not do any treatment to the must. No clarification, no enzyme, no sulfite, no yeast, or nutrient addition. And naturally, no chaptalization or dilution. If the ambient temperature is too warm, however, he might have to cool the juice as it comes out of the press. Thus his fermentations are exclusively wild-yeast based. He has no rule for the management of the fermentations except to encourage a slow evolution and so, if necessary, he may rack to reduce the speed. Some ferments are left to go to dryness, and others are stopped with some residual sugar by cooling to 2°C (35°F) and racking. For maturation, again there is no rule: As some batches are left to mature on their lees while others are racked to separate the cider from the lees. And some batches are left for maturation in wood barrels while others are put in standard tanks. These decisions are taken individually for each batch based on experience and taste. The maturation may be quite long because there is no post-fermentation clarification treatment; hence he waits until the cider clarifies naturally. The whole fermentation and maturation process may, for some batches, need as much as a year and a half to complete.

Figure 5.17. A bottle display for tasting at the cidery Obsthof am Steinberg, demonstrating that not all producers adhere to the usual bottling standards mentioned in the text.

Figure 5.18. A display of bottles at Weidmann & Groh: First on the right is an Apfelschaumwein, then an apple-quince pétillant cider (*Apfel-Quittenperlwein*), followed by an Apfelperlwein, and different cuvées of still, modern-style ciders.

The final processing at Obsthof am Steinberg is done by contract, which is fairly common among German producers. The contractor picks up cider tanks at the farm, does a cross-flow filtration, and adds sulfite to obtain 15 to 25 ppm free SO_2, and this is followed by the bottling. There is no back-sweetening. For the pétillant ciders (*Perlwein*), carbonation is done by the injection method. For the traditional-method sparkling ciders (*Schaumwein*), again this contractor does the processing. After bottling the dry cider with a liqueur de tirage, the cider is left for a very long maturation that may be up to four years before riddling is performed (other producers would normally have a much shorter maturation period, however). A liqueur de dosage is added at disgorging, most of the time for about 8 to 12 g/L of residual sugar, thus giving an off-dry cider.

It should be noted that the cider making at Obsthof am Steinberg as described here is not really standard procedure among German cider makers. Most will make use of modern wine making technologies that permit them to complete their fermentations in less time. To illustrate this, we visit Weidmann & Groh, a producer of fine modern-style Apfelwein, where Norman Groh is in charge of the cider making. His methods are more conventional and representative of the way many producers work. He starts with an enzymatic depectinization of the must, which he lets settle overnight. He then racks and adds a selected cultured wine yeast. He keeps the temperature at about 15°C (60°F) and manages the fermentation so that the cider reaches dryness in approximately three weeks. He then lets the cider sit on its lees for a month, racks it, and gives it another month of maturation to clear. He says he doesn't normally need fining but that the addition of speierling helps the clarification. He is typically ready for bottling about three months after starting the fermentation. Prior to bottling, he does a filtration with a plate filter and adds sulfite to obtain 35 ppm of free SO_2. The cider then goes to a contractor for bottling. The bottles are clear glass bordelais-type of a volume of 750 mL (or sometimes 1L) with screw-cap closure. Such bottles are used by a majority of producers. Most of the ciders at Weidmann & Groh are fermented to dryness, but when a non-dry is desired, the fermentation is stopped and sterile filtration is used to ensure stability with residual sweetness. It may be noted that other producers may use back-sweetening for some of their ciders.

If we now look at the making of traditional Apfelwein, the Schoppen, we see that this is quite straightforward. No special care is given to the handling of the apples and to the blend, and most producers simply use all the available apples, including non-premium dessert apples, and mix them all together at milling. They then simply let the must ferment naturally, most often without any yeast addition or clarification treatment, until dryness. The time required to complete the fermentation will vary from producer to producer depending on the temperature of the cellar, and on the natural concentration of nitrogenous nutrients in the apples. In the case of Obsthof am Steinberg, since the apples are grown organically and contain less nutrients from fertilization, these fermentations take longer than for most other producers, and may need three months to complete. A good portion of the traditional Apfelwein output isn't packaged, as many producers sell it by the liter at the cidery as a dry, still, and unfiltered Schoppen to customers who bring their own bottles or growlers to fill. Another part is kegged for selling to restaurants and bars. The traditional Apfelwein may also be bottled: brown-colored glass, 1-liter bottles are mostly used, with the content generally identified either as Apfelwein or as Schoppen.

Plate XXX

1. Oldfield.

2. Moorcroft.

3. Thirston's Red.

4. Holmer.

5. Taynton Squash.

6. Chaseley Green.

7. White Squash.

G. Severeyns, Chromolith. Brussels.

Edith E. Bull. del.
for The Woolhope Club.

PART II

TRADITIONAL PERRIES

During my travels on the Cider Planet, I've had the chance to visit three important traditional perry production regions in Europe: Herefordshire in the United Kingdom, Domfrontais in France, and Mostviertel in Austria. This isn't to say there aren't other places in the world where perry is produced in a traditional way, but these three regions have in common a much greater concentration of large, old trees than we can see anywhere else. It is important to note that the perry pear trees that we can observe nowadays are remnants of much larger populations that covered a great part of Europe 100 to 150 years ago. In the nineteenth century, perry pear trees numbered in tens of millions, while we now talk about a few hundred thousand for the regions that have the most—that is about one tree out of 100 that remains. And it was only about 50 years ago that perry pear trees began to be planted again, mostly in the three regions mentioned above. Fortunately, the pear tree is long-lived, and this is what has permitted many varieties to reach us. Some trees are estimated to be over 300 years old. This also gives a good indication that perry traditions are pretty ancient. In fact, there are historians who believe the perry pear tree was grown in Europe quite some time before the cider apple tree was introduced.

Whatever the region of origin, however, all traditional perry makers face some common challenges that are different from those associated with cider. The first is the extreme harshness of perry pears, due to their combination of acidity with very strong astringency. We may think of some cider apples as "spitters," but this is nothing compared to many perry pears—they are among the most unpalatable of any fruit one would try to eat fresh, and some actions need to be taken to reduce the astringency in the perry. A second challenge is that perry is notoriously more difficult to clarify. And very often there will remain particles that may flutter around the glass. The French have a nice word for these—they call them *voltigeurs*, which unfortunately doesn't have a good equivalent in English. A third challenge comes from the ripening of pears: perry pears stay green and hard and seem way underripe, until, all of the sudden, they become overripe and

Figure 1. Large perry pear trees are the most majestic of all fruit trees, and they are especially spectacular during bloom. This specimen is in Domfrontais; photo by Gérard Houdou.

blet (soft and brownish flesh)—within just a few days. Pears are much less tolerant than apples in this respect, and thus the perry maker needs to know his fruit well and judge the optimum moment to process it. And a fourth challenge comes from the presence of citric acid that gives a characteristic lemony flavor to the perry, but may transform more easily into volatile acidity (acetic acid), which would be objectionable. Another specificity of perry is the presence of sorbitol, which is sweet but does not ferment. It increases the density of the dry perry and gives a slight sweet taste. It also has a laxative effect, which has contributed to a bad reputation for perry when drunk in excess. Given all this, one could ask the question: Why bother making perry when one can make cider? According to many perry makers, the question does merit asking: the rewards from a great perry certainly compensate for the difficulties in making it.

Figure 2. Large perry pear trees are also spectacular when fully loaded, such as this giant specimen in Mostviertel, estimated to be about 300 years old. It may yield between 1 and 2 tons of pears.

The first two challenging issues that were noted, harshness and difficult clarification, are mainly due to the tannins present in the perry pears, which are different from those found in cider apples. The main compound in the perry pear is a polyphenol named leucoanthocyanin. This is a very astringent tannin, and it sometimes causes hazes and precipitates that are not easily predictable or avoided (hence the voltigeurs).

Perry pears are not classified the same way as

cider apples. Thus there is no such thing as sweets or bittersweets. This is simply because they would mostly be bittersharps, as all varieties have medium to high acidity combined with high tannin (note, however, that dessert pears could classify as sweets). In fact, it could be more appropriate to say perry pears are astringent-sharp, as their tannins are mostly not bitter. The result is that blending isn't as important as it is for cider apples, and much more often we will see single-variety perries that will naturally be well balanced. Another consequence is that, when planning an orchard, it is not necessary to balance the number of trees of the different classes as it is with apples, and so a lesser number of varieties is required.

We will now discuss the specificities of perries from the three selected regions, and for this the knowledge and experience from well-known perry makers will be used. These perries do have some common characteristics, as they share their base material—the perry pears from the different regions have quite similar flavors even if they are not the same varieties—but also some noticeable differences. The perries from Domfrontais are always sparkling and generally sweeter. From Herefordshire, many are sparkling but we also find some that are still, and they are generally drier than the French ones, but not as dry as the Austrian ones. And from Mostviertel, we mostly have still and dry perries that are very elegant and somewhat like white wines.

CHAPTER SIX

The United Kingdom
Perry

In the U.K., the most important traditional perry production is in Herefordshire, in the West Midlands, with smaller volumes being produced in the neighboring counties of Gloucestershire and Worcestershire. Perry is also produced in Wales, especially in the county of Monmouthshire adjacent to Herefordshire. There are approximately 75 to 80 producers in total, nearly two-thirds of which are in Herefordshire. The three English counties each have their own PGI label (for example, Herefordshire Perry), and there is also one for Traditional Welsh Perry.

I visited the region in August 2017 and had the pleasure to discuss quite a bit with Tom Oliver, of Oliver's Cider and Perry in Ocle Pychard, a most respected and well-known perry and cider maker. A lot of the information presented here comes from these discussions, and from those I had with producers

Figure 6.1. Tom Oliver (*left*) with the author, in a young semi-intensive pear orchard in Ocle Pychard. Photo by Mark Gleonec.

Mike Johnson (Ross on Wye Cider & Perry Company), James Marsden (Gregg's Pit Cider & Perry), Simon Day (Once Upon a Tree), and Mike Penney (Troggi Seidr, in Wales). Tom additionally revised this presentation on Herefordshire perry to ensure its accuracy, and he also has provided some of the photos used to illustrate the varieties; I thank him gratefully for his generosity. For those who wish to read further, the classic book *Perry Pears* by L. C. Luckwill and A. Pollard is certainly the best reference, if you can find it as it is a bit old (published in 1963 by the University of Bristol) and has been out of print for a while. The following two books are more recent and also provide excellent information: *Pears of Gloucestershire and Perry Pears of the Three Counties* by Charles Martell (Hartpury Heritage Trust, 2013); and *The Book of Pears* by Joan Morgan, published in 2015 by Ebury Press (in the U.K.) and Chelsea Green Publishing (in the US).

The Orchard and the Pear Varieties

The perry pear orchards of the West Midlands declined tremendously during the twentieth century. Censuses from the Ministry of Agriculture indicate a population of 118,000 trees in 1951, and this number had fallen to 75,000 in 1957, these being the remaining population from what was estimated to be in the millions a century earlier. Most of these trees would have been planted by the beginning of the nineteenth century, and thus are now about 200 years old. Since those censuses were done, we have seen new plantings of standard trees, so nowadays there are a good number of trees that are up to 50 years old, attaining their maturity of production. More recently, there has been some plantings of smaller trees in bush orchards. However, according to Tom Oliver, the fruit quality from these young bush trees is not on par with that of older trees. He finds the sugar content is lower, and the juice is blander, and consequently he now exclusively uses fruit from trees that are at least 20 years old to obtain the highest-quality perry.

Approximately 100 known perry pear varieties are in the West Midlands, to which we may add a small number of varieties that are local to Wales. Of these, 54 are fully described in Luckwill and Pollard's *Perry Pears*, and maybe about 40 are propagated by nurseries. When asked which varieties he would most highly recommend for planting, Tom Oliver suggested Thorn, Blakeney Red, Gin, and Oldfield, with the same number of trees of each variety. He added: "These all make great single-variety perries but also blend well. Thorn has acid and is early. Blakeney Red and Gin might need some acid. Oldfield is balanced. Blakeney Red can be a big tree, but the others are smaller. Pollination should be fine. They are all reasonable pears to grow and harvest and make tasty but accessible perries." Other producers have

Figure 6.2. An old perry pear orchard where young trees have been planted in empty spots, in Ocle Pychard.

their own favorite varieties. For example, James Marsden of Gregg's Pit Cider & Perry has a local variety named from the pit that is on his property, Gregg's Pit, which also gave its name to his cidery.

The following pear varieties are the most often seen. Note that pretty much all traditional varieties of perry pears are centuries old, as there has never been any breeding programs for them—hence their origin and pedigree is generally uncertain. To note again, perry pears are not classified the same way as cider apples, so sweets, bittersweets, and so forth are not shown in this list because they would all be astringent-sharp.

Figure 6.3. Blakeney Red pears. Photo by Tom Oliver.

Blakeney Red is a variety that probably arose in the village of Blakeney in Gloucestershire. It was planted in many districts, and since the end of the nineteenth century has been the most common in the West Midlands. It may not be the highest quality for the making of perry, but it is good for many purposes, including cooking and canning. Add that it provides year after year an abundant crop, and its success is easily understood. The juice contains good sugar, medium acidity, and medium tannin. Its astringency and acidity are not as marked as in other varieties, which permits its use for purposes other than perry.

Gin is a favorite with many craft producers for its distinctive aroma and flavor. It contains more citric acid than most varieties, a factor that contributes to its typicity. According to Luckwill and Pollard, the tree shows little sensitivity to scab and canker, and the fruit keeps well, which is a quality rarely seen among perry pears. The acidity is low to medium and the tannin content is medium.

Figure 6.4. Gin pears. Photo by Tom Oliver.

Figure 6.5. Winnal's Longdon pears from the author's orchard.

Oldfield is well liked by producers Tom Oliver and James Marsden, even though it is more susceptible to scab and canker than other varieties. According to Luckwill and Pollard, it is only in some districts that the tree succeeds well. The juice has high sugar and acidity, and medium tannin.

Thorn is the earliest high-quality variety of the season. It makes a smaller tree, which is an advantage to some. This tree is extremely winter-hardy (it certainly produces well in my orchard in Quebec, a cold Canadian location). The variety has been known for a very long time, and it was mentioned as early as 1676 by Worlidge in his *Vinetum Britannicum*. The juice is astringent and has good sugar and medium to high acidity.

Winnal's Longdon is a variety that Tom Oliver told me about: "It is great for perry but not so great as regards harvesting. It tends to blet heavily from the inside out and often needs shaking off the tree." For these reasons he wouldn't recommend planting much of it, but he nevertheless considers it as one of his personal favorites for the quality of the perry it produces. For sure this is an extremely cold-hardy variety, as it is one of the few to succeed (along with Thorn) in my Canadian climate. The pear is very nice looking, and the juice is sharp and astringent, with medium sugar.

Some other varieties often seen include Barland, Brandy, Hendre Huffcap, Moorcroft, Taynton Squash, and Yellow Huffcap.

Perry Making

For most varieties, the fruit is collected weekly from the ground as it falls naturally when ripe. For some other varieties, however, the fruit tends to stay too long on the tree and would be overripe and blet by the time it falls naturally. It is then necessary to shake those trees when the pears are at optimum ripeness.

For the early varieties that ripen in September, the pressing of the pears is done rapidly, within 24 hours of collection. Late varieties may be kept up to two weeks. Tom Oliver mentions the importance of processing the pears at the optimum time, as they just come ripe. This optimum period is short, which makes it more difficult to blend at pressing time because the different varieties the maker might want to blend may not be at the right maturity at the same moment.

After milling, Tom Oliver leaves the pomace for maceration during 24 to 48 hours before pressing, as this reduces the strong natural astringency of perry pears. Milling and pressing is done with the same equipment used for apples, and many types of presses may be seen in the region: Tom uses a belt press, Mike Penney and James Marsden have traditional twin-screw rack and cloth presses, while Simon Day uses a horizontal pneumatic press.

One tricky part of perry making is with blending because the short optimal period for pressing is a constraint. Tom Oliver mentions that while some varieties do blend relatively well, in some cases the blending of incompatible varieties may cause hazes, which is very difficult if not impossible to clarify. It is not uncommon to see the blend of two perfectly clear perries develop a haze within a few days after blending. Obviously, experience is the key here, and the perry maker needs to know the pear varieties very well and which are compatible for blending. With fully fermented perries, tests may be done on small volumes to ensure the blend won't cause a haze. This is also a reason why perries will more often be made as single-variety.

On fermentation management, most of the techniques used for cider may also be used for perry. Tom Oliver uses the keeving process, when conditions are favorable, for part of his perry production. The keeve is done the same way as for cider, with the addition of PME enzyme, followed by a calcium salt, as described in chapter 1, page 28. Once the chapeau brun (brown cap) has formed and raised, the clear must is racked and fermentation starts naturally. The fermenting perry is left at ambient temperature, which might get quite cool in winter. It will be racked a number of times as needed to control the fermentation speed, the aim being to observe a gravity drop of one degree per week when the time comes in spring to bottle the perry. For the keeved perries, Tom uses the ancestral method and will typically bottle at a specific gravity (SG) of 1.020 to obtain a finished perry at about 1.015. No additions are done at bottling time, and the sediments are left in the bottle. In the U.K., such perries are said to be bottle conditioned.

When the conditions are not suitable for keeving and processing as described here, Tom Oliver lets the fermentation go naturally, without any pre-fermentation clarification and without racking. Tom exclusively does wild yeast fermentations, and he doesn't add sulfite or nutrients to the must. Other producers, however, may sulfite the must, add nutrients, and use a selected yeast. Many options are then possible for the process to use. Tom will select one or another from his experience and depending on what sort of product he wishes to make:

- To obtain a perry with good natural residual sugar, he would rack when the fermenting perry approaches the desired SG, typically around 1.014 to 1.024, and then filter, sulfite, bottle, and pasteurize. Such perries may be left still, or they may be carbonated (injection method).
- Some cuvées are left to ferment all the way until completion. From these we may get dry or back-sweetened perries, which may be still or carbonated. Tom sometimes blends with some of

Figure 6.6. *From the left,* a carbonated perry from Oliver's Cider and Perry, bottles of ancestral method keeved cider and perry from Oliver's Cider and Perry, and bottles of traditional method perry and cider from Once Upon a Tree.

his keeved perry instead of back-sweetening. Pasteurization or sterile filtration is used to ensure stability of such perries, and sulfite is added at bottling time.

- Finally, some cuvées are processed using the traditional method. These perries are fermented to dryness, and then bottled with a liqueur de tirage that contains sugar, yeast, nutrient, and bentonite clay (a clarifying agent). Once the in-bottle fermentation is complete, the perry is allowed to mature for many months, after which riddling and disgorging is performed. A liqueur de dosage that contains sugar may be added while disgorging to bring some residual sweetness. In the U.K., such perries are said to be bottle-fermented.

It is interesting to note that the PGI for Traditional Welsh Perry is more stringent than those for the three English counties. In effect the Welsh PGI specification doesn't permit back-sweetening or carbonation. Only three forms may then be produced: still, bottle-conditioned, and bottle-fermented.

As for packaging, the bottle-conditioned and bottle-fermented perries are normally presented in 750 mL champagne-type bottles, with either crown caps or mushroom corks with wire cages. For the still and carbonated perries, a variety of lighter-weight bottles of different formats may be used. For deliveries to pubs, bag-in-box is quite standard, as well as kegs for carbonated perries.

CHAPTER SEVEN

France
Poiré

The Domfrontais is a region located in the southwest of Normandy, and it surrounds the beautiful medieval city of Domfront. Perry and calvados are two of the specialties, and in fact, the calvados from Domfrontais usually contains a good part of pears in addition to apples. For the perry, there is a PDO label (AOP in French), *Poiré Domfront*, which protects the name and specifies many parameters for its production. There are about 15 producers that are part of the PDO, and a number of others who produce perry but without the label. Most producers make cider and calvados in addition to perry.

A good part of the information presented here was obtained from discussion with a respected PDO producer that I visited during the summer of 2016, Stéphane Leroyer, of Ferme de la Poulardière at Saint-Fraimbault. He produces about 25,000 liters of perry per year, and about the same quantity of cider, all of which is organic. I also visited the well-known cider and perry maker Éric Bordelet, who is located in Mayenne, just south of the Domfrontais, and is not part of the PDO region. A good number of Norman cider producers also have small plots of pear trees and a limited perry production, but the better part of the perry production remains in the Domfront area, with an estimated 60 percent of the total number of perry pear trees of France. Other good sources of information (in French) are the PDO specification itself and two recent books: The first is more specifically about the PDO perry producers, written by François Lemarchand and titled *Poiréculteurs en pays de Domfront* (Orep éditions, 2016), and the second, *Le poiré et les vergers du Domfrontais* (Orep éditions, 2011); is a collective work from Maison de la pomme et de la poire, and is more about pear orchards than pear varieties. Unfortunately, however, there is no document that I know of that contains a good directory with descriptions of the French perry pear varieties (the second book mentioned above only gives a list of varieties found in Domfrontais). For those interested in visiting this beautiful region, there is a museum, the Musée du poiré in Barenton, which is well worth a stop.

Some of the photographs in this chapter were graciously provided by the journalist, author, and talented photographer Gérard Houdou, who lives in the Domfront area and has an amazing collection of photos related to Domfront pear trees and perry.

The Orchard and the Pear Varieties

It is estimated there are over 100,000 large perry pear trees in Domfrontais. For new plantings, it should be noted the PDO specification only permits high-stem standard trees, hence we will not find many higher-density orchards of smaller trees. The maximum permitted planting density is of 150 trees per hectare (60 per acre), and a "high-stem" tree is defined as having its first branches at a height of 1.8 meters (nearly 6 feet) or more. In practice, nowadays these trees are formed in three parts: the root, on which is grafted a special pear variety to form the trunk, and then the fruiting variety grafted at the height of the first branches. At Leroyer's Ferme de la Poulardière, there are 150 trees of 150 years of age or more in addition to newer plantings of trees that

Figure 7.1. A classical spring landscape sight in the Domfrontais with Norman cows grazing in a blooming perry pear orchard. Photo by Gérard Houdou.

are up to 25 years old and spaced 15 × 15 meters apart for 45 trees per hectare (50 × 50 feet, 18 trees per acre). It is interesting to note the old trees are not normally seen in a standard square grid pattern, but are rather planted all around a cultivated plot. Very often the traditional orchards of Domfront (as in the rest of Normandy) serve the double purpose of providing grazing for cattle in addition to fruit.

The main perry pear variety in the Domfrontais is the Plant de Blanc. In addition, the PDO specification lists 29 complementary varieties that may be used in blends, and a total of approximately 100 known varieties are in the region. Many are, however, used exclusively in distillation for calvados production. Some producers make their perry as single-variety Plant de Blanc, but most blend that variety with some of the 29 other accepted varieties so that the final blend contains somewhere between 40 and 80 percent of Plant de Blanc (the PDO specification requires a minimum of 40 percent of Plant de Blanc in the blend). Following are brief descriptions of a few of the most often seen varieties.

Antricotin is a small pear with a firm and very juicy flesh with good acidity and sugar. It is harvested by the end of October to be processed mid-November. The tree is very vigorous, hardy, healthy, and productive in alternate years.

De Cloche is an old variety known in all parts of Normandy and in Perche. The tree is very vigorous, hardy, and productive in alternate years. The fruit is medium size and bell-shaped (hence the name). It is among the latest to ripen and keeps fairly well. The flavor is acidic and astringent.

Fausset is a medium-size pear-shaped fruit with reddish cheeks on the sunny side. It ripens late, falling from the tree in November,

Figure 7.2. A young plantation of high-stem perry pear trees at Éric Bordelet.

and may be kept three weeks before processing.

Plant de Blanc is considered the king of the orchards in Domfront and in most of Normandy. It is the best known and most cultivated variety. The fruit is small, round, and green-yellow with brown spots. It ripens mid-October and is processed by the end of October. Its juice is naturally well balanced between sugar, acid, and astringency. This is the only variety that may be used for a single-variety PDO Domfront perry.

Figure 7.3. Plant de Blanc pears. Photo by Gérard Houdou.

Rouge vigné, also written as Rouge de Vigny, is often described in pomological works of the nineteenth century. The tree is remarkable as it lives long and may become very large—comparable to oak trees. Some specimens exceed the height of 20 meters (65 feet), with trunks 1 meter (3 feet) in diameter. It is not one of the most productive varieties, however. The fruit is medium size, juicy, with plenty of acid. It ripens earlier than most varieties, by mid-October, and is processed by the end of that month.

For perry pear trees, orchard management is reduced to a minimum. With large trees that may reach 20 meter, it makes no sense to even try to spray anything. The orchard soil is grassed, and many producers let their grazing animals in the orchards during the summer. The pears are harvested on the ground as they fall naturally (the PDO specification forbids shaking fruit from the trees), and they are regularly collected, at least once a week. They are not kept for long and are processed as soon as there is enough for making a cuvée.

Perry Making

At the Leroyer's farm, the pears are milled in the afternoon and the milled pulp is left to macerate overnight in a conquet. Stéphane mentioned the maceration is very important for perry pears as it softens the strong astringency, and it also helps a lot for the clarification later on. The pressing is done the next morning in a horizontal pneumatic press (many producers, however, still use the classic rack and cloth hydraulic press). The SG of the must is usually around 1.055 to 1.060, and the acidity is in the range of 6 to 7.5 g/L as malic acid, with the target pH around 3.4 to 3.5. The must is not sulfited unless the temperatures are very warm during the pressing, in which case about 60 ppm SO_2 may be used, mainly for protection against volatile acidity production, which may happen when the temperature is too high. Stéphane notes that for the organic label, total SO_2 may not exceed 50 ppm, and he prefers not to use it on the must so he may have the possibility of adding it to the perry at bottling time for improved stability.

Figure 7.4. Éric Bordelet in his tasting room.

Stéphane Leroyer doesn't keeve his must but leaves it to decant for a couple of days, and then he racks and filters it before the beginning of fermentation. He mentioned some other producers do keeve their perry pear musts, but not systematically, and the decision as to whether to keeve or not depends on the variety and the terroir. He says his soil is rather rich and the musts contain quite a bit of nitrogen, and because of this, he needs to monitor closely the fermentation to control it. The temperature is conditioned to 8 to 10°C (45 to 50°F) in the tank room. To start the fermentation, some dry yeast may be used if the wild yeast

Figure 7.5. Éric Bordelet's Poiré Granit of the 2009 cuvée was still excellent when drunk in 2016, although it was somewhat deeper in color than a younger perry.

count is too low. He doesn't normally use yeast nutrients. He racks and filters when the SG has fallen to about 1.035 to reduce the yeast biomass and the speed of fermentation, and additional stabilization rackings may be done if required. Fining is usually necessary to ensure a good clarification before bottling, and for this he uses a combination of gelatin at a dosage of 20 to 30 g/hL (grams per hundred liters) followed with silica solution (Kieselsol or similar) at 5 to 10 mL/hL. He notes that if he didn't do a maceration of the pulp and a decantation of the must, the dosages for fining would have to be increased substantially.

The Poiré Domfront is always sparkling and presented in a champagne-style bottle, with a mushroom cork and wire cage. It may be brut (dry), demi-sec (medium), or doux (sweet), but the most common is the demi-sec. The PDO specification requires that the sparkle be obtained by in-bottle fermentation without any sugar addition, and thus the Charmat method can't be used, and artificial carbonation as well as pasteurization are strictly forbidden. Most perry makers use the ancestral method and will bottle at an SG of about 1.022 to 1.027 to obtain a demi-sec. Lower or higher SG at bottling time would produce a brut or a doux, respectively.

During the in-bottle fermentation, the perry loses about 4 points of density as the internal pressure of CO_2 rises. Note the true resulting residual sugar will be lower than what is suggested by the density because of the sorbitol, which increases the density of the dry perry. As mentioned in the description of the ancestral method in chapter 1, page 39, such perries may not be perfectly stable over the long run and have some sediment in the bottom of the bottles, which may cause a haze in the last glasses poured. In order to overcome this, Stéphane Leroyer told me he had conducted trials at riddling and disgorging the bottles with the neck frozen (à la glace), but as yet he hadn't mastered the technique well enough to use it for his production perries. I do, however, strongly suspect that Éric Bordelet uses a similar method for his perries, or possibly the transfer method. However, I didn't have the opportunity to get a confirmation of this from Éric. In any case, the fact is that his perries do not have any sediment in the bottles and are very stable: He had given me a seven-year-old bottle of his Poiré Granit that was still perfect.

Figure 7.6. A typical bottle of Poiré Domfront PDO, from Stéphane Leroyer's Ferme de la Poulardière.

CHAPTER EIGHT

Austria
Birnenmost

In 2015, I received an invitation to attend the Salon des Mostes and the Birnenleben conference on perry pear orchards in Amstetten, in the Mostviertel region of Austria, to be held in late August of that year. I must say that at that time I had no idea this region had such a rich cider and perry tradition. I did hesitate, as my agenda was quite busy for that period, with a scheduled trip to Australia just a few weeks later, not to mention I had to attend to my own apple harvest and cider production. After checking a bit on the internet, I read interesting things about the Mostviertel region, and so I decided to go—a decision I never regretted, as I found there fantastic people, a beautiful country, and a cider tradition that made me think upon return that Mostviertel was the best-kept secret on the Cider Planet.

Mostviertel spreads approximately 200 kilometers (120 miles) west of Vienna in the direction of Salzburg,

Figure 8.1. A beautiful perry pear tree specimen with the Hansbauer cidery in the background.

between the Danube, which constitutes its northern border, and the mountains in the south. The fundamental feature of this region is the uninterrupted presence of large, majestic perry pear trees. It is estimated there are between 150,000 and 200,000 such large trees in Mostviertel. Some of the larger specimens may be between 250 and 300 years old and make fabulous trees that can reach nearly 40 meters (130 feet) in height. Most of the older trees date from the reign of the Habsburg empress Maria Theresa, who ordered their planting by law. The pear is so important that not only do we see them in trees but also in numerous pieces of artwork spread everywhere, most strikingly in the center of roundabouts, which is quite unique to the region. It may go as far as to giving a pear shape to an ornamental tree!

Figure 8.2. One of the numerous roundabouts featuring pear artwork in Mostviertel, near Amstetten.

The main product of the region is the *Mostviertler Birnenmost* (also spelled *Birnmost*), or for short, simply *most*. Apple cider is called *Apfelmost*, and an apple-pear blend is called *Apfel-Birnenmost*. For a person who has drunk perries only from France or England, the first contact with the *most* is somewhat surprising:

Presentation. *Most* is served in a fancy crystal wine glass (see appendix B). It is still, perfectly clear, and with very little color. The appearance is like a classic white wine.

Bouquet. It is characteristic of perry: very clean, fruity, fresh, without any lactic notes or volatile acidity noticeable.

Figure 8.3. *Most* glasses ready for a tasting. This is the standard model of glass used by producers in their tasting rooms.

Taste and flavor. Acidity is quite present, more or less depending on the variety. Astringency is also present, characteristic of perries. It is generally dry or very dry; even the sweeter *mosts* give an impression of dryness.

All in all, *most* is delicate and fancy, fresh, fruity, and clean with a sharp flavor and characteristic perry bouquet.

The total annual production of *most* is of the order of two to three million liters. There are 130 producers in the region, most of them having an annual capacity in the range of 5,000 to 60,000 liters, while the largest may produce as much as 300,000 liters. The region also has an important production of distilled fruit spirits, or schnapps, while another specialty is *Mostello*, a blend of pear schnapps with partially fermented *most*, aged four years in wood casks. The most important center of perry making activity is around the town of Amstetten, which is well situated in the heart of Mostviertel.

This chapter was written with the help of Toni Distelberger, a senior Most Baron who with his family runs the Distelberger cidery in Amstetten. They also run a *Heuriger*, a restaurant where simple, traditional food is served. The cidery's production is approximately 20,000 liters of perry and cider. They additionally produce fresh juice, different kinds of schnapps, liqueur, and vinegar. I also wish to acknowledge the collaborative support provided by the Moststraße organization,* the input I received from Bernhard Scheiblauer, and the help given me by the great producers I visited during my stay: Bernhard Datzberger (Seppelbauer),

---

* The Moststraße is an organization that supports the producers. It created a "Perry Route," and provides information, marketing support, and other services.

Hans Heibl (Hansbauer), Josef Zeiner (Mostg'wölb), and Ferdinand Litzellachner (FERDL). And I thank Christian Haberhauer (Moststraße), who did a wonderful job as a guide and interpreter.

The Most Barons

The Most Barons are certainly a unique feature of Mostviertel. They are an association of producers, enologists, tasters, and restaurant owners dedicated to the promotion of the *most* culture and tradition. Their role includes the establishment of quality criteria for the *most* and the protection and conservation of the pear tree heritage for future generations. They are also responsible for the introduction of the fancy glasses that are used by most cideries for the tastings. In addition to this, they meet in an annual ritual to do blind tastings of their finest cuvées. The best ones will then be blended together to elaborate three flagship products, the *Gourmet Mosts*: Brous, Preh and Exibatur. The Most Barons are easily recognizable when they wear

Figure 8.4. Bernhard Datzberger (*right*) in his tasting room with Christian Haberhauer.

their black hat with a red ribbon and white feather. There are currently 21 of them, but this number may change as new members join the association. In Austria, there are no labels such as PGI or PDO for the perry. Although a request had been made to introduce a PGI for Mostviertler Birnenmost, this was abandoned in 2018. In fact, the term "Most Barons" plays a similar role to the label: when customers see "Most Baron" printed on the bottle, they are assured of a certain style and quality.

Figure 8.5. Most Baron Reikersdorfer with a display of some of his products at the Salon des Mostes. Note the characteristic hat of the Most Barons.

The Orchard and the Pear Varieties

As in all the rest of Europe, the perry pear orchard of Mostviertel has seen a drastic reduction in the number of trees during the twentieth century: Censuses made in 1938 and in 1994 indicate the number fell from 7.5 million to slightly under 200,000 trees. In other words, 39 trees out of 40 trees disappeared in half a century! These trees are generally not planted in a typical square pattern but rather as lines of trees, often along roads or lanes, with a spacing of 10 to 15 meters (35 to 50 feet) between trees. Fruit from these is always fully organic. In addition to the old trees, modern plantations of standard trees may now be up to 30 years old. Perry pears are also grown in semi-intensive orchards, usually on quince rootstock, but some producers use Fox 11 and Farold rootstocks. IPM techniques are not generally used, although some growers are looking into this. Density may be on the order of 600 or 700 trees per hectare (240 to 280 per acre). There is no real experience here of growing pears at higher density than those numbers.

Figure 8.6. Nice specimens of old perry pear trees. Note the trees are planted in lines rather than in a typical orchard grid pattern.

Figure 8.7. The page featuring the Grüne Pichlbirne pear in the Moststraße book *Äpfel & Birnen, Schätze der Streuobstwiensen*, by Gerlinde Handlechner and Martina Schmidthaler, with some perry made of this variety.

Mostviertel has the richest perry pear pomona of all producing regions: It is currently estimated there could be some 200 to 300 different varieties, of which to date only approximately 150 have been adequately analyzed, characterized, and catalogued. An important book was published in 2019 by the Moststraße (the Perry Route) organization: *Äpfel & Birnen, Schätze der Streuobstwiensen* by Gerlinde Handlechner and Martina Schmidthaler. Moststraße has permitted me to use photos from this book, and I thank them very much for this. The following are some of the most ubiquitous varieties used for perry making in Mostviertel.

Dorschbirne is a well-liked, earlier-maturing, and high-acidity variety. It is often used for single-variety perry. The fruit is yellow, very juicy, rather small at 4 to 5 cm (1½ to 2 inches) in diameter, and doesn't keep long. The variety is very productive.

Figure 8.8. Rote Pichlbirne pears from the book *Äpfel & Birnen, Schätze der Streuobstwiensen*. Photo by Moststraße.

Grüne Pichlbirne (also written Pichelbirne) is late-ripening, with high acid, a lot of tannins, and a full-bodied flavor. The variety is ancient, dating back to before 1700, and the very large trees are productive but alternate bearing. The fruits are juicy, of medium size, and greenish in color, with a round shape.

Rote Pichlbirne is a pretty pear of a good size with reddish-yellow skin, mild in acid, and early ripening. It is excellent for making dried pears, schnapps, fresh juice, and perry. Often the ripest fruits are used for drying and for schnapps, while firmer fruits are used for perry.

Speckbirne, a very popular variety, is a larger fruit of up to 8 cm (3 inches) across that has milder acidity but quite harsh, bitter tannins. This variety is not as ancient as others, as it was first recorded in 1888 in Carinthia (southern Austria). In addition to perry, it is used for drying, schnapps, and juice. Ripening is in October and the fruits keep fairly well. Although it is used by many producers, Toni Distelberger would not recommend this variety for a hobbyist as he says it is difficult to work with.

Wasserbirne (Schweizer Wasserbirne) is an important, not-so-sharp variety with low tannins, which originated in Switzerland in the early 1800s. The fruit is fairly large, barrel-shaped, and green-yellow. The name means "water pear." According to Toni Distelberger, the fruits may be eaten fresh, give a juice with a wonderful peary nose, and produce a very fragrant, graceful perry. Being lower in tannins, the perry will clear more easily and fining is usually not necessary.

And to a lesser extent, the Stieglbirne, Winawitzbirne, Landlbirne, Scheiblbirne, and Knollbirne varieties are used. Toni Distelberger's favorite varieties are Dorschbirne and Rote Pichlbirne as early-ripening varieties (by mid-September), and Knollbirne and Stieglbirne as later ripening in October. He says they all bear rich fruit and are easy to process.

In Germany and Switzerland, many other important perry pear varieties are available, among which we note the following.

Champagner Bratbirne is an old German variety that originated in Swabia and was already well known by the 1760s. The variety has been traditionally used for more than 200 years in the production of sparkling perry that was served at the court of nobles as well as during festivities in Swabian villages. The juice of this pear is high in sugar and has a medium to high tannin content. Nowadays it is used by the well-known German cider and perry maker Jörg Geiger, and there is an interesting story about it. Geiger produces a traditional-method sparkling perry that he markets under the name Champagner Bratbirne. French champagne producers tried to stop him from using this name, claiming the name could create confusion with true Champagne sparkling wine. In court, it was however judged that since the name is that of the fruit used, and considering it is over two centuries old, Geiger could keep on calling his perry Champagner Bratbirne.

Gelbmöstler is a variety of Swiss origin, and it is grown in that country as well as in Austria and Germany for making perry and schnapps. It is also known in the United States, as it is part of the perry pear collection at the NCGR Corvallis (the National Clonal Germplasm Repository in Oregon), and a few producers in the US use it. The author U. P. Hedrick

Figure 8.9. Champagner Bratbirne perry pears. Photo by Jörg Geiger.

describes it briefly in his book *The Pears of New York* (1921), writing that it is very astringent and quickly becomes overripe. The name simply means yellow perry pear. The fruit ripens in September and doesn't keep long. It is medium size and yellow. The flesh is juicy and has good acidity and tannins.

Perry Making

The pears are harvested from early September until the end of October. Most are hand-collected on the ground as they fall, but a few producers use mechanical harvesting machines. Toni Distelberger mentioned that the temperatures have been very warm in September these last few years, and as a result, the pears need to be processed rapidly after they are collected. Only the latest-ripening varieties may be left for maturation.

A large fraction of the pears is processed variety by variety to produce single-variety perries. As an example, Hans Heibl told me that he does over 85 percent of his perry production as single-variety. For the blended perries, the fruit may be blended before milling, and also,

Figure 8.10. Bernhard Datzberger and his antique traditional press.

fermented perries may be blended. Milling is by standard grater or centrifugal mills. Maceration is not done systematically, but some producers let the pulp macerate for an hour or two before pressing. Old traditional presses, such as shown in figure 8.10, are of a lever type with a heavy concrete counterweight, and resemble somewhat a giant nutcracker. A few were still in use until the end of the last century. They have mostly been replaced by hydraulic rack and cloth presses, which in turn are now being superseded by horizontal pneumatic presses, which require much less manual work. A few larger producers use a belt press. Typical properties of the fresh juice may be as follows: The target pH would be 3.4 to 3.6, but may rise to 3.8 when some fruit is overripe; the total acidity expressed as malic acid equivalent would be around 5 g/L for the lower-acidity varieties, and up to 9 g/L for the higher-acidity varieties such as Dorschbirne.

The producers wish to obtain a very clean, fragrant perry, and for this they have adopted some modern wine making technologies, which they mix with the ancestral tradition. Thus, the perry making technique in Mostviertel is quite unique and is fairly different from what is done by their colleagues in France and England. The pre-fermentation processing of the must is crucial and has two purposes: First, it controls the microorganisms and makes sure all acetic and lactic acid bacteria as well as *Brettanomyces* and other wild yeasts are eliminated; and, second, it reduces the tannins and the harshness of the perry pears. For this, the producers most often do a pasteurization of the must, using an inline flash pasteurizer that raises the temperature of the must to 80°C (176°F) for a short period of time (such pasteurizers are also called HTST, for high temperature short time). After heating, the must goes through another heat exchanger with cold water for rapid cooling. Producers also clarify the must either before or after the pasteurization, depending on the temperature and the risks of having a spontaneous fermentation, which they want to avoid. This clarification, a débourbage, is quite elaborate, and the exact procedure varies depending on the conditions and on the producer. Toni Distelberger's would go as follows: First, an enzyme is added to degrade the pectins. This is followed by a gelatin fining, which, according to Toni, is the most efficient for working with the pear tannins. Either pure gelatin is used, or a product such as Erbslöh Mostgelatine, which also includes casein and is more efficient in decreasing the astringency of the juice. After which a silica solution such as Blankasit or Kieselsol is added. And, finally, he may complete the fining process with bentonite. This whole clarification procedure may last for two days if the temperature permits, the objective being to obtain a perfectly cleared must before starting the fermentation. When the clarification is successful, he is quite assured everything will go smoothly and the resulting perry will be crystal clear and have the ideal tannin balance. Otherwise, he might try a filtration, or hope the perry will clear naturally after fermentation. Toni also mentioned that fining after fermentation is not something he likes to do because the high dosages of gelatin that are then required might affect the perry aroma. He believes that the pre-fermentation fining gives much better results.

The pasteurized must is stable and is sometimes kept for months before being used. It is usually stored in tanks that are steam-sterilized before filling. Some producers prefer to wait until winter before they start their fermentations, as there is less farm work to do at that period. Additionally, this permits them to make successive batches in the same

Figure 8.11. Most Baron Distelberger and some of his products at the Salon des Mostes. Note the typical 1-liter glass bottles with screwtop closures, and a bottle of traditional method sparkling perry on the right.

fermentation tanks. It may be noted that some larger producers, such as FERDL, have juice storage facilities that can be rented to smaller producers. Hence, producers can press the pears in September and October, and fill their fermentation tanks with a first batch of must, while the rest is sent to the storage tanks. And when the first batches are complete, the producers can fetch some more of their must from storage and start again.

Most producers use stainless steel fermentation tanks, often with temperature control, and follow modern practices for the fermentation. Sulfiting of the must prior to fermentation is not necessary when the juice has been pasteurized. If a batch hasn't been pasteurized, then sulfiting at a dosage of about 50 ppm is done. The must is inoculated with a strain of white wine yeast (*Saccharomyces cerevisiae*). Nutrients are normally used as recommended for the yeast strain. The temperature is kept relatively high, between 14 and 18°C (57 to 64°F), depending on the particular yeast strain used. The fermentations are fast, and they are usually carried all the way to dryness in about three weeks. A racking is done at the end of the fermentation to separate the perry from its lees.

At this stage, the perry may be left a couple of months for maturation, and during this time it will complete its clarification. The perry will then be ready for bottling. By far the most common procedure is to bottle a still perry in which juice or sugar may be added to give some residual sweetness. The stability would then be insured by a sterile filtration and addition of sulfite at a dosage of 35 to 40 ppm. Many small producers don't have the equipment for this and will contract the bottling and related processing. The standard bottles are 1-liter, clear glass with a screw cap closure. The Austrians have a quite elaborate nomenclature for categories of residual sweetness and acidity in the perry, which are defined as follows:

Extra trocken. Extra dry, no residual sugar.
Trocken. Dry, around 4 g/L sugar and may be up to 9 g/L sugar if the acidity is also high to balance the sugar.
Halbtrocken. Semidry, up to 12 g/L sugar.
Lieblich or Halbsüß. Semisweet, 12 to 45 g/L sugar.
Süß. Sweet, over 45 g/L sugar (this is rarely seen in practice).
Kräftig. Tannins are dominant, even if residual sugar is high, and acidity is low.
Resch. High acidity, over 7.2 g/L as malic acid equivalent. Typical of the varieties Dorschbirne, Landlbirne, and Grüne Pichlbirne.
Halbmild. Medium acidity, between 5.8 and 7.2 g/L. Tannins are not dominant; residual sugar either equals acidity or is lower. Typical of the varieties Stieglbirne, Speckbirne, Rote Pichlbirne, and Knollbirne.
Mild. Low acidity, less than 5.8 g/L. No significant tannins, either low in acidity or at least a balancing high residual sugar content. Typical of the varieties Wasserbirne and Winawitzbirne.

A few alternative processes may be seen. In order to retain some natural residual sweetness, a few producers stop the fermentation by cold shock before dryness is reached, then they rack and filter. Small quantities of pétillant and sparkling perry are also produced. Pétillant perries, called *Frizzante*, are usually obtained by the injection method to approximately 2 bars (29 psi). Only a couple of producers make some true sparkling perry by the traditional method. Toni Distelberger is one of them, but he has the processing done under contract.

Plate XI.

2. Cherry Norman.

3. Red Norman.

1. Redstreak

5 Strawberry Norman

4. White Norman.

8 Pym Square

7. Black Norman

6. Handsome Norman.

Alice B.Ellis del

for The Woolhope Club.

PART III

NEW AND EMERGING CIDERS AND PERRIES

We will now explore craft ciders that are produced in nontraditional cider regions. These regions are in the Americas and Australia, and also in Asia and in parts of Europe where there is not a long tradition for making cider, such as in Scandinavia. In a number of cases, some craft cider making activity existed long ago but had stopped for different reasons. And in some of these regions a cider industry has been present for quite some time, but there was no (or no more) craft cider until a recent revival. Exploration of these ciders is fascinating, in great part because in those regions there are no established rules and no traditions to which cider makers have to adhere. This is then an open invitation to diversity, to experimentation. What will strike us most is the lack of homogeneity in style. If we take for example French or Spanish traditional ciders, they will be quite easily recognizable, and a moderately knowledgeable person in a blind test would correctly identify the style. Not so with the ciders from these newer-producing regions where a huge range of styles, from very European-like to fruit or spiced flavored, may be found. Yes, we saw, for example in Spain and in Germany, that traditional and modern styles coexist in those regions, but these modern ciders are nevertheless made according to the country's cider tradition, just being slightly less *wild* than their traditional counterpart. This is not the case anymore on this scene of the new and emerging ciders.

Another important aspect of these ciders is movement and dynamism. We may see the traditional European cider as being static: Often the cideries have been established for a long time and they are passed along to the next generation; processes don't change much and evolution is slow; and cider apple pommages are well known and established. It is just the opposite in this new scene where there is a rapid evolution of cider making practices, a search for the discovery of new cider apple varieties, and the general quality of the cider gets better year after year. Everything is young, with an overwhelming majority of the producers having less than 5 or 10 years of experience in cider making. They are still experimenting, and they are eager to learn how to make better cider.

We'll start this exploration with Australia and New Zealand in chapter 9, then move to North America, and conclude with visits to a few cider makers in unlikely cider places.

CHAPTER NINE

Australia and New Zealand

In January 2015, I received a completely unexpected email message from Jane Anderson of Cider Australia, inviting me to visit Australia during two weeks in September/October of that year, to be a guest international judge at their annual Australian Cider Awards and participate in their Australian Cider Festival. I almost fell out of my chair, and soon after recovering from my surprise and having read the email a second and a third time, I asked my wife: "How about a trip to Australia?" We immediately agreed this was the opportunity of a lifetime to travel in this country, which for us is the antipode, and where I hadn't even dreamed I would visit one day. Plus, Tasmania, that large island south of Melbourne that is sometimes referred to as the Apple Isle, had represented one of the most exotic destinations I could think of. I must say I was very impressed by the organizational talents of Jane Anderson, who did all the planning for this visit in Australia. I discovered a very dynamic cider community that makes every effort to bring Australian ciders to the highest level.

The cider history in Australia starts at the beginning of the 1800s with some records of cider making near Sydney by 1803, and in Tasmania during the 1820s (I visited a cider mill at the Woolmer's Estate museum in Tasmania that dated back to 1843). During the 1850s, cideries were set up near gold mines to supply the miners, in addition to a commercial producer that operated in Melbourne. The industry slowly increased in size and then boomed during the 1960s and '70s, with large Australian producers and even Bulmers from the U.K. producing some of their ciders in Australia at that time. This popularity, however, fell drastically in the 1980s and '90s, to the point where there remained only a few local craft producers and a couple of brands of industrial cider by the turn of the millennium. In the introduction he wrote for *The Australian Cider Guide* (2013),* Max Allen mentions the year 2007 as being a turning point where the modern cider boom started: "Even as recently as 2007, when the first Cider Tasting Australia competition was staged in the Adelaide Hills, it attracted entries from just a dozen local producers—and that pretty much covered everybody involved in the industry at the time." From then on, things started to accelerate. The Cider Australia organization was established in 2012 by a group of producers to represent the interests of the industry. Thirty of them became members of the organization at its founding, and by the end of 2018, there were some 80 members of Cider Australia out of an estimated total number of 140 cider producers in the country. The annual growth of the industry has been very strong, peaking at more than 20 percent around 2012. In more recent years, there has been a slowdown of the growth, with a shift from large-scale industrial cider to more crafty cider produced by smaller players.

The 2007 Cider Tasting Australia competition was not repeated in the following years, and a few years later the Australian Cider Awards

---

* *The Australian Cider Guide* is a promotional booklet edited by Max Allen that was first published in 2013 by Barrel Media. An updated version was published in 2020 by Cider Australia. Max Allen is a well-known journalist, wine and cider writer, and author.

competition was established under the leadership of David Pickering and producers James and Gail Kendell of Small Acres Cyder. This new competition was first held in September 2011 in Orange (west of Sydney). In 2014, the organization was handed to Cider Australia and it was moved to Melbourne. It has seen steady growth since then, with 260 entries in 2018. One remarkable characteristic of this competition is that every year the organization invites an international guest judge to be part of the judging team to bring some international perspective. I had the honor of being this guest judge in 2015, and a few other people mentioned in different parts of this book have also received this invitation. It is interesting to note the competition is open to internationally produced ciders, as long as they are available for sale in Australia. In the early years, the award for best cider or perry had mostly been won by imported products. In 2015, when I was judge, this award was given to a cider produced in Australia, and since then, except for one year, it is an Australian cider that has earned the grand prize, thus demonstrating the increase in quality of Australia-produced ciders.

One problem that craft cider makers face in Australia and New Zealand is that there are no regulations concerning a minimum apple juice content. This means that a beverage can be made with only a minimal use of apples or apple juice and still be labeled as a cider. The Cider Australia organization is currently asking for a reform of the definition of cider and perry in the Australia New Zealand Food Standards Code so that it should include a minimum apple juice content. Additionally, they introduced in October 2018 a Trust Mark to clearly identify ciders made with 100 percent Australian-grown fruit. The Trust Mark also requires a minimum juice content. It is not as rigorous or stringent as a PGI or PDO certification label, as it doesn't impose any rules in the cider-making process, but Cider Australia considers this Trust Mark as a first step to help customers select the right cider for them.

Portraits of a Few Australian Cider Makers

I would like to introduce here a few of the cider makers I met during my stay in Australia. I chose them because I had the opportunity to get to

Figure 9.1. Lynne Uptin and Clive Crossley picking from their medium-density orchard at Red Sails in Tasmania. Note the beautiful view of the sea. Photo by Red Sails Cider.

know them better, and I think they have had an important influence on the development of the Australian cider industry.

One of the first modern-era, Australian cidermakers to make use of true cider apples for commercial production was Drew Henry (Henry of Harcourt cidery). My wife and I had the pleasure to visit Drew and his family in 2015, and they gave us the warmest welcome. Unfortunately, a farm accident claimed Drew's life in 2017, and this was a shock for all of the Australian cider community. His son Michael continues the good work. Drew, who had made a career as a geologist, acquired the property in Harcourt in 1994, which included orchards of commercial dessert apple and pear varieties. He started experimenting with cider in 1997 and replaced most of the dessert varieties (except a few that he kept) by top-working the trees and grafting cider apple varieties. The Henry of Harcourt cidery officially opened in 2003. His favorite varieties were Bulmer's Norman, Michelin,

Kingston Black, and Improved Foxwhelp. He also liked the dessert varieties Pink Lady and Sundowner, of which he used the non-premium fruit for cider. Drew was a very competent orchardist who had some of the best managed high-density orchards that I have seen.

Another pioneer of the Australian cider revival is Clive Crossley. He and his wife Lynne Uptin run the Red Sails cidery in the south of Tasmania, not far from Hobart, where we were hosted for a few days during our 2015 stay. Clive started planting his orchard in 1987 while he was still active in his professional career as a cell biologist, but it was only when he retired in 2010 that he started to produce cider commercially on a small scale. Right from the start his trees were true cider apple varieties, planted on midsize rootstock in a medium-density orchard that is managed without the use of pesticides. Red Sails's orchards now contain more than 30 varieties of cider apple, as well as a few varieties of true perry pears. About half of his apples are bittersweet varieties, and half are varieties that contain more acid (sharp and bittersharp), which he says make perfect blends for him. His favorites are Yarlington Mill, Kingston Black, Somerset Red-streak, Dabinett, Foxwhelp, Fréquin rouge, and Blanchet. The Red Sails cidery is one of the few in Australia to use the traditional method of keeving in the production of some of their ciders.

Tim Jones was head cider maker at William Smith & Sons, in the Huon Valley, Tasmania. William Smith planted his first orchard in 1888 and founded the company, which is nowadays directed by his great-grandson Ian Smith. This company is firstly a large commercial grower of market apples, with 50 hectares (125 acres) of orchards. They converted their fruit-growing operation to organic in 1997 and started the production of cider in 2012. In the beginning, the cider operation was mainly aimed at using the nonpremium fruit for making light, modern-style ciders. However, along came Tim Jones in 2014 as head cider maker. Tim happens to be married to a woman from Brittany in France who enjoys serious traditional cider, and he was exposed to the *cidres Bretons* when he visited his in-laws. He enjoyed those ciders so much that he convinced his boss to start planting true cider apple varieties and to make ciders inspired by the European tradition. He succeeded in this venture indeed: His first cuvée, which was a blend of 18 cider apple varieties, was the one to

Figure 9.2. Tim Jones at the 2015 Australian Cider Festival in Melbourne, displaying his award-winning 18 Varieties cider.

which we awarded the Best in Show prize during the 2015 Awards. And it didn't stop there: His French Blend won the same prize in 2016, and a single-variety Kingston Black won again in 2018! And while the mainstream modern-style ciders still make up the bulk of the production at William Smith & Sons, these cuvées of traditional European inspiration certainly have put the cidery on the short list of the great ones. Tim's favorite apple varieties are Yarlington Mill, Kingston Black, Cimetière de Blangy, and Crémière.

In addition to the individuals just noted, I would like to mention and thank here the following persons who have contributed to my understanding of the Australian cider scene by discussions or by inviting me to visit their cidery: Max Allen, Jane Anderson (Cider Australia), Warwick Billings (LOBO Cider), Nyall Condon (Flying Brick Cider Co.), Lisa Cresswell (Seven Oaks Farmhouse Cider), Karina Dambergs (Red Brick Road Cider), Wayne Hewett (Cheeky Rascal), Behn Payten (Napoleone Cider), David Pickering, and Damien Viney (Spreyton Cider Co.).

New Zealand Cider Scene

The cider scene in New Zealand evolved in a rather different way from that of Australia. In effect there are no records of commercial cider making during the nineteenth century, and during the twentieth century, it is rather the fruit wine industry that took the market. Some of the fruit wine producers also had a cider offered in their portfolio, but it was never given a high priority and was rather seen as a low-cost sweet drink for nondiscriminating consumers. An association, the Fruit Wine and Cider Makers Association of New Zealand, was formed in the 1980s to represent the interests of fruit wine, cider, mead, and liqueur producers, and it has held an annual combined competition for all those products.

Since about 2005, New Zealand has seen a steady growth of the cider sector, initially mostly due to large brewers or fruit wine producers that added cider to their product line, industrially made either from concentrates or from surplus market apples. During the early 2010s, the Rekorderlig cider from Sweden was launched in New Zealand and there was subsequently a "boom" in that style of ultra-sweet, fruit-flavored ciders. In the same period, the Magners brand from Ireland was also introduced, which became very popular served on ice. With this increase in cider activity, the Fruit Wine and Cider Makers Association of New Zealand decided to have a separate section for cider, Cider NZ, which was born in 2015 with the aim to promote the many styles of cider created by New Zealand cider makers, through the annual NZ Cider Awards and by supporting and promoting the NZ Cider Festival. Hence, nowadays the NZ Cider Awards competition is held separately from the fruit wine competition. The first NZ Cider Festival was held in 2016 in Nelson. As of the end of 2018, there were 31 commercial cider and perry producer members of Cider NZ. Of these, 14 are dedicated cideries (although some are owned by major breweries), and 17 are breweries that have cider in their portfolio of products. (It is interesting to note that no fruit wine producers still make cider.) Only a handful of cider makers, however, would be considered "craft" producers of traditional-style cider. A good number of future producers are currently in the experimental or pre-commercial stage, and we can expect some growth in the number of small craft cideries in the coming years.

Unfortunately, I haven't been able to visit New Zealand yet. I hope I'll be able to go one day, but in the meantime I was able to gather the information presented in this chapter from good contacts I have in the country:

David Sax is chairman of the Cider NZ association. He works for Redwood Cider Co., which is the largest cider producer in the country, with an annual production of 10 million liters of modern-style cider made from dessert apple varieties.

Paul Paynter is from a family of fruit tree growers who currently manage 700 hectares (1,730 acres) of orchards in Hawke's Bay. He and his team started Paynter's Cider in 2013, making the cider using modern cider making practices, and blends of richer-flavored dessert apples with traditional English, Spanish, and French cider apple varieties.

Alex and Caroline Peckham run Peckham's Cidery and Orchard, a small craft cidery near Nelson that has earned the Champion Cider prize at the NZ Cider Awards in 2015, 2016, 2017, and 2018! They mostly use English cider apple varieties, sometimes blended with dessert varieties such as Jonagold or Russets. (With sadness, I just learned that Alex Peckham passed away in April 2022.)

Trevor Fitzjohn is a radiologist who has had a longtime passion for English cider apples and for traditional West Country cider. He recently launched TeePee Cider in Wairarapa, making a very small production of craft ciders inspired by the English style.

The Orchard and the Apple Varieties

Most apple orchards in Australia and New Zealand are of the semi-intensive to super intensive (high-density) types. In Australia are some of the highest densities of planting that I have seen anywhere, and just

Figure 9.3. A high-density orchard at Henry of Harcourt, north of Melbourne. This V-shaped planting system is called the Tatura Trellis and was developed in Australia.

Figure 9.4. At Spreyton Cider Company in Tasmania is a recently planted block to experiment with cider apple varieties in an ultra-high-density system. Note the irrigation pipes that run from tree to tree.

about no large apple trees or traditional extensive orchards. As summers are dry and hot, irrigation is the norm in most locations. Orchard management is typical of what is usually seen in intensive fruit growing with fully dwarfing rootstocks, including the use of IPM techniques and herbicide strips on tree rows. The majority of the larger orchards use conventional pest management, but there are exceptions and some have converted to organic management. Among the smaller producers managing lower-density orchards, we see more that are fully organic or even zero-spray.

Older orchards of the semi-intensive type, planted on medium-size rootstocks, are also there. Generally, these mature orchards were originally planted with standard market varieties, but many cider makers are now top-grafting these trees to cider varieties. One exception I have seen is the orchard at Red Sails, which was planted with true cider varieties right at the start in the 1990s.

A large part of the cider produced in Australia and New Zealand is made from standard market apple varieties, as both countries are major dessert apple growers and exporters, and a large supply of apples rejected at the packing houses are available for a low cost to the cider producers. The most widely grown and seen in cider making

Figure 9.5. At Napoleone in the Yarra Valley, hectares of orchards are fully covered by nets for protection against hail, birds, and bats.

Figure 9.6. Top-grafting a semi-intensive orchard to cider apple varieties at Seven Oaks Farmhouse Cider, on the Mornington Peninsula.

are as follows. In Australia, the varieties are Granny Smith, Red and Golden Delicious, Pink Lady (Cripps Pink), Fuji, Gala, Jonagold, Braeburn, and Sundowner (Cripps Red). In New Zealand, the varieties are Braeburn, Royal Gala, Fuji, Jazz, Envy, Smitten, and Sonya. There are also some richer-flavored heritage dessert varieties that aren't grown much anymore for the market, but have become popular with some craft cider makers. Examples of such are the Cox Orange Pippin, Newtown Pippin, and Sturmer Pippin. More information on the varieties used for cider in Australia may be found in Cecilia Thornton's *Cider Apples* (2013).

In addition to the varieties already noted, which are mostly sharp apples, Australia and New Zealand are fortunate to have good collections of true cider apples that were imported from Europe at different times during the twentieth century. Nowadays, these two countries have very stringent regulations regarding the importation of vegetal material, which makes it difficult and very costly to import new varieties.

In Australia, the European cider varieties were kept in different collections across the country, and they were not always accurately identified. Among these collections, two of the most important were at the Orange Agricultural Institute in New South Wales, and in Tasmania at the Grove facility of the Department of Agriculture. Australian cider makers are fortunate that David Pickering got interested by the matter. He started in 1984 to collect the cider cultivars that he could find from these government collections and also from private owners, and to graft them in his orchard in Orange, with the goal to collect all the cider apple varieties in existence in Australia.

Then the challenge was to make sure these were true to name when the Australian name was known in England or in France, or to seek an equivalent or synonym when the Australian name didn't match a known cultivar name in Europe. He made a study trip to visit English and French cider apple collections in October of 2007, thus confirming the identity of a number of varieties in existence in Australia. By the end of 2018, he was able to confirm that 34 cider apple varieties of English or French origin that were present in Australia were identical to their European counterparts bearing the same name. His work has also permitted the correction of the spelling of some variety names.

Figure 9.7. David Pickering in his orchard. Photo by Bill Bradshaw.

And in addition to these confirmed varieties, he also has collected an additional nine varieties that have cider apple names and could be useful in cider making but for which he hasn't been able to confirm the identity. It is interesting to note that, as a side effect of this work, he has discovered a few apples in Australia that had been lost in England. Thus, the English were able to reintroduce these in England! Currently, David Pickering's orchard is one of the very few to contain all the confirmed cider apple varieties present on the Australian territory, and he has been an important source of grafting wood for nurseries, growers, or hobbyists who want to propagate or grow these apples. I will add that David has been a great resource and helped a lot with the writing of this chapter.

The 34 identified cider varieties are spread within all standard cider categories (bittersharp, sharp, bittersweet, sweet).* Among the most important varieties, we may note, from England: Brown Snout, Brown's Apple, Bulmer's Norman, Dabinett, Kingston Black, Somerset Redstreak, Stoke Red, Tremlett's Bitter, and Yarlington Mill; and from France: Antoinette, Bedan, Cimetière de Blangy, Fréquin rouge, Michelin, and Tardive de la Sarthe.

In New Zealand, the core collection of cider varieties is quite similar, with varieties such as Kingston Black, Chisel Jersey, Yarlington Mill, Porter's Perfection, Harry Master's Jersey, or Major widely grown among producers of traditional-style cider. However, there are some identification problems: Paul Paynter indicated that at least three different apple varieties share the name Kingston Black! And he thinks that others might not be true to name—although they nevertheless make good cider. Paul also grows some less common varieties such as the C'hwervruz, a bitter variety from the Fouesnant region of Brittany.

Following are descriptions of a few varieties that are quite unique to cider making in Australia or New Zealand.

Blanchet (sharp to bittersharp) is a cider apple of French origin that is highly praised by Clive Crossley in Tasmania. Although it is described in the French reference book by Boré and Fleckinger (*Pommiers à cidre – variétés de France*), it is not grown much anymore for cider making in France. It is a late-ripening, mostly yellow apple of varying size. The juice of Blanchet is quite well balanced, with moderate concentrations of sugar, acid, and tannins.

Crémière (bittersweet) is obviously of French origin by its name, but it is no longer known in that country. Records indicate it had been grown in Somerset during the first part of the twentieth century but was considered lost until rediscovered in Tasmania. Material from the variety was returned to the U.K. in 2005 so that

* A complete listing may be obtained from the website CiderOz (www.cideroz.com).

it may be propagated again. Crémière has a nice flavor and good tannins. It is a favorite of Tim Jones.

Lady Williams (sharp) is from a wild seedling found in Donny-brook, Western Australia, that bore its first fruits in the early 1940s on Boronia Farm. It is thought that Granny Smith could be one of its parents. This apple is medium size and bright pink-red. This is a very late apple that keeps well. On the website of Boronia Farm, it is said the apples ripen in June or July and hang on the tree until August.* Now, this is the southern hemisphere, so their August is like February in the northern hemisphere! This is late indeed. For cider making, Lady Williams is quite sharp, but after hanging on the tree for a sufficiently long time, the sugar-acid ratio improves a lot. It is mostly used in Western Australia.

Pink Lady (sharp) was bred in 1973 in Western Australia by John Cripps (hence its official cultivar name of Cripps Pink) and intro-duced in 1979. It is a cross of Golden Delicious and Lady Williams. Pink Lady is an important commercial variety in Australia, and it is also grown in New Zealand. It is appreciated by many cider makers who consider it higher-flavored than most other market apples. Drew Henry liked it very much. The apples ripen very late and require a lot of heat to develop their proper flavor. I have heard people saying the quality is poor, but apparently the fruit quality depends a lot on the growing conditions, and when these are right, this apple becomes superb for eating and for cider. The variety is very susceptible to scab.

Smitten is a modern commercial variety that was bred in New Zealand and introduced in 1995. Its official cultivar name is PremA17 and is a seedling of (Falstaff × Fiesta) × (Braeburn × Royal Gala). It is well liked by Paul Paynter who says it takes after its Falstaff and Fiesta highly flavored grandparents.

---

* "Lady Williams Apple," Boronia Farm (website), last accessed April 12, 2022, https://boroniafarm.com.au/lady-williams-apple.

Figure 9.8. Pink Lady apples.

Sturmer Pippin (sharp) is an old English variety that possibly came from a natural cross of Ribston Pippin × Nonpareil, introduced during the 1830s. It was extensively grown in Tasmania and in New Zealand by the end of the 1800s for export to the U.K. and is still a popular variety for cider making among craft producers in those areas. It has a rich, sweet, and aromatic flavor, and its acidity is quite high and its tannins are low. It keeps very well and develops its sugar and aromatics after a good period in storage.

Sundowner (sharp) is from the same breeding program that released Pink Lady but is not as well known internationally. It is also a cross of Golden Delicious and Lady Williams, introduced in 1979, and its official cultivar name is Cripps Red. It requires a lot of heat and a very long growing season to ripen its fruits properly. The harvest period is late May to early June in the southern hemisphere, later than Pink Lady but not as late as Lady Williams. Paul Paynter considers it as one of the best among the modern market varieties for cider-making purposes, and it was one of the favorites of Drew Henry.

In Australia, a true effort has not been made to develop a genuine cider apple pomona by a selection of seedlings of Australian origin. In New Zealand, Paul Paynter has a small personal breeding program for obtaining cider apple varieties. He hasn't yet named a variety, but he has obtained some promising selections that he uses in his ciders.

Cider Styles and Cider Making

We find in Australia and in New Zealand two quite distinct styles of cider: the mainstream ciders, which are of a modern style, often made by larger producers; and the farmhouse and more traditional ciders, which are usually made by smaller craft producers.

Modern-Style Cider

The ciders of the modern style are often qualified as "easy drinking," as they are light in color and flavor, perfectly clarified, refreshing, fruity with a good acidity, and without perceptible astringency or bitterness. The mouthfeel is rather light, without much persistence. These ciders should have a clean flavor and none of the funkiness usually associated with malolactic fermentation. Most are made sparkling, and although their sweetness may range from dry to sweet, they are often on the sweeter side. They may be made from Australia-grown or New Zealand–grown commercial dessert apples, or from imported concentrates in the case of some industrial ciders. This style is defined as follows in the two countries:

- Australia—in the 2018 Style Guide of the Australian Cider Awards, this style is called "New World cider" and is defined as follows: "New World cider is made primarily from culinary/table apples. Typically, these ciders are generally lower in tannin and higher in acidity. New World ciders serve well as a 'session' drink, and suitably accompany a wide variety of foods." The guide additionally gives descriptors for aroma, flavor, appearance and color, and mouthfeel. The style is divided into four classes for different sweetness levels, and a fifth class is designated for ciders made sparkling with the traditional method.

- New Zealand—from the documentation of Cider NZ, this style is called "Contemporary Cider" and is defined as follows: "Contemporary NZ Ciders are simpler in style than Traditional Ciders and may be reminiscent of English East Country Ciders or French Ciders. They can be made using either cider apples, heritage apples or dessert apples. Contemporary NZ Ciders tend to be fruity, clean, straw color, light to medium body and have varying degrees of tannin and sweetness."

These ciders are usually made with commercial market varieties. Many producers don't grow their own apples and get them as non-premium fruit from large orchards or from packing houses. They can also buy the juice in bulk. Other producers do, however, manage their own orchards, and in that case they sell the premium fruit for the market and use the non-premium fruit for cider.

The cider making process for this style uses modern technologies, which are more fully described in chapter 1. We won't see here a description of the industrial process that uses concentrates, but only the techniques used by producers that make their cider from apples.

- Fruit handling and juicing varies greatly depending on whether the producer grows the fruit or buys it. The

Figure 9.9. The Flying Brick Cider Co. is in Geelong, about an hour south of Melbourne, and has one of the nicest tasting rooms that I have seen. It is owned by a winery, Leura Park Estate. This is a quite common situation in Australia. Their head cider maker is Nyall Condon, an important figure in the Australian cider scene. The cider is typical Australian modern-style, pale in color, and offered in beer-style bottles.

apples are usually tree-picked before complete maturity, as is commonly done for market fruit, and the maturation is completed in storage. The apples then are washed and sorted prior to milling. Maceration of the pulp between milling and pressing is not normally done. Belt presses are the most common type. The juice needs to be cooled at press exit, as it is usually quite warm during fall.

- The pre-fermentation procedure includes complete enzymatic depectinization and sulfite addition. Some blending and corrections for acidity and sugar (chaptalization or dilution) may be done.
- Fermentation is done using a selected yeast strain, with controlled nutrition, at temperatures that may range between 15 and 18°C (59 and 64°F). Such fermentations are usually completed to dryness in three to six weeks, and they are followed by a maturation of varying duration.
- The final processing consists of a clarification treatment by fining or filtration, blending, and back-sweetening. Prior to bottling, sterile filtration is most often used to ensure in-bottle stability. The cider is usually sulfited to 25 to 40 ppm of free SO_2.
- Sparkling ciders are produced by the CO_2 injection method, but some producers make modern-style ciders using the traditional method.
- Packaging is "beer style," either in 300 to 500 mL crown-capped glass bottles or in cans, and are sold as four- or six-packs. Some cider is also kegged for distribution to restaurants and bars.

Traditional-Style Cider

The traditional-style ciders are usually produced by smaller-sized cideries, and the apples are most often grown on the farm, which means these would be farm-based cideries. The main feature of this style is that some tannin-rich cider apples are used in the blends, which may also include a variable fraction of commercial or heritage dessert and culinary apple varieties. These ciders are complex and rich in aroma and flavor, which is described as follows in the Australian Style Guide: "Can range from subtle or perhaps no overt apple character, but with various flavors and esters that suggest apples or transformation of apples, through to fruitier apple character/aromas from slow or arrested fermentation. There may be some malolactic fermentation which contributes to desirable spicy/smoky, phenolic, and farmyard/old-horse characters." To the eye, these ciders may be hazy or well clarified, and their color is deeper than the modern style, ranging from yellow to amber. The mouthfeel is medium to full, with some astringency or bitterness from the tannins, and a long finish. The sweetness may range from bone-dry to medium sweet, but most are on the drier side.

The fundamental difference in the making of this cider compared to the modern style is, as already mentioned, the type of apples used in the blend. Apart from that, many producers will use less of the modern technologies in their process. Sometimes we'll see wild yeast fer-

Figure 9.10. The traditional-style cider produced by Borrodell Vineyard near Orange (west of Sydney) is made with Kingston Black, Foxwhelp, Somerset Redstreak, and Pink Lady apples. This is a dry and well-balanced cider of very high quality, packaged in beer-style bottles.

mentations, or ciders that haven't been perfectly clarified. Sulfite is generally used in smaller dosages, and this may permit the malolactic fermentation to proceed and impart more *funky* flavors. The fermentations will need more time before reaching dryness. A few producers use the keeving process to retain some unfermented sugar and achieve medium or sweet ciders without back-sweetening, and also a few pasteurize their bottles to insure stability.

Sparkling traditional-style ciders may be obtained by either the injection, traditional, or Charmat method. And in the case of keeved ciders, it would be the ancestral method that is used. The packaging is quite similar to what we see for modern ciders, although there are more of the 750 mL champagne-type bottles.

Additional Cider and Perry Styles

In addition to the modern and traditional ciders, we find perries that may also be of modern or traditional style, depending on the type of pears used to make them: traditional perries made with special perry pears, which are of English origin; and modern perries made with commercial dessert pear varieties. The other important style is the flavored cider, called "Cider or Perry with Fruit" in the Australian Style Guide, and "Cider Blend" in New Zealand. These ciders are produced from a modern-style cider base to which is added some other fruit, honey, hops, or spices. In New Zealand, it is said this is possibly the biggest category of cider sold in the country. These ciders should have a good balance between the blending components and the underlying cider character to make a harmonious and well-rounded drink.

CHAPTER TEN

United States and Canada

During the eighteenth and nineteenth centuries, there was a very strong cider culture in the United States. Many documents testify that cider was the main drink of rural people, and a number of eminent personalities, for example, President Thomas Jefferson, were known to be cider lovers. Jefferson even had his own cider orchard and cidery at his property at Monticello in Virginia. In New England, it is sometimes said that people drank more cider than all other drinks combined, including milk, water, tea, beer, and wine. Pomology references of that period also describe many apple varieties that were primarily used for cider; and Todd Little-Siebold, who teaches the history of agriculture at the College of the Atlantic in Maine, has started to compile a list of early American cider apples from old nursery catalogs and treatises. His list, at the moment of writing this, contains about 100 varieties and is still growing as he often finds new ones.

The cider industry, however, started to decline by the end of the nineteenth century, with the advent of temperance movements and gains made by the beer industry. Commercial cider making eventually came to a complete stop with the Prohibition (1920–33), and most cider orchards were cut down during that period. After Prohibition, it was beer that gained the hearts of Americans, in part because it was much quicker to grow grain than it was to wait for the production from newly planted apple trees. As a result, for the best part of the twentieth century, commercial cider making in the United States remained extremely marginal. An interesting peculiarity of cider in the United States is that it is often called *hard cider*, while *cider* by itself would refer to freshly pressed apple juice. A possible explanation for this would be that during Prohibition, as alcoholic beverages were banned, the juice was seen as a replacement for cider, and the name stayed.

In Canada the cider history has been completely different: Since the beginning of the French regime in the 1600s, beer has been the main drink of the people and cider never became important. Additionally, there is no record of specific apple varieties for use in cider making.* The reasons why these two neighbor countries evolved so differently (relative to cider) are not really understood, considering there was quite a bit of exchange between them, and that apple trees do grow well in both countries.

If we now look at the modern cider scene in North America, it is in the Canadian province of Quebec that craft cideries first started sprouting by the end of the 1980s. This was triggered by a small group of apple growers and cider makers that included the late Pierre Lafond of Cidrerie Saint-Nicolas, Michel Jodoin, and Robert Demoy of Cidrerie du Minot, who pressed the government and obtained a change in legislation that permitted artisanal cider production and sale. The decade of the 1990s then saw intense cider activity in Quebec, with the advent of many new cideries, the foundation of the

---

* This is quite well documented by Alain Boucher, in his book, *La petite histoire du cidre au Québec* (Quebec: Éditions Trois-Pistoles, 2011) and in a chapter he wrote in the collective work *La transformation du cidre au Québec* (Presses de l'Université du Québec, 2017).

association Cidriculteurs artisans du Québec (CAQ) in 1992, and also the development of ice cider. In 2002 in Quebec, there were already 30 active craft cideries members of the CAQ. The association was recently renamed Les producteurs de cidre du Québec.

During that same period in the United States, the cider scene remained rather calm, but a few pioneers laid stones for the revival of cider: Terry and Judith Maloney started West County Cider in 1984 in Massachusetts and cofounded the annual CiderDays festival in 1994, which eventually had a huge influence on the development of cider in the country and is still one of the major cider events on the continent; Steve Wood in New Hampshire was the first, in 1989, to plant a commercial orchard of true cider apple varieties, and founded Farnum Hill Ciders in 1995; Joe Cerniglia and Greg Failing made in 1991 the first batch of Woodchuck Hard Cider in a Vermont garage; and in Oregon, Alan Foster planted an important orchard of European cider apples and perry pears, and was probably the first in the country to produce commercially a single-variety Kingston Black cider. However, it took another 5 to 10 years after the turn of the millennium before the cider activity that we saw in Quebec reached the other provinces of Canada and the United States. But from then on, the cider industry in the United States has grown very rapidly to become nowadays one of the most important in the world—although in absolute numbers, the cider market is still quite small relative to other drinks like beer. US producers created the United States Association of Cider Makers (USACM) in 2013 (renamed the American Cider Association or ACA in 2019), a very dynamic association that among other things organizes every year the biggest cider event worldwide, CiderCon (short for "cider conference"). The most important cider competition, GLINTCAP (Great Lakes International Cider and Perry Competition), was initiated by Gary Awdey in 2005 and after a modest start now establishes year after year new world records for the number of entries. A large number of all sorts of cider events are now all around the continent—salons for tasting, festivals, and workshops. Some of them are very local, while others have national status.

At the beginning of 2019, a survey made by Cyder Market included 910 makers of cider or perry operating in the United States, while this number was just 40 in the year 2000; thus the number of cideries has multiplied by more than 20 times in 18 years. In fact, the number of US cideries has really exploded during the decade between 2008 and 2017. With a population on the order of 325 million in the country, this would now make approximately 2.8 cideries per million of population. That same survey informs us that the states hosting the largest number of cideries are New York, Michigan, and California, with just about 100 each. But the state that would have the greatest number of cideries relative to its population is Vermont, with 25 cideries for a population of about 600,000.

In Canada, it is in the province of Quebec where we find the greatest number of cideries, with more than 100 in 2020. In Ontario, 60 cideries were members of the Ontario Craft Cider Association (OCCA) in 2019, a number that has grown very rapidly from the 10 members at the founding of the association in 2012. British Columbia in the west also has a dynamic cider industry, and in the east a movement is starting in the Maritime provinces.

We will not find PDO or PGI certification labels in the United States, but there is one PGI label in Canada for Quebec Ice Cider. We will, however, find a number of ciders that have an organic certification. And also, a certification in California, Certified Real California Cider, ensures the cider is made 100 percent from apples grown in California.

Cider Styles

Classifying the cider styles in North America is certainly a difficult task because of the great variety of different products. We will find very traditional-type ciders that may be influenced by the traditional European ciders, or that may try to reproduce the American ciders that were produced during the nineteenth century, as well as very modern-type ciders, and everything in-between. We'll also find a panoply of flavored ciders, for which the American producers are certainly the world leaders. In the United States, the American Cider Association has made a number of trials to put some order in this, and thus help the customer to have a better knowledge as to what really is in the bottle. They first published the *Cider Style Guidelines*, of which a second version was issued in December 2018. But then, in November 2019, they replaced these styles to define five families of cider as follows:

Cider: made with only fermented apples.
Perry: made with only fermented pears.
Fruit Cider: made with apples (or pears) and another fruit either co-fermented or added post-fermentation.
Botanical Cider: made with apples (or pears) and one or more other botanical ingredients such as hops or spices.
Dessert Cider: includes drinks one would imagine having after a meal, such as ice cider, pommeau, eau-de-vie, or apple brandy.

The GLINTCAP competition also provides some style guidelines. In order to make judging possible, the ciders need to be entered in a certain category so that each will compete against other ciders of similar style. It is, in effect, nearly impossible to judge a traditional Spanish sidra against a fruit-flavored cider in the same flight. These style guidelines have changed through the years, and possibly will change again in the future, but in 2020 they define three broad categories: Standard Styles, Specialty Styles, and Intensified and Distilled Styles. Within the Standard Styles, they are defined further:

Modern Ciders: made primarily from culinary/table apples.
Heritage Ciders: made primarily from multiuse or cider-specific bittersweet/bittersharp apples, with wild or crab apples sometimes used for acidity–tannin balance.
Traditional Ciders: encompasses those produced in the West Country of England (notably Somerset and Herefordshire), Northern France (notably Normandy and Brittany), and other regions in which cider-specific apple varieties and production techniques are used to achieve a profile similar to traditional English and French ciders.
Natural Cider: intended for ciders from Asturias, the Basque Country, and other regions in which similar apple varieties and production techniques are used to achieve a

typical Spanish cider profile. In Asturias these ciders are known as *sidra natural*. In the Basque Country these ciders are known as *sagardo naturala*.

Rosé Cider: intended for any Standard Style cider whose coloration is derived entirely from red-fleshed or red-skinned apples.

Modern Perry: made from culinary/table pears.

Traditional Perry: made from pears grown specifically for perry rather than for eating or cooking.

It should be noted that since GLINTCAP is an international competition, the Traditional Cider and Natural Cider classes are specifically intended for ciders produced in Europe, or for some American offerings that reproduce the characteristic flavor of these. More typical American ciders would then correspond either to the Modern Cider or to the Heritage Cider style. Let us then look a bit deeper into these:

Modern Ciders are made primarily from commercial apples that have been grown in high-density orchards intended for the production of market fruit. It is then the non-premium fruit that is used to make the juice. The cider making generally follows modern practices as described in chapter 1. These ciders are low in tannins, which means there is no bitterness or astringency in the mouth, and little persistence of the flavor. They usually have a medium acidity, making them refreshing but not harsh or biting. The sweetness may range from dry to sweet. The color is typically pale to yellow.

Heritage Ciders are made from apples that contain more tannins or acid than standard commercial apples. The fruit is often grown in medium-density bush orchards specifically managed for the purpose of cider making. Producers of Heritage Ciders may use modern or traditional practices. The presence of tannins gives more mouthfeel and flavor persistence to these ciders, with some bitterness or astringency. Compared to Modern Cider style, the flavor is of an increased complexity and the coloration is deeper, more toward the amber. The acidity–tannin balance may range from low acid–high tannin to high acid–low tannin (see appendix A), and the sweetness usually ranges from bone dry to medium dry, and occasionally we see sweeter ciders.

The second broad category in the GLINTCAP competition is for Specialty Styles. These include Fruit Cider, Hopped Cider, Spiced Cider, Wood Aged Cider, Wood Aged Specialty Cider, Specialty Cider and Perry, and Unlimited Cider and Perry. The third broad category for Intensified and Distilled Styles includes Ice Cider, Fortified Cider, and Spirits.

It is interesting to look at the 2019 GLINTCAP results, and in particular at the number of commercial entries in the different broad categories. For the Standard Style ciders and perries, there were a total of 529 entries; for the Specialty Styles, there were 636 entries; and for the Intensified and Distilled Styles, there were 52 entries. This for a grand total of 1,217 commercial entries that year. We see that the Specialty Styles account for more than half of the total, and this certainly gives a very clear indication of the importance of these fruit-flavored, botanical, and specialty ciders and perries in the

Figure 10.1. The Spanish sidra natural style has become very popular in United States. We see here Ryan Burk of Angry Orchard in front of wooden vats he uses for this production in Walden, New York.

North American cider industry. It should be noted that the flavored ciders are normally based on Modern Style ciders. In effect, flavoring the cider may be seen as a way to compensate for the lack of character from the commercial table apples that are used in these ciders. Also, since many producers have very similar (if not identical) raw material to start with, they can express their creativity by some original flavoring. I must say I have seldom met a producer of a heritage-style cider that felt the need to add flavoring to the ciders he produced (one exception to that may be with hopped ciders that are made by some of them).

Apple Varieties

The pommages used in North America are very diverse and include commercial dessert varieties, heirloom varieties, and true cider apples. There are great variations among producers, depending on the region and climate, and on the style of cider they produce.

Standard Market Varieties

The apple varieties that we generally find in stores and that are used for the making of modern-style ciders include McIntosh, Golden and Red Delicious, Goldrush, Honeycrisp, Cortland, Idared, Jonagold, Granny Smith, Gala, and Fuji. None of these varieties are considered cider apples—they are strictly table, dessert, or cooking apples. When used for cider, they generally provide low to medium acidity and very little tannin. Most would be classified as sharps, while some lower-acidity varieties could be sweets. These apples are generally mass-produced in large intensive orchards that are managed in such a way as to produce good-looking table fruit, and it is the non-premium fruit that is available at low cost and used for cider making. However, sometimes the same varieties are grown on larger-sized trees with little fertilization in low-spray orchards, and in such cases these apples have improved properties for cider making purposes. An example of this is with Eve's Cidery in New York, where the Idared is highly prized. And as for myself in Quebec, I use Cortland a lot in my blends. We will not discuss these varieties further, as they are well known. Except for one, however, which I think deserves a special mention.

> **Goldrush** (sharp) is highly prized among many producers of heritage-style ciders, although it is a modern market variety. It gives a lot more substance to the cider than the other varieties of this group. The Goldrush apple was introduced in 1993 as a scab-resistant variety. It is a cross of Golden Delicious and a disease-resistant selection. The apple matures very late; the Golden-type flavor is rich, slightly spiced, with a high sugar content, a good acidity, and more tannins than most dessert apples. This is an apple for districts with a favorable climate with a lot of summer heat and a long growing season. It is a favorite of Ryan Burk of Angry Orchard and of Fabio Chizzola of Westwind Orchard, both in the Hudson Valley, New York.

European Cider Varieties

A number of bittersweet and bittersharp varieties that have been introduced from England, France, and Spain are nowadays under trial in North America. And some of the better-known varieties have been planted by a number of growers for cider production. Steve Wood of Farnum Hill Ciders in New Hampshire was a pioneer in the culture of these apples in the United States, having planted his first commercial orchard of European cider apples in 1989. Most of these varieties had been imported by the 1960s and '70s and kept in conservation orchards such as the New York State Agricultural Experiment Station in Geneva, New York, and the Canadian Clonal Genebank in Harrow, Ontario. They are now readily available from a number of nurseries in both countries. It is only very recently, however, that some Spanish varieties went through the US import process, and a few are now available.

According to a document published by Cornell University in 2018, the European cider apples that have the greatest acreage in the State of New York are Dabinett, Kingston Black, Porter's Perfection, Harry Master's Jersey, Geneva Tremlett, Brown Snout, Ellis Bitter, Chisel Jersey, Michelin, Brown's Apple, Yarlington Mill, and Somerset

Redstreak.* In the Pacific Northwest, growers tend to have more of the French varieties like Fréquin rouge, Bedan, Binet rouge, Bramtot, Médaille d'or, and Kermerrien. Descriptions for many of these varieties are presented in chapters 2 and 3.

Heirlooms

Heirloom is a word often used for an older apple variety, that is not mass-produced for the market. Generally, we talk about varieties that originated in America, but some were introduced from Europe. Most heirloom varieties fall into one of these broad categories:

- Dessert, table, or cooking apples that are rather sharp and are mainly eaten as fresh fruit and used for pies and cooking.
- Sweet apples that are low in acidity and mostly used for baking or making apple syrup.
- Cider apples that would for most be of the bittersharp, sharp, or bittersweet classes.

As for dessert apples, many are still popular as regional varieties, and customers who appreciate them can get them at a pick-your-own farm or at a farmers market. Some were the reigning varieties during their heydays a century or more ago, and have been intensively grown and even exported overseas. (However, at that time the term *intensive growing* didn't have the same significance as today because production orchards then consisted exclusively of widely spaced large trees.) So we may ask: What is fundamentally different between an heirloom dessert variety and a modern market variety? Not much in fact, and in many cases the distinction isn't clear. It is not just a question of age: Some of the common varieties, for example, the McIntosh, are just as old as most heirlooms. Many heirlooms are varieties that never became popular or fell out of favor for one reason or another. The falling out of a variety may have been because of a lack of hardiness or because it

---

* Lindsay Pashow, *Hard Cider Supply Chain Analysis*, Cornell Cooperative Extension, Harvest New York (March 23, 2018): https://harvestny.cce.cornell.edu/uploads/doc_48.pdf.

didn't adapt well to the new high-density orcharding techniques of the twentieth century. Taste was also a factor in many cases, in that the flavor of newer varieties was sweeter and more fashionable. But the fact remains that the heirloom varieties most often used in cider making, when compared to market varieties, show more intense flavors, and when we analyze their juice, we generally measure higher contents of sugar, acid, and tannin. This makes them more apt to produce a quality cider in the heritage style that has some good structure, mouthfeel, aroma, and flavor. As for their classification for cider making, these apples would be considered as sharps because their tannin content, although higher than that of common market varieties, is still insufficient to rank them as bittersharps.

Baldwin originated in Massachusetts as a wild seedling discovered around the 1740s. This old New England favorite was the queen of the orchards until the extreme winter of 1933–1934, when successions of warm and cold killed millions of trees. It was thereafter replaced by the hardier McIntosh as the dominant market variety. It is a heavy bearer, but only in alternate years. The fruit is large and mostly red. It ripens late and keeps well. The juice has good sugar content, and acidity is medium to high. Baldwins have always been used in New England for cider making, and the variety is still highly regarded by some producers. West County Cider makes a fine single-variety cider from Baldwin.

Esopus Spitzenburg is a beautiful medium-sized apple, and it is one of the most flavorful that can be tasted. It is packed with sugar and acidity and gives a lot of punch to a cider blend. But no matter how great its flavor, it never really was grown on a large scale because the tree isn't very productive and is sensitive to many diseases, including fire blight, making it a challenge for the grower. The variety originated at Esopus near the Hudson River in New York, but the date is not documented. It probably originated sometime during the second half of the eighteenth century, as it was known well enough by the early 1800s to be planted at Monticello in Virginia by President Thomas Jefferson, who considered it as one of the best apples. A favorite at Farnum Hill Ciders.

Golden Russet is among the most highly regarded North American apples for making cider. For the writing of *The New Cider Maker's Handbook*, I did a survey on the favorite varieties of seven preeminent cider experts in different regions of North America, and the Golden Russet was, by far, the most often mentioned. And the story repeated itself when I interviewed more producers for the writing of this chapter: Almost all of them mentioned Golden Russet as among their favorites. The variety was first described in the United States in 1845 by A. J. Downing, so it probably appeared on the continent during the first half of that century.* But its origin is uncertain: It could have been imported from Europe or it could have sprouted as a seedling. In the beginning, it was mostly grown in central and western New York, but it has since conquered the whole continent, proving its great adaptability to diverse conditions, from the mild West Coast all the way to cold Quebec. The strong assets of Golden Russet for making cider are its very high sugar content and its good flavor and aroma, which are combined with a reasonable acidity.

Newtown Pippin, known in Virginia as Albemarle Pippin, is the emblematic variety of one of the oldest cideries in Virginia: Albemarle CiderWorks, owned by the Shelton family. The variety arose as a seedling on Long Island during the first half of the eighteenth century. It became an important variety in the orchards of the Hudson Valley and also found a favorable ground in Albemarle County, Virginia. About 100 years after its introduction, it could be found successfully growing in some districts on the West Coast. This is a fruit that ripens late and is a great keeper. Large quantities were exported to England during the 1800s. At the 2018 CiderDays festival in Massachusetts, we had the rare opportunity to taste side-by-side single-variety ciders made with Newtown (Albemarle) Pippin apples that had been grown in different regions of the country: from the Hudson Valley of New York in two ciders by Angry Orchard; from Albemarle County, Virginia, in a cider by Albemarle

* Downing is an American pomologist whose best-known work is titled *The Fruits and Fruit Trees of America*.

Figure 10.2. Golden Russet apples growing in the author's orchard.

CiderWorks; from Washington State in a cider by Dragon's Head Cider; and from California in two ciders, each featuring a different orchard, by Tilted Shed Ciderworks. This was truly an interesting tasting that showed this variety has all that is needed to make very fine ciders. In fact, its quality for cider has long been recognized, as S. A. Beach wrote in *The Apples of New York*, published in 1905: "Cider made from it is very clear and of high quality, and in the early days, large quantities of the fruit were used for this purpose." He also wrote that it is not an easy variety to grow, and that it doesn't succeed as well in districts other than those noted here.

Northern Spy appeared in New York State at the beginning of the nineteenth century and remains a favorite with cider makers in that state (mainly in the Hudson Valley and Finger Lakes regions). It is also appreciated in the Great Lakes, the Pacific Northwest, and in the Canadian Maritime provinces. The apples ripen late and keep well, but a fairly long season is required for perfect ripening. The juice has average sugar content and high acidity. It gives a flavor to the cider that can be somewhat peculiar for those who are not accustomed to it. Northern Spy is a favorite at Eve's Cidery, which makes a highly praised single-variety cider. It is also a favorite of Ryan Burk at Angry Orchard.

Wickson was introduced in 1944 by Albert Etter, who was a plant breeder active in Northern California during the first half of the twentieth century. There is some ambiguity about its genealogy, but according to the plant patent that was filed for it, Wickson is a cross of Newtown Pippin × Spitzenberg Crab.* Wickson is therefore a fairly modern variety, but it is nevertheless generally considered as being in the heirloom category. It is a beautiful, small red apple, very cold hardy, rich to very rich in sugar and in acidity,

---

* The US Plant Patent #724 was issued for Wickson in 1947, where we can read: "The crab apple tree is a cross between the Newtown and Spitzenberg crab." We can find in Daniel Bussey's *The Illustrated History of Apples in the United States and Canada* (Mt. Horeb, WI: JAK KAW Press, 2016), that Spitzenberg Crab is either a *Malus baccata* cross or selection.

with good tannin. Steve Wood of Farnum Hill Ciders was probably the first to grow it at a commercial scale for cider making, and now it is among the 10 most widely grown cider varieties, mostly in New England and in the Pacific Northwest.

We may add to this the Ashmead's Kernel, an English apple already described in chapter 2. It is well liked among American producers, and a favorite at Black Diamond Cider and at Farnum Hill Ciders. And we could additionally mention Gravenstein, an old classic from Continental Europe introduced to the United States around the end of the 1700s, which found an ideal bioregion in the California's Sonoma County, where it is a favorite variety for Tilted Shed Ciderworks.

The second group is sweet apples. This class of apples was very important for rural people 150 to 200 years ago, as they could boil the juice to make a sweet syrup that served the same purpose as, nowadays, sugar (imported refined sugar wasn't widely available then). Their low acidity makes them unappealing to eat fresh, as they lack the characteristic freshness of apples, but it made them ideal for making a concentrated syrup that wasn't overly acidic. In a cider blend these apples mellow the high acidity of the dessert varieties described previously. Sweet apples fell out of favor, however, as sugar became an inexpensive commodity; their cultivation became pointless. Sweet apples of note include the following varieties.

Pumpkin Sweet or Pound Sweet is an old, classic American sweet apple. This is a large green apple that develops a nice yellow coloring with sometimes a bit of bronze when it's fully ripened. The variety originated in Connecticut around 1800, and it was first described in 1834. It ripens in late mid-season and doesn't keep much past December. It is especially esteemed for baking, and there are numerous accounts of it being used for cider making. It makes a thick syrupy juice, very sweet, and slightly astringent. Cidrerie Michel Jodoin in Quebec grows it, and Michel, being quite fond of it, is planning to plant more.

Tolman Sweet is a variety of uncertain origin, but some authors have speculated that it appeared in Massachusetts before 1800 because it was described in 1822 by James Thacher in *The American Orchardist*. In 1905, S. A. Beach wrote in *The Apples of New York* that it "has gained the reputation of being one of the hardiest of the old New England varieties." This is a medium-size, mostly green-ish-yellow apple that ripens late and keeps well. The flesh is, however, quite peculiar, completely lacking acidity. Some astrin-gency is readily noticeable when eaten, and there is a long persistency of the flavor, thus indicating a non-negligible amount of tannins. For my part, by tasting it I think it could be classified as borderline between sweet and bittersweet. However, I haven't as yet seen results of juice analysis, which could confirm this impression.

There were at one time quite a number of other varieties in this class of sweet apples. Just the name Pumpkin Sweet may refer to two or three other varieties of large sweet apples. We may additionally add the Sweet Bough, which has also been used for cider, but being more of a summer apple, it matures too early to be really useful.

The third group of heirloom varieties is for true cider apples, variet-ies of American origin that were mainly used for cider making during the heydays of US cider production in the seventeenth to nineteenth centuries. Most varieties of the past are now lost, unfor-tunately, but a few have been rediscovered in old orchards and identified by apple experts. I wish to highlight here the important role played by Tom Burford for the identification and propagation of some of these varieties, in particular the Harrison and the Hewe's Virginia Crab. Without him these apples would not have the dis-semination they now have. Burford came from a family of Virginia farmers, operated a nursery for many years, and is the author of a number of publications, among which is his *Apples of North America* (2013). He has worked closely with pioneer cider makers in Vir-ginia (Diane Flynt of Foggy Ridge Cider, and Chuck and Charlotte Shelton of Albemarle CiderWorks) to make sure these apples would not be lost a second time, and he tirelessly sent free scion wood to all who showed interest in these varieties.

In the following descriptions, I often refer to comments written by William Coxe in his book, *A View of the Cultivation of Fruit Trees, and the Management of Orchards and Cider*, published in 1817. This is one of the first American pomological works of importance, and it also contains information about cider making. (It may be noted that Coxe was a well-known cider maker in New Jersey.) Coxe doesn't give much information about the origin of the varieties he describes, but because his book was published in 1817, all the varieties had to have been well established by that date.

> **Campfield** (bittersweet) and **Graniwinkle** (sweet) are two varieties that have a somewhat comparable story. They were used a lot by New Jersey cider makers during the 1800s, and Coxe wrote about them in similar terms, saying about Campfield: "This apple is next in reputation as a cider fruit to the Harrison; and usually mixed with that apple in equal portions when ground." And about Graniwinkle: "The cider produced from this apple resembles a syrup in its taste and consistence. . . . [I]t is usually mixed with the Harrison for making cider of a superior quality." So we see both were used in blends with Harrison, and we may assume that such blends permitted a reduction of the acidity coming from the Harrison, thus making better balanced ciders. Beach wrote in 1905 about Campfield that it was then becoming obsolete—which is understandable as by that time cider had lost most of its luster. I haven't been able to find information on how these varieties have gone through the twentieth century and how they reappeared on the modern cider scene, but nowadays we see them here and there in the catalogs of a few specialized nurseries. As far as I know they haven't yet been planted on a large scale, but they have been tested at Washington State University where the measured properties would classify Campfield as a bittersweet, and Graniwinkle as a sweet.*

---

* Carol Miles, et al., *Annual Report 2011: Hard Cider* (Mount Vernon, WA: Washington State University, 2011): https://s3.wp.wsu.edu/uploads/sites /2167/2017/04/Cider-Apples-Annual-Report-2011.pdf.

Figure 10.3. A watercolor representation of a Harrison apple from the US Department of Agriculture (USDA) Pomological Watercolor Collection, dated 1899, and identified by the eminent pomologist W. H. Ragan as the true Harrison of Coxe. This collection contains over 7,500 fruit reproductions in watercolors (of which 3,807 are apples), painted by the end of the 19th and beginning of the 20th centuries.

Harrison (sharp to bittersharp) was the reigning cider apple variety two-hundred years ago in the eastern counties of New Jersey, which were then among the most important cider production regions on the continent. All conditions were met for the development of this industry: a good terroir and the proximity of the important market that was New York City. The Harrison apple appeared in the region of Newark in the early 1700s. It could be used as a single variety or blended with sweeter varieties such as those mentioned previously. Coxe wrote: "This is the most celebrated of the cider apples of Newark in New Jersey.... [I]t produces a high colored, rich, and sweet cider of great strength, commanding a high price in New York." However, as cider declined in the second half of the nineteenth century, the Harrison apple wasn't planted anymore and slowly sank into oblivion. Case in point, in 1905 Beach didn't even mention it in his *Apples of New York*! The variety was long thought to be lost until the mid-1970s when an old tree standing by an ancient cider mill in New Jersey was identified as a Harrison. Cuttings were taken. Some time later, under the influence of Tom Burford, it is in Virginia that the Harrison made its first real comeback, more specifically in the orchards of Foggy Ridge Cider and Albemarle CiderWorks. They were the first to commercially make cider with it. Nowadays, important blocks of Harrison are being planted in all cider districts of the continent, and many cider makers are starting to use it as the trees grow older and the production increases. Analysis results of the juice show very high sugar content with medium to high acidity and low to medium tannin.

Hewe's Virginia Crab (bittersharp) may have its origin in Virginia in the beginning of the eighteenth century. This apple also has been grown in the Canadian Prairies, where it has shown great winter hardiness. Interestingly, the eminent Canadian pomologist W. T. Macoun places its origin in Iowa.* Some authors suspect it could have the indigenous crab species, *Malus angustifolia*, as an ancestor.

---

* W. T. Macoun, *Apple in Canada: Its Cultivation and Improvement*, Canada Department of Agriculture Bulletin #86, 1916.

Figure 10.4. Hewe's Virginia Crab. The three apples on top were picked in Virginia by the end of August 2018 and kept refrigerated until the photo was taken. Those on the lower row were grown in the author's orchard in Quebec and harvested at the beginning of October. It is interesting to note the difference in coloration from the terroir.

Whatever its true origin and genealogy, we have many accounts of this apple being the most widely grown variety in Virginia for cider during the late 1700s and early 1800s, and that President Thomas Jefferson was very fond of it, and of the crab cider his people made for him in Monticello. The juice of the Hewe's Virginia Crab has a high content of sugar, high to very high acidity, and medium tannin that is rather soft and astringent. It's a favorite at Albemarle CiderWorks for making a fine single-variety cider.

In addition to the varieties noted here, I will mention two other old cider varieties that may still be found in some nursery catalogs, but for which very little information is available: Smith's Cider, a variety that would be borderline between sweet and mildly sharp that is from Pennsylvania; and Taliaferro, a quite obscure and almost mythical sharp or bittersharp variety that is said to have been cultivated by President Thomas Jefferson at Monticello.

Redflesh Apples

The use of redflesh apples to make ciders that keep a rosé or bronze color started in North America relatively recently. At least two importations of pink or redflesh apples in the United States are documented. The first is with a pink-fleshed variety of unknown origin that had spread in Western Europe and was called the "Surprise apple" in England around 1830, and subsequently brought into the United States, most likely by German immigrants. It was used by Albert Etter in his breeding program in California, and one of the best-known varieties from this program is the Pink Pearl. The second introduction is by Niels E. Hansen in South Dakota, who upon returning from a trip to Russia in 1897 brought into the United States some scion wood of *Malus niedzwetzkyana*, a red-leafed and red-flowering subspecies of apple that had been found growing wild in the Tian Shan mountains of central Asia by the Russian botanist Vladislav Niedzwetzky. After these introductions, many red-flesh varieties were bred by Hansen, Etter, and other breeders in United States and Canada, but those varieties that inherited the redflesh trait from the Surprise apple do not show as deep of a red juice as those that come from *M. niedzwetzkyana*. In cider making, two of the most often used redflesh varieties are the Redfield and the Geneva.

Geneva (bittersharp) was bred in Canada at the Ottawa Central Experimental Farm and introduced in 1928, within a program that was aimed at the development of decorative crabapple varieties with pink or red flowers, using *M. niedzwetzkyana* as the seed parent. It was first used for cider making purposes during the 1970s by Cidrobec, a company in Rougemont, Quebec, that produced industrial ciders. But that effort didn't last for very long. In 1988 Michel Jodoin, also in Rougemont, started using it in experimental cider batches and planted a few blocks. He released his first commercial rosé cider made as a single-variety Geneva using the traditional method in the mid-1990s. He still does it the same way, and that cider has won numerous prizes, among which was a gold medal in the heritage style at the 2018 Cidercraft Awards. At about the same period, another producer in Quebec, Robert Demoy of Cidrerie du Minot, also used the Geneva for making a rosé cider. The juice of Geneva is of a beautiful red color, is relatively low in sugar content, medium to high in acidity, and quite astringent.

Redfield (bittersharp) is a large apple obtained from a cross of Wolf River × *M. niedzwetzkyana*, and it was introduced in 1938 by the New York State Agricultural Experiment Station in Geneva. The variety wasn't successful at first, because its taste as fresh fruit isn't very good. But it bakes well and the tree is great: beautiful and healthy, with bronze-red leaves and pink blossoms. The Redfield as a cider apple was discovered by the late Terry Maloney (cofounder of West County Cider in Massachusetts) at the beginning of the 1980s: As he was visiting the orchards in Geneva, he noticed this tree with its striking, large red fruits, and upon tasting one he thought it should be tried for cider making. His intuition was certainly correct, as this apple has now become a true American classic. The cider produced by West County Cider with the Redfield has a beautiful copper-rose color, a very pleasant red berry

Figure 10.5. Redfield apples grown in the orchard of West County Cider.

aroma, a nice, slightly astringent and persistent mouthfeel, and a very good acidity–tannin balance with medium-dry sweetness. This cider has won numerous prizes, including a Best in Show at the Eastern States Exposition cider competition in 2018.

Since these two varieties have been rediscovered by Jodoin and Maloney respectively, many other growers and cider makers have started planting and using redflesh varieties in Canada and United States, to the point that rosé ciders have now become quite common and, in fact, very *cool*. It should, however, be noted that not all rosé ciders use redflesh apples to obtain their color. For example, at Cidrerie Milton in Quebec, they extract the red pigment from the skin of Dolgo crab apples by warm maceration. Other cideries may add some red berries, sometimes concentrated, to a normal cider.

Foraged Apples

In recent years, a number of cider makers have searched the woods, roadsides, and abandoned orchards for apples suitable for cider making. Such apples are often called "foraged" or "wild" apples. Generally unnamed, they are either natural seedlings or rootstocks that have survived or outgrown a grafted tree, or they may be a grafted variety whose identity has been lost. Foraged apples are usually quite rich in tannins. Most are also rich in acid and would be classified as bittersharps; but occasionally some are found that may be classified as bittersweets. Foraged or wild apples are now raising a lot of interest from many cider makers in all parts of North America, and there was a workshop specifically on that subject during the CiderCon of 2019: Cultivating Wild Apples, with preeminent cider makers from all around the country, such as Ellen Cavalli of Tilted Shed Ciderworks in California, Matt Kaminsky of Carr's Ciderhouse in Massachusetts, Steve Selin of South Hill Cider in New York, and Tierney Schipper Rouston of Stoic Cider in Arizona as speakers.

Some of the foraged apples have been found to have really superior qualities year after year, and they have been named by their respective discoverer. This effort has the objective to develop a native pommage, a collection of varieties that may eventually replace the

European varieties used by many producers to provide the tannins required for a great heritage-style cider. In effect, the use of European varieties may be seen as a transitional period before the advent of native varieties that no doubt will have many advantages. First, these local varieties have a good chance of being better adapted to the terroir. And, second, their flavor will be different from that of the imported varieties and, with time, this will permit the development of true North American pommages and cider styles. Following are a few foraged apple varieties that have been named by their respective discoverers. Note that this list is far from being exhaustive—it simply exemplifies the work that has been accomplished so far.

Andy Brennan of Aaron Burr Cider in the Hudson Valley, New York, is one of the better-known cider makers who use foraged apples. His ciders are highly praised and he has contributed a lot in increasing the popularity of foraged apples in cider making. He estimates that he has tried approximately 400 different apples that he found in all the locations he forages. Of these, he grafted about 100 in his orchard for further evaluation. He has named the following varieties.

> **Denniston Red** (bittersharp) was brought to his attention in 2013 by the owner of the property where the tree grows. It has medium sugar, medium acid, and high tannin content. The apple is medium size, round, deep red with some green where in shade. The season is mid to late. The tree has shown some resistance to fire blight and to rust, and is apparently a regular bearer.

> **Bitter Burr** (bittersweet) unexpectedly grew on Brennan's property from the rootstock of a tree when the grafted part died. It bore its first fruits in 2015. The apple is yellow, tannic, and low in acid. The flavor is somewhat similar to some bitter cider apples in France.

Bill Mayo is an orchardist in Franklin County, Vermont. He discovered a prolific seedling tree growing wild on his property. Mayo isn't a cider maker, but he had the intuition it could do well for that purpose, and he gave some apples to cider makers he knew so they could test the apple in their blends. After getting some positive comments about the apple, he went through the process of making it a named variety:

Figure 10.6. Franklin Cider apple. Photo by Bill Mayo.

Franklin Cider (bittersharp) was discovered by Mayo in 2008. Reports indicate it to be extremely productive, with the juice having high sugar, acidity, and tannin contents. The variety has been patented and is now distributed by Stark Bro's Nurseries & Orchards Co. It was officially introduced in 2017 under the name Stark Franklin Cider. This is the first among the newly discovered or foraged varieties to be propagated at such a large scale and to be made available for general planting.

Eric Shatt runs Redbyrd Orchard Cider in the Finger Lakes, New York. Eric is an accomplished orchardist who also manages the experimental orchards of Cornell University at Ithaca. Here is one variety among his finds:

Gnarled Chapman (bittersweet) is a late variety and was introduced in 2015. It is now offered by the Fedco Trees nursery, with the following description in their catalogue: "Large, roundish-oblate and

Figure 10.7. Douce de Charlevoix apples from the author's orchard.

Figure 10.8. Cornell University in New York is testing ultra-intensive management for cider apples. This system is called super spindle, and the density is 5,000 trees per hectare (2,000 per acre).

outrageously beautiful. Yellowy-green skin with a glowing orange blush, netted and dotted with russet. Eric named this seedling in honor of America's most famous apple guy, John 'Appleseed' Chapman. Vigorous upright tip-bearing tree. Recommended for trial in all cider-apple growing districts. Blooms midseason. Zone 4–7."

Other discoveries named by Eric include Barn Hill Sharp, Redbyrd Bitter, Searsbury Cherry Bomb, and Texas King Crab.

And as for myself, in Charlevoix County, Quebec, Canada, I've found quite a few apples that appear to have a good potential, among which I have named the Banane amère, Bilodeau, Douce de Charlevoix, and Maillard, which are now available from a few specialized nurseries in North America, and are undergoing formal testing in standard orchard conditions by RECUPOM in Frelighsburg (Quebec). There is also a number of still-unnamed varieties that I am evaluating. Meanwhile, here is a description of my favorite named variety.

Douce de Charlevoix (bittersweet) is an early midseason apple that blends very well with other apples that ripen by mid-September for the making of first season cider. This variety has a good potential for marginal regions with cold winters and short summers. It has become my own emblematic variety, and I use it at up to 60 percent in blends (not more because some juice with higher acidity is needed for balance). It gives a very fragrant aroma to the cider.

There are many more native varieties from cider makers in all parts of the continent. In fact, millions of naturally occurring seedling apple trees are in North America. Each of them is unique, following the laws of genetics. And although only a small fraction of them have the potential to become a good cider variety, this small fraction nevertheless represents a great number of potentially excellent apples that go unnoticed and whose fruit at present only feeds wild animals. Naturally, only time will tell if any of the varieties noted here will become important enough to be grown at a commercial scale. It should be noted that most are still not available from nurseries and can only be obtained as scion wood from their respective discoverer. There is also a

Figure 10.9. Ian Merwin of Black Diamond Cider in New York is one of the few people I have met to combine expertise in intensive orchard management with high-quality heritage-style cider making.

need for lots of testing in real orchard conditions. Those that successfully pass this test period will be propagated by nurseries, to be eventually distributed to apple growers.

The Orchards

The type of orchard varies considerably depending on if it is for a modern- or heritage-style producer. Orchards for modern-style ciders are typically large, high-density, intensive orchards managed for the production of market fruit. Often the cider maker is firstly an apple producer who uses the better part of his production for market apples or for a pick-your-own operation, while the non-premium fruit is used for the making of cider. Such a strategy permits the grower to give additional value to non-premium fruit that otherwise would be nearly worthless. Also, many producers of modern-style ciders and of specialty styles don't grow the apples themselves and would rather buy bulk juice from large suppliers.

In the case of heritage-style cider makers, the operation is most often farm-based and the orchard will typically be smaller in terms of surface area. Most often, these producers want their products to represent their particular terroir, and for this reason they will work closely with local orchardists to procure apples when they don't grow them all themselves. Heritage-style cider makers most commonly utilize a medium-density, bush-type orchard, where the trees are grafted on medium-size rootstocks. Some even go for the traditional orchard with full-size trees planted in low densities. Only a minority of heritage-style cider makers successfully grow their apple trees in

Figure 10.10. Top-grafting standard trees to cider varieties at Westwind Orchard & Cidery in New York.

high-density, intensive orchards. This is mainly because these orchards require a lot of expertise in orchard management that most cider makers don't have, or don't really care to undertake. I have also seen a number of producers that have top-grafted orchards of commercial eating apples into cider-specific or heirloom varieties.

Cider Making

An 1841 painting by William Sidney Mount, *Cider Making*, tells us a lot about traditional cider making practices in the United States in the middle of the nineteenth century. On the left side of the painting (figure 10.11), we can see the crushing of the apples in a circular trough

Figure 10.11. Traditional cider making in 1841. *Cider Making* by William Sidney Mount, Metropolitan Museum of Arts, New York.

with a large wooden wheel driven by a horse. I've wondered why we don't see in America stone troughs and wheels like we often see in France and England. This painting might bring the answer: They were made out of wood, so they rot too quickly for posterity. The press is also interesting: It is a twin-screw press of quite large size, with wooden screws. Apparently the screws were tightened alternately, one after the other—note the man with a lever who is tightening the right side. We also see that the pomace was formed into a "cheese" that had a square shape, built with straw to provide drainage for the juice. The barrels are also worth an examination, as their hoops were made of wood rather than steel as is now standard. The juice flowing from the press was poured into the barrels and was most likely left to ferment naturally to dryness without further processing.

Naturally, nowadays, things are a bit different. Although we can find in North America a few producers who work very traditionally, most follow more modern practices in their cider making. We will review here the basic cider making processes, and not those used for making flavored or other specialty ciders, as this could become the subject of a complete book by itself!*

Fruit Handling and Juicing

In North America, the apples are mostly picked on the trees, as opposed to Europe where the apples are more often gathered from the ground. Postharvest ripening, or sweating, is done either in cold storage or at ambient temperature. In warmer climates like Virginia, cold storage is essential. Maceration of the pulp between milling and pressing is not standard practice and only occassionally seen. This is because the juicing lines are often designed so the mill discharges the pulp directly to the press. Hence, some important modifications would be required to include a buffer volume for maceration before pressing. Most midsize and larger producers use a modern juicing

---

* The methods for making flavored and specialty ciders are well covered in the recently published title by Christopher Shockey and Kirsten K. Shockey, *The Big Book of Cidermaking: Expert Techniques for Fermenting and Flavoring Your Favorite Hard Cider* (North Adams, MA: Storey Publishing, 2020).

line with a belt press. With the very small producers, there is a trend to use hydropresses, as they are relatively inexpensive. Rack and cloth hydraulic presses are still popular with intermediate-size producers. One press type that is unique to North America and that we see in intermediate and larger-size operations is the Goodnature Squeezebox, which has a very clever accordion-like design that permits a substantial labor reduction as compared to a traditional rack and cloth press.

Fermentation and Final Processing

In North America, fermentation is in general done in stainless steel tanks. Both fixed- and variable-volume models are used. However, the cider industry is in a fast-growing mode, and many producers have a shortage of tanks. They then may use less expensive plastic tanks and IBCs (intermediate bulk containers, commonly called totes) as temporary fermenting vessels or for short-term storage. Wood barrels are not commonly used for fermentation, but many producers do use them for maturation.

For the modern-style ciders, it is expected the product should be very clean, fruity, and without any of the flavors brought by malolactic fermentation. Additionally, the cider should be perfectly clear. Hence pre-fermentation clarification will be performed, and the fermentation as well as the final processing are generally managed according to standard modern practices as described in chapter 1. If a sparkling cider is produced, the injection method is most often used, and the cider is then packaged. Naturally, some producers will use different processes, but the traditional method is the standard for the production of high-end sparkling ciders. Most modern-style ciders are back-sweetened, but a few producers, such as Citizen Cider in Vermont, use the cold-shock method to retain some of the natural sugars.

We see more variations from producers of heritage-style ciders. Firstly, on the question of balance of the musts, there exists a very wide spectrum. Many makers mostly use heirloom sharp varieties and will thus work with blends that are relatively high in acid and low in tannins. Others mostly use bittersweet and bittersharp

Figure 10.12. Hydropresses are popular with smaller producers. They are often worked in tandem: as one is under pressure, the other gets filled. These hydropresses are at Bear Swamp Orchard in Massachusetts.

Figure 10.13. An old rack and cloth press in action at Farnum Hill Ciders in New Hampshire.

Figure 10.14. Brite tanks are often used for the carbonation of modern-style ciders by the injection method. Bottle filling is then done with a counter-pressure filler. This setup is at Blake's Orchard & Cider Mill in Michigan.

varieties and thus obtain blends that are rich in tannins and low in acid. Then there are those who use approximately equal proportions of high-acid heirlooms and high-tannin apples for blends that will have medium concentrations in both acidity and tannins. And if we add the makers who use crabs, redflesh, and foraged apples we can observe a huge diversity of blend properties and balance points within this style (see also appendix A). For pre-fermentation treatments and initiation of fermentation, many producers won't add any sulfite or pectic enzyme and will simply let the must ferment on its natural wild yeasts. Others have an approach similar to that of the modern-style makers as just described. There is no rule here because it is more acceptable for heritage-style ciders to have slightly funky flavors and some haziness. The fermentation itself is seldom managed and generally goes to dryness. There are exceptions to this, however. In particular, a recent trend is seen in the Pacific Northwest where a number of producers use the keeving process as done in France to obtain ciders that retain some of their natural sugars for residual sweetness. Final processing of heritage-style ciders often involves less technology than for modern-style ciders. Most of the time, and more particularly with smaller producers, the ciders are sold dry and thus do not require any filtration or stabilization. However, for the ciders that are back-sweetened, sterile filtration is the most common stabilization technique used, and some sulfite is added at bottling. Most sparkling ciders are obtained by the traditional method, the injection method with a brite tank, or the Charmat method, while the use of the ancestral method or the basic method may be occasionally seen, usually with smaller producers.

Packaging

The packaging of cider in North America has gone through important changes these last years. Since marketing studies have shown that the largest potential growth of the cider market would be with younger people and beer drinkers, many producers have started to package their products in a similar way to beer, using more and more cans and smaller beer-size bottles in four- or six-packs. The trend was started with modern-style producers, but recently I have seen that even highly regarded heritage-style producers such as Farnum Hill Ciders and Eden Specialty Ciders now offer some of their products in cans. This leaves the traditional 750 mL champenoise bottle to higher-end and more expensive ciders, to ciders produced with the traditional method, and to the ciders of smaller makers who mostly sell directly at the farm. Kegging is used a lot for selling to bars and restaurants.

Many smaller producers contract the final processing and packaging. This is mostly seen for canning, as only very large producers can afford a canning line. But also this is seen for bottling when the producer reaches a size that makes it impractical to bottle manually while the cost of an automated bottling line would be prohibitive. Another area where external contractors are often used is for the traditional method processing, because to insure the stability of these ciders, the processing must be flawless.

Ice Cider Making

Ice cider is a style that was developed in the Canadian province of Quebec during the 1990s. It is a very sweet or syrupy cider, obtained by fermenting freeze-concentrated apple must, that may be consumed at dessert or as an aperitif. The historical landmarks of its development were recently covered in detail by Anaïs Détolle in a well-documented paper,* and I will give here only a very short summary. Most of the credit for this development may be attributed to two men who worked independently during the 1990s: Pierre Lafond of Cidrerie Saint-Nicolas near Quebec City and Christian Barthomeuf of Clos Saragnat in Frelighsburg. In 1999 the official designation *cidre de glace* (or ice cider in English) was given to the product. In the following years, ice cider quickly gained in popularity. Many cideries in Quebec started making it, and now approximately 50 producers of ice cider are in the province. In the beginning, two cideries distinguished themselves, La Face cachée de la pomme and Domaine Pinnacle. They became the largest producers and leaders of the industry, exporting their ice ciders to many foreign countries. This popularity then reached the United States, where some producers in colder districts also started its production. In particular, Eleanor and Albert Leger of Eden Specialty Ciders in northern Vermont were the first, in 2007, to make it using the natural winter cold (as in Quebec) and with a federally approved label. Eden Specialty Ciders did a lot to promote ice cider in the United States, as their product was of high quality and competed on par with the best from Quebec in some international competitions. Since December 2014, Quebec ice cider is recognized by a PGI certification label that defines the process and establishes norms of quality. Ice cider making has now spread to the whole of the Cider Planet, as we can find producers in such countries as the United Kingdom, France, Spain, Germany, Sweden, the Czech Republic, and even Australia (although it is not done with natural winter cold in all those countries).

---

* Anaïs Détolle, *Un regard chronologique sur le cidre de glace au Québec*, in the collective work under the direction of L. M. Cloutier and A. Détolle, *La transformaition du cidre au Québec: Perspective écosystémique*, Presses de l'Université du Québec, 2017.

Figure 10.15. Frozen Cortland apples hanging in a tree in the author's orchard. This variety is one of the most popular in Quebec for on-tree freezing, as it hangs longer than other varieties. Once the apples have lost their color and have become uniformly brown, they are ready to harvest and process into ice cider.

As Quebec is the world leader in the development, production, and marketing of ice cider, the government has published regulations to protect the name and the product from lower-quality imitations. In 2008, the following definition and standard was adopted:

> *"Ice cider": cider obtained by the fermentation of juice of apples that has a pre-fermentation sugar content of not less than 30° Brix achieved solely by natural cold, producing a finished product with a residual sugar content of not less than 130 g per litre and an actual alcoholic strength of more than 7% by volume but not more than 13% by volume.**

Furthermore, some additional requirements must be met: It is forbidden to add sugar, alcohol, artificial color, or flavor, for example.

---

* Regulation respecting cider and other apple-based alcoholic beverages: an Act respecting the Société des alcools du Québec , C.Q.L.R. c S-13, r 4, https://canlii .ca/t/556p8.

Artificial cold as in a freezer is not permitted to obtain the freeze-concentrated must.

The specification for the PGI label is more stringent than the base definition. In effect, the initial sugar concentration is raised to 32° Brix (rather than 30°), the minimum residual sugar is 140 g/L (rather than 130), and the alcohol strength is set at a minimum of 9 percent by volume (rather than 7 percent). The specification additionally defines a geographical zone and requires the product to conform to some criteria on color, texture, aroma, and flavor that are controlled by professional tasters.

Ice cider making differs from normal cider making in two fundamental ways: The first is that we start with a concentrated must that is obtained by freeze concentration. And the second is that we need to stop the fermentation and stabilize the cider while there is still a high sugar content in it. The principle of freeze concentration relies upon the fact that a solution containing sugar will freeze at a lower temperature than pure water. And when the two phases (liquid and ice) are simultaneously present in the same medium, the liquid will always have a higher sugar concentration than the ice. Two methods are used in the production of ice cider:

Cryo-extraction. This process consists of freezing apples, which will be pressed when partially frozen. Water remains trapped as ice crystals in the apple flesh and the extracted juice thus has a greater concentration of sugar. Freezing of the apples is done in two ways: The apples remain on the trees and are picked once they are frozen; or the apples are harvested in the fall and kept in cold storage until the outside temperature is cold enough and the bins are then brought outside to freeze.

Cryo-concentration. In this case, the juice is extracted in the usual manner from the apples that have been kept in storage until the outside temperature is cold enough. After pressing, the juice is brought outside to freeze. Upon melting, the first juice to flow will have a higher concentration of sugar.

In commercial operations, the cryo-concentration method is by far the most widely used, and may account for about 90 percent of all the ice cider produced. Its implementation is quite simple: The juice is extracted from the apples by milling and pressing in the usual way. Optional treatments may be done on the fresh juice such as depectinization or sulfite addition. The containers are filled, leaving a sufficient headspace for expansion. Most often the containers used are IBC totes with a capacity of about 1,000 liters. The filled containers are brought outside until they are sufficiently frozen. This may need more or less time depending on the size of the container and outside temperature, but for a 1,000 liter IBC, a good month when the temperatures range between -15° to -10°C (5° to 14°F) is normally required. Some producers leave the IBCs outside from December to March. After that, the containers are brought in a heated space for melting and draining. Again, this takes more or less time depending on the size of the container. In the beginning, juice will flow at a very high concentration that gradually decreases as the ice melts. Draining is stopped when the target initial concentration is reached. As a quick rule of thumb, about a quarter of the original quantity of juice that was frozen will be obtained at a concentration suitable for making ice cider.

The cryo-extraction method is not as widely used, but most experts claim it produces a cider of superior quality; hence the method is usually kept for the high-end and more expensive products. Very few producers use exclusively apples that are left to freeze on the trees because of the uncertainty whether the apples will actually hang—this will depend on the apple variety and on the meteorological conditions. Some years, most apples might hang, but in another year maybe only a small fraction could be usable. Christian Barthomeuf of Clos Saragnat is one of those few producers, as he firmly believes that this is the way to obtain the best quality ice cider. The other method—harvesting the apples in the fall and keeping them in cold storage until the outside temperatures are cold enough—is definitely more reliable. Nowadays, the trend in Quebec is to press the apples whole, without grinding, when the core temperature is measured at around -10° to -9°C (14° to 16°F). A high-pressure hydraulic basket press is most often used. Some producers, however, prefer to mill the frozen apples and press them in a standard rack and cloth press. Because the apples are frozen, the pressing is very long, and many producers conduct more than one press to obtain a sufficient quantity of concentrate. The first juice that flows from the press is at a higher concentration, and this concentration decreases with time as the ice thaws in the press. The juice is collected until the desired must concentration is attained. After that, there is still some lower-concentration juice coming from the press and this may be used for other purposes.

Fermentation of the concentrated must is quite similar to that of a normal modern-style cider: The nutrients are adjusted and the must, after it has warmed up, is inoculated with a selected wine yeast strain. It is important, however, to consider that this fermentation will have to be stopped when the density reaches the target set for the finished cider. Thus a regular monitoring of the speed of fermentation is required to keep it under control. Stopping the fermentation requires more or less intervention depending on the speed of fermentation. Slow ferments are much easier to stop, and often all that is required is to fine the cider and do a racking with filtering. Fast ferments often require being cold-shocked. Many producers have jacketed tanks for this. An alternative is to have an outdoor tank to which the cider is transferred. Naturally, the exterior temperature has to be cold enough, but not excessively so. The cold causes the fermentation to stop, and a good part of the suspended solids settle in the bottom of the tank with the lees. Fining can then be done, which will improve the clarification and facilitate the filtration. The cider is finally racked and filtered. After that, the cider may be bottled right away, but more often it is transferred to some other vessels for aging or until it is blended with another batch. Some producers use oak barrels for aging, which may give a slight woody character to the cider.

Bottling of the ice cider has to be done with perfectly sanitized material, as any in-bottle refermentation would be catastrophic considering the amount of residual sugar present. The cider goes through sterile filtration, and this is generally complemented by chemical stabilization, before going to the bottle filler. The standard bottles for ice cider are clear glass, with a capacity of 200 or 375 mL. The closures are normal wine corks.

CHAPTER ELEVEN

Craft Cider Is Booming All Around the Planet

This chapter is dedicated to all cider makers who work hard in the many parts of our Cider Planet that are not considered a traditional cider region. These are often pioneers in their respective countries, as they have to start everything from scratch. When there are no cider apples, and no cider tradition, one has to start by finding the apples, which often means evaluating the existing varieties to see if some are appropriate for cider making, or planting trees of foreign varieties for testing—and waiting 5 to 10 years to get a sizeable production. Then these cider makers need to create a style for their country or region—a style that will depend on the apples that can adapt well, be it imported varieties or locally found; on the process that will best fit the apples; and finally on local taste preferences (more or less sweet, tannic, acidic, or sparkling). Sometimes they even need to lobby their governments in order to have some laws changed to make them compatible with cider making and selling. In short, it is no easy task. Nevertheless, it is happening in almost all places where the apple tree can grow.

In this chapter, I present portraits of some cider makers whom I have had the chance to meet, and I will try to highlight the work they have done and the challenges they have overcome. We start this tour in Europe, then head east to Asia, followed by journeys to Central and South America, and finally Africa. We will see that, in some regions, industrial cider making has been going on for a long time but that craft cider making had been entirely lost and is now being revived. Naturally, this is only a partial portrait of all that is happening on the Cider Planet: Much more is going on and things are evolving rapidly!

Italy
Gianluca Telloli, Maley Cider

I met Gianluca Telloli in 2015 at the Salon des Mostes in Austria, where he was presenting his ciders. After this first encounter, he invited me to

attend, in 2016, a cider festival, Sicera, in his home region at Antey-Saint-André in the Aosta Valley. This was a very friendly festival, where I was able to meet a few other Italian cider makers, but overall, there wasn't really more than about half a dozen of them for the whole of Italy.

Gianluca's work is a perfect example of an important trend that I have seen in many parts of the Cider Planet, where ancient and often abandoned orchards are rejuvenated, and their apple production is used for the making of cider. Most often the

Figure 11.1. Gianluca Telloli at his stand during the Salon des Mostes in Austria.

Figure 11.2. A gigantic tree of the variety Raventze in an alpine orchard in the village of Seissogne, near the town of Aosta.

varieties are old standards of the region, which may have been used for cider a century or two ago. In the case of Maley Cider, we are talking about a number of alpine orchards that are at altitudes of 1,000 to 1,500 meters (3,500 to 5,000 feet) above sea level, often with very large trees. Gianluca explained that many orchards were cut down during the times of Mussolini because it was decided that wine had to

Figure 11.3. Raventze apples growing in the Seissogne orchard.

be the national drink of Italy, and thus there was no place for orchards and cider. What is now left are the few orchards that were salvaged from this destruction.

One of Gianluca's emblematic apple varieties is the Raventze, which would be classified bittersweet borderline to bittersharp. It has become the base variety in Maley's ciders. We were also introduced to the Renetta di Antey, a local variety that was in a small orchard planted in 1902 near the town of Antey-Saint-André. And on the other side of the valley, in the small village of Torgnon, was a tree of the variety Barbelune. The story says this tree was planted in 1795; it was one of only three remaining of the variety. However, Gianluca has taken cuttings and there are now many young trees of Barbelune in his orchards. In addition to these varieties, apples from Haute Savoie in France, mainly from the Chamonix Valley, are used in the ciders. Gianluca insists on using only historical alpine apple varieties.

Maley ciders are greatly influenced by Gianluca's past experience as an enologist for an important winery in Gattinara, a region that produces some of the finest Italian wines. The first time I tasted the cider, I thought it was almost like champagne, with a similar sort of biscuity flavor that comes from long aging over the lees, some minerality, a good acidity, and quite dry. This was the Jorasses cuvée, which is made with the Raventze apple using the traditional method, and which remains my own personal favorite within Maley's ciders. Some other of Maley's ciders are made using the Charmat method, or the ancestral method with different blends of apples coming from the Aosta and Chamonix Valleys. The cidery is located in Neyran-Dessus, in the region of Brissogne.

Ireland

Mark Jenkinson, The Cider Mill (Slane)

Ireland is a country of cider drinkers, where individual consumption is among the highest in the world. I like to consider Ireland as an island, but there are in fact two political entities: the Republic of Ireland, which covers some 85 percent of the land, and Northern Ireland, which is part of the United Kingdom. In the Republic, the annual cider market is about 60 million liters for a population just short of 5 million, thus making some 12 liters *per capita*. In Northern Ireland, the drinking habits are quite similar, but the actual numbers would be included with the statistics for the U.K.

I would like to thank my collaborator Mark Jenkinson, who has been a great help for information on Irish cider and its history. He owns with his family The Cider Mill in Slane, which started commercial production in 2012. This is a small farm-based cidery in County Meath (Republic of Ireland) with 5 hectares (12 acres) of orchards where they grow some 120 varieties that include traditional Irish apples as well as cider apples and perry pears from England and France. The production of the cidery is 30,000 liters, and one specialty of theirs is keeved cider—a forgotten tradition in Ireland that they are reviving. Mark is a founding member of Cider Ireland and has authored the history section on the website of the association. I have also had the pleasure to meet and talk with the Irish producers Daniel Emerson and David Llewellyn, who were both at the CiderWorld'18 fair in Frankfurt.

Historically, the evolution of cider making activity in Ireland followed a path similar to what we have seen in chapter 2 for England during the seventeenth and up to mid-nineteenth century. During

Figure 11.4. A bottle of Bulmers/Magners Champagne Cider from the early years of the cidery. Photo by Mark Jenkinson.

those times, Ireland was mostly under English dominance and control, and this naturally resulted in some exchanges between the two islands, and some mutual influence concerning the apple varieties and cider making practices. Irish cider gained some fame during that period, with writers both Irish and from abroad commenting on its excellent quality. However, this stopped with the Great Famine (1845–52), which was so devastating that it wiped out many agri-food traditions, including cider making.

Later in the nineteenth century, cider making activity started again, and several producers emerged: some larger makers near towns, and some smaller, farm-based makers in the countryside. Then in 1935, William Magner founded a cidery which was subsequently bought by the large U.K. producer HP Bulmer. This initiated a movement of consolidation with Bulmers/Magners buying out their competitors until they became the sole producer on the island by the end of the twentieth century. Nowadays, the Irish cider market is still outrageously dominated by this one producer, which is not connected anymore to its former owner HP Bulmer (UK). In the Republic of Ireland, their cider is sold under the brand name Bulmers Irish Cider, while in the rest of the world (including Northern Ireland), it is sold as Magners. So while cider never ceased to be produced in Ireland, the only cider for a number of decades was this industrial cider. Craft cider making, for its part, was totally wiped out.

It is only at the beginning of the twenty-first century that craft cider making started a revival. Among the pioneers, we may mention the Armagh Cider Company in Northern Ireland, and David Llewellyn of Llewellyn's Orchard in the Republic of Ireland. A few others started operating during the following years, and an association, Cider Ireland, was founded in 2012. Currently, some 12 producers can be considered as "craft" in the Republic, and 8 in Northern Ireland, which together occupy less than 2 percent of the market share.

The government of the Republic of Ireland published a *National Apple Orchard Census* in 2017, where we can read that there were 50 commercial apple growers operating in the country in 2017, exploiting a little over 700 hectares (1,750 acres) of orchards, for a yield that varies between 24 and 29 tons per hectare (10 to 12 tons per acre).* The total production may reach 20,000 tons in good years, and this is split between culinary apples for 42 percent, dessert apples for 30 percent, and cider apples for 28 percent. I haven't seen equivalent information pertaining to Northern Ireland, but according to my collaborator Mark Jenkinson, there would be three to four times as many apple growers, for a total production of over 50,000 tons. There is no significant production of cider-specific apple varieties, however, and the Bramley's Seedling is by far the most widely grown.

Yet, there is no well-defined style for Irish craft cider. Historically, by the beginning of the nineteenth century, it seems most descriptions point to a more acidic style of cider, possibly a bit like the English eastern–style. Historic references to Irish cider mention a similarity with white wine. It was made with dessert and culinary apples that contained mild tannins. High-tannin bittersweet apples such as we see in the West Country and in France were not known in Ireland in those days, although a few bittersharp varieties were used in cider making, and one of these, the Cockagee, was highly praised. In more recent years, some English bittersweet apple varieties have been

---

* This report may be downloaded from the Bord Bia, Irish Food Board: https://www .bordbia.ie/globalassets/bordbia.ie/industry/irish-sector-profiles/horticulture -censuses/national-apple-orchard-census-2017.pdf.

introduced and now account for a substantial fraction of the apple crop. We can thus see among the craft makers some that produce a cider with a high proportion of tannic apples as in the West Country, some who mostly use culinary and dessert apples as in the southeast of England, and some others who would be positioned in between both styles.

The most widely grown apples besides Bramley's Seedling are Jonagold, Dabinett, and Michelin. In particular, Bramley's are the pride of County Armagh in Northern Ireland and account for well over half of total apple production of the island. The Dabinett is the most grown of the cider-specific varieties, accounting for about half of the category, followed by the Michelin, and a few others grown to a much lesser extent. By far and away, the main buyer for these apples is the Bulmers/Magners cidery, which processes about half of the island's total commercial apple production. Most of the smaller and craft makers also work with these varieties, with more or less of the bittersweet type depending on the style of cider they make. It is interesting to note that there are no native Irish varieties that are grown commercially on the island. Historically, approximately 150 Irish varieties were recorded. Many are lost, but a number have been saved from extinction and are now being propagated again. Some of those were known for their good properties for cider, such as the Cockagee, Gibbons Russet, Valentine, White Moss, April Queen, Dockney, and Irish Russet. These would mainly be classified as sharp to mild bittersharp. There are nowadays only a handful of apple growers and cider makers putting effort into the reintroduction and use of native Irish varieties, but there is good hope that the movement will spread.

The Cockagee is an emblematic variety for my collaborator Mark Jenkinson, who markets some of his cider under this name. It is a bittersharp that is also used for cooking as it has good acidity. The oldest known written records for it date back to the 1660s. The variety was introduced in England quite early and became important, as it was described (as Cocko Gee) in Hugh Stafford's *A Treatise on Cyder-Making* (1753). It was popular in Devon at the beginning of the nineteenth century, and we also find it noted in Hogg and Bull's *Herefordshire Pomona* (1878). Since the beginning of the twentieth century, the variety was thought extinct, but it was recently rediscovered in England and is now being propagated again in Ireland. Mark recently wrote an article for the Irish Seed Savers Association on the whereabouts of this variety. He wrote:

The Cockagee was once the most famous and highly regarded of Irish cider apple trees on these shores and beyond. This fame was

Figure 11.5. Plate 72 from the *Herefordshire Pomona* showing a number of cider apples of the time, including the Coccagee (note the slightly different spelling). Photo courtesy of Cornell University Libraries.

due to the exceptional quality of the cider its fruits produced, being compared to the finest of white wines and often referred to as Cockagee Champagne Cider. It reached such high repute that it gained an almost cult or celebrity status in its heyday appearing in dozens of Poems, Novels, Plays and writings of the 18th and 19th centuries. Ship manifestos show it was exported worldwide long before Guinness sent its first barrels abroad, and probably most telling of all are the records of it being sold into the Royal household in London for four times the price of fine French wine.

Latvia
Māris Plūme and Dace Smiltniece-Plūme, Mr. Plūme sidra darītava

The Baltic countries include Latvia, Estonia, and Lithuania. Beer is the main drink but, historically, these countries have had a tradition of fruit wine making: a type of fairly sweet dessert wine made with locally grown fruits and berries. Cider as we understand it is something quite new and growing fast. It should be said, however, that many of the commercial cider makers simply use the available commercial apples for making their ciders, and only a few really focus on finding the most appropriate varieties for making high-quality craft cider that is representative of their terroir. In this last category, I mention in Estonia Alvar Roosimaa of Jaanihanso Siidrivabrik, and in Latvia the Mr. Plūme team, whom we will meet just now.

I met Māris Plūme and Dace Smiltniece-Plūme in 2015 at the Salon des Mostes in Austria, the same event where I met Gianluca from Italy. Māris is quite at ease in Austria as he has learned his craft with the Most Baron Toni Distelberger (see chapter 8). Dace and Māris run Mr. Plūme sidra darītava, a small craft cidery in Lielvārdes novads, a county approximately 60 km (37 mi.) east of the capital city Riga. They started in 2010 to build the cidery on a very low budget, and entered commercial production in 2013. They are still a husband-and-wife business and they do everything by themselves. They have planted a 1.5-hectare (3.7-acre) orchard and also use apples they

Figure 11.6. Māris Plūme (*right*) with Dace Smiltniece-Plūme and a Most Baron, at their display during the Salon des Mostes 2015 in Austria. Note the artwork on the labels, which is very original.

procure from what they call "apple safari"—looking for interesting natural seedling trees in the wild—and also surplus fruit from apple farms in the region. In their orchard, they have planted a mixture of local and historical varieties, some English and French bittersweet and bittersharp apples, some wild varieties discovered as natural seedlings in the region, and some crabs. They also grow some Austrian perry pears. When asked about his favorite or emblematic varieties, Māris answers: Lietuvas Pepiņš, Sīpoliņš, Safrāna Pepiņš, Dabinett, Yarlington Mill, Three Counties, Kerr, Hyslop, and Antonovka. He says there is still a lot of work and experimentation ahead in order to establish the best cider pommages for the region.

The cider making practices at Mr. Plūme are quite typical of small craft makers, using some traditional processes intermixed with more modern practices, but in general their cider is produced with the least intervention and additions possible. Some batches are fermented with wild yeasts, while others are inoculated with cultured strains. Some are keeved. The total production remains under 20,000 liters annually, split between naturally sparkling ciders made with the ancestral method, and bottled still ciders.

Nordic Countries

In Finland, Sweden, Norway, and Denmark, there is a tradition for fruit wines like in the Baltic countries, and in a similar fashion there is a young craft cider industry that is growing. One major difference, however, is that some of the biggest worldwide selling industrial cider brands are from this part of the world: Rekorderlig and Kopparberg are both Swedish, while Somersby is Danish, being part of the Carlsberg Group. Their products are mostly very sweet fruit-flavored ciders, and quite far from the type of craft cider that raises our interest in this book.

As in many emerging cider regions, we can find a variety of styles. Producers on the island of Fejø (Denmark) produce organic keeved cider from French cider apple varieties, and elsewhere we can find some who use quite acidic cooking apples such as Bramley's Seedling or Boskoop. In Finland, Jean-Marc Hering brought the techniques from his native Champagne in France to make fine sparkling wines and ciders using the traditional method. It was a pleasure to meet him at CiderWorld'18 in Frankfurt and chat in French. . . . At that same event, there was also Gjermund Åkre, who makes Edel Sider in Norway, high-quality sparkling ciders made with either the Charmat or the traditional method. Let's note too that the southwestern coast of Norway is home of a PDO label, Sider frå Hardanger. But let's spend here a bit of time with Andreas Sundgren of Sweden.

I haven't yet been able to meet Andreas in person, but we have exchanged correspondence for many years. In the beginning of his cider adventure, Andreas was looking for bittersweet apple varieties that could thrive in such harsh climates, and naturally we got to contact one another because we both face fairly similar challenges with the cold and snowy winters, the short length of the summer season, and the winter hardiness (or lack thereof) of cider apple varieties. We exchanged ideas and experiences on the most appropriate varieties, how to grow them, and so on. He did take a different track, however, finally orienting himself to making ice cider with local Swedish apple varieties, which are mostly sharp eating apples, and some crabs. Ice cider, because of its high residual sugar, is particularly apt to be made with sharp apples, the high acidity being in balance with the sweetness. He has now become one of the most successful makers of ice cider in Europe, and I can testify his Brännland Iscider is among the best in the style.

———

There is a lot more going on in Europe, from promising cider projects in Portugal to emerging cider industries in Poland, the Netherlands, and the Czech Republic. In Belgium, apart from the Stassen industrial cidery, we find a true craft producer, Cidrerie du Condroz, where they use ancient regional varieties and traditional methods for making a fine *cidre bouché* (sparkling cider) that has a distinct personality.

Russia
Dmitrii Tikhomirov, Bullevie Cidre

Now heading northeast, we'll find craft cider in Russia, where the apple tree is omnipresent but where cider has never had the importance it should have deserved. Dmitrii Tikhomirov has done some research on the history of cider in Russia and found a few mentions in the nineteenth century literature about cider production, and sporadic pomological references that mention some native apples as being good for cider. However, at best these are only anecdotal, and cider in this country never was widely consumed—no more during the Soviet era than during the Russian Empire. We all know that vodka has been the main drink of the people for a long time, while the wealthy often prefer imported wines and spirits. An important traditional drink is kvass, which is an effervescent sour beverage made from fermenting bread soaked in water. Beer and mead are also common low-alcohol drinks.

Figure 11.7. A display of Bullevie Cidre bottles where we can easily identify some ciders of French, English, and Spanish inspiration. Photo by Bullevie Cidre.

And there is a tradition in the countryside of making fruit wine from apples and all other fruits available mixed with water and sugar for fermentation. During Soviet times, Georgian wine was popular, as well as "Soviet champagne" (of which my wife, who spent the first part of her life in the Soviet Union, has found souvenirs). Some cider has been produced, but according to Dmitrii, the quality was questionable and the production never important.

It is in the early 2000s that the company Yablochniy Spas was formed and started to produce the St. Anton cider near Moscow, the first modern pure-juice craft cider in the country and still the leading brand. They have been joined by a few other makers among which I may mention: DaDa Cider from Moscow, which was present at the exhibition at CiderWorld'19 in Frankfurt; Toksovo Cidrerie in St. Petersburg, highly praised by the renowned French producer Antoine Marois; and Bullevie Cidre, presented here with more details. All in all, currently fewer than 10 producers of craft cider are in this huge country, but this number will certainly grow rapidly in the coming years.

Dmitrii Tikhomirov got the cider bug after traveling in Normandy. He also was in the cider-making regions of Spain and England, and developed his craft with Peter Mitchell (Cider and Perry Academy) and Étienne Dupont (well-known maker of cidre and calvados). In 2015, he started his company, Craftier Ltd, in St. Petersburg and acquired a piece of land that had been in the family for many generations in the village of Oleshno, 200 km (125 mi.) south of the city, to plant 8 hectares (20 acres) of apple and pear orchards. Among the varieties, there are old native Russian apples that give unique character to the ciders. The production started in 2017, and the cider is marketed under the brand Bullevie Cidre, a name that sounds very nice in French, as *bulles de vie*, meaning bubbles of life. . . . In 2020, when last checked, the annual production had already reached 200,000 liters, and the company offers a nice portfolio of craft ciders, some of them inspired by traditional European styles, while others seek to be truly Russian.

Kazakhstan
Alexander Thomas and Aizhan Bekzhanova, Apple City Cider

As we keep on going east, we reach where the steppes of Kazakhstan meet the Tian Shan mountains, and the city of Almaty, former capital of the country. We saw in the introduction of this book that this is the place of origin of the apple species. We may wonder why cider is not part of the culture in such a place, but this is now being corrected with the foundation of Apple City Cider. I have already introduced Alex Thomas and Aizhan Bekzhanova as they were our hosts for our trip to the wild apple forests in 2017. They founded this new cidery in 2018, the first commercial cidery in the country. One objective of Apple City Cider is to use apples of the species *Malus sieversii* in the making of cider as a way to protect the wild apple forests. In effect, the reasoning is that if the wild apples are given some value by their cider potential, it becomes much more natural to protect them. They have been working on this project for quite a

Figure 11.8. Alex Thomas and Aizhan Bekzhanova, owners of Apple City Cider.

while now, and they had the good idea years ago to have some trees started for eventually transplanting into the cidery orchard. These are from selections of *M. sieversii* that are mostly bittersharps, with some bittersweets.

The name of the cidery, Apple City Cider, comes from its proximity to the city of Almaty, which has always been considered the City of the Apples because it is surrounded by mountains that hosted wild apple forests. (Unfortunately most of those trees closer to the city have been cut down to make room for new housing developments.) The former name of Almaty in the times of the

Figure 11.9. Planting the first *Malus sieversii* cider orchard. Note the Tian Shan mountains in the background. Photo by Alexander Thomas.

Soviet Union was Alma-Ata, which means "grandfather of the apple" in the Kazakh language.

Although Kazakhstan is a place where the apple tree naturally thrives, a commercial cidery had never been in the country. And from its past as a republic in the Soviet Union, it retained some aspects of the Soviet bureaucracy. As a result, obtaining all the permits for the establishment of this cidery was probably more challenging than in most other places of the world. Add to that the difficulty of procuring the cidery equipment when there are no suppliers within thousands of kilometers and we have just a slight idea of what the owners had to go through. It took them over four years to bring the project to completion, but now all of this is behind them, and the cidery began selling their first batches in 2020.

Asia

From Kazakhstan, we first head south and cross the Himalayas to arrive in northern India and Nepal. In those areas located at the foothills of the Himalayas, there is a good climate for apple growing and, yes, cider makers are there. In India, cideries are found in the region of Himachal Pradesh, and some of the better-known brands are Tempest and Himachal. In Nepal, I heard about one ambitious producer located at an altitude of 3,500 meters (11,500 feet) above sea level. They use eating varieties such as Golden Delicious, Fuji, and Gala grown in the region for the making of cider, as is often the case for modern-style cider.

If we continue our journey going east, we will cross China, the largest apple producer in the world. Most of the cider consumed there is imported, but the first cidery appeared in 2018: Ping Dynasty Cider. Another cider I heard about is Malan Mountain Cider. I know very little about these products, but I have no doubts that in the coming years, China will see an important growth of its cider production.

One more step, and we are in South Korea, where a Frenchman, Dominique Herque, founded the first Korean cidery in 2017, Domaine les Dom. He makes what he calls a natural cider, fermented by wild yeast and made sparkling using the ancestral method followed by disgorgement. He has difficulty finding proper apples locally to make cider, Fuji being the main variety grown. He manages by making an early fermentation with summer apples that contain more acidity, and then he blends this back with the Fuji bulk cider. He also has access to some redflesh apples of the Swiss-bred Redlove varieties, which are quite sharp and tannin-rich. He uses them for making a rosé cider and also for blending in his main cuvées. Dominique says that since he started, more cideries have popped up in the country, but these are more industrial-like producers.

Our last Asian stop is Japan, where there is a small cider industry concentrated around the main apple growing regions: Aomori, Nagano, and Yamanashi. Japan is well known for its production of extremely high-quality dessert apples grown on small-scale farms. These apples are so perfect, it is almost as if each apple has been individually petted during its growth up to harvest. And they go as far as bagging the apples while they grow on the tree to protect them. The problem with such high-quality apples is that they become much too expensive to use in cider making. Thus, finding proper apples at a reasonable price becomes a challenge for the cider makers. One interesting anecdote in Japan is that the word *cider* is used for a sort of lemonade that mostly children drink, hence proper cider is called by its French name *cidre*, in part because during the 1950s some French cider experts came as consultants to help start a new industry. So we can see that cider has been around for quite a while in Japan, for longer than in many other countries. However, it still remains little known and its production level is relatively low. It is nevertheless important enough to justify the existence of a bilingual magazine dedicated to all things cider and called *inCiderJapan*.

A number of good producers are in Japan, but I have had the opportunity to meet only one of them. Shoji Tamura founded Tamura Cidre in 2014 in Hirosaki (Aomori Prefecture), after having worked in different fields of the fruit business. He now runs a 12-hectare (30-acre) orchard that produces 240 tons of apples annually, which are used for a number of processed apple products, including cider. The varieties grown are typical Japanese dessert apples such as Fuji, Mutsu, and Orin. In 2016, Tamura Cidre was the first from Japan to win a Pomme d'or in the CiderWorld fair in Frankfurt, and since then, Shoji has been

Figure 11.10. Shoji Tamura (*left*) presenting his cidre at the CiderWorld'18 fair in Frankfurt.

a regular exhibitor at the fair. I met him there in 2018, but I must say communication between us wasn't easy as we don't speak the same language. The cider is typical modern style, rather light, very well crafted using the traditional method. A few other well-regarded Japanese producers are Toshiko Moriyamaen who makes the Moriyamaen Tekikaka Cidre in Aomori, and two wineries in Nagano that also produce high-quality ciders, Mashino Winery and St. Cousair Winery & Vineyards.

Latin America

Let us now cross the Pacific Ocean to land in Mexico before visiting South America. Cider has been around for a long time in these countries, the habit of drinking it coming from the Spanish. A part of their cider is imported from Spain, but there are some local centers of production. In most of Latin America, sparkling cider is the traditional drink for Christmas and New Year festivities, but it is seldom consumed during the rest of the year except when there are special occasions such as weddings. It should be said also that this traditional cider is rather on the sweet side. Latin America isn't really the place of choice for those who enjoy dry ciders, but there are a few exceptions.

Mexico has had cider making activity since as early as the 1600s and the national consumption (including imports) amounts to approximately 12 million liters per year. Traditional Mexican cider is made sparkling by carbonation and presented in champagne bottles. It is relatively high in residual sugar, low in tannins, and made with mostly well-known table apple varieties with sometimes the addition of some old varieties that are specifically used for cider. Mexico is not seeing a cider boom as in other countries. Most of the cideries were established during the first half of the twentieth century, and this is a fairly stable market with few new players. Because of the seasonality, many producers do not solely make ciders but also make other types of beverages such as wine, wine coolers, and many different flavored ciders (in Mexico, 50 percent apple juice is required for writing the word *sidra* on the label). We often see *sidra rosata*, which is generally produced by mixing grapes or red wine with cider.

Apple growing is in cooler and higher-altitude locations, mainly in the states of Chihuahua, Puebla, and Hidalgo, while the main cider production centers are in the state of Puebla, in Zacatlán, Huejotzingo, and Cholula. This last town is home of one of the largest producers, Copa de Oro, which was founded in 1936. They still use large oak vessels to age the cider for over a year. In Huejotzingo, which is near the volcano Iztaccíhuatl at an altitude of over 2,000 meters (6,500 feet), we can find five major cider production facilities plus a number of smaller, traditional producers. Most are family owned, for example, Sidra San Francisco, which maintains the artisanal way of making the cider that has been going on for generations. But probably the best-known Mexican cider outside of Mexico is the Zemilla Mexican Hard Cider, produced by Bodegas Delicia in Zacatlán, which is exported to the United States and thus has more international visibility.

We will now head south to reach Argentina and Chile. These countries are both important producers of apples and of many other fruits, and they share quite similar situations relative to cider, although it should be said that Argentina is probably the country with the richest cider tradition in Latin America. As is the case in Mexico, cider is very seasonal, being mostly consumed around the Christmas period and for some traditional fiestas. But marketing efforts are in place to bring the people to drink it in other periods of the year. Apples are grown, and cideries may be found, in the south of both countries where the climate is cooler.

In Argentina, the main regions for apple production are in the provinces of Mendoza and San Juan, located west of Buenos Aires in the foothills of the Andes. This region is also famous for wine production. More to the south, apple production can be found on the plateaus of Río Negro and other regions of Patagonia. There are many large cideries that use typical industrial processes to make sweet, carbonated ciders, and these generate the bulk of the production. Among those is Sáenz Briones, which is probably the best known in the country and has a very wide portfolio of products, from traditional champagne-style to more modern offerings. La Farruca is a century-old cidery in the Uco Valley in Mendoza, located at 1,500 meters (5,000 feet) of altitude. And Sidra Real, also a century old, is in the Alto Valley of Río Negro.

In Chile it is mainly in the regions of Los Lagos, Los Ríos, and Araucanía where we find apple orchards and cider. Among important cideries, we find Sidra Punucapa in the province of Los Ríos, which is a Denominación de origen (equivalent to PDO), and Gran Sidra Antillanca in Los Lagos. One interesting form of cider popular in the south of the country is what's known as *chicha*. This beverage is lightly fermented and is drunk very fresh and young.

The main varieties grown and used for cider making in both countries are typical commercial international apples such as Pink Lady, Granny Smith, Royal Gala, Red Delicious, and other similar market varieties. But before these varieties became dominant, there were some old local and traditional varieties. These are now being sought out by some cider makers. One of these is the Limona, from the region of Los Ríos in Chile, which is a small yellow apple that combines sweetness and acidity. According to the story, it was brought by the conquistado-res some 400 years ago. Let us now meet a few craft producers.

Quebrada del Chucao is a very small craft cidery with a production of under 10,000 liters and uses apples from century-old orchards of almost forgotten or even unknown ancient varieties that were intro-duced by the first settlers of the region. The cidery was founded in 2010 by Matías Nahrwold and Diego Rivera, and it is located in the heart of the Chilean province of Araucanía. They take pride in using no commercial apples in their ciders, and they have initiated a program to rescue these old ancestral varieties and propagate them to preserve the apple diversity found in southern Chile. The ciders are sparkling, made using the traditional method, and stand out for their very low (by Chilean standards) level of residual sugar.

An interesting initiative in Argentina is the Txapela Sidra Vasca Natural, a cider inspired by the sagardoa style. This was born in 2016 from the collaboration of Xabier Aguirre, a Basque descendant living in Buenos Aires, with the cidery Petritegi Sagardotegia located in Astigarraga (Spanish Basque Country). The Argentine cidery is based in the Río Negro Valley in Patagonia, and they make cider from apples grown in the region, mostly of the Pink Lady variety.

Another craft cidery worthy of our attention is Alai, which was founded by a French enologist, Laurence Real. She came to Chile some 25 years ago to work in the wine industry, and her interest switched to cider in 2013. One particularity of her work is the use of quince blended with apples. She says Chilean quinces are of very good quality, and that they add a lot of perfume and some tannins to the ciders. The cidery makes their ciders naturally, without sulfite or yeast additions. Some of their pét-nat ciders are produced with the ancestral method, and the fully sparkling with the traditional method. As Laurence has some roots in the Basque Country, the cidery also produces a cider inspired by the sagardoa style.

South Africa

We will end our 'round-the-Cider Planet tour after crossing an ocean again to land in South Africa. This might come as a surprise to some, but South Africa is a major cider market, being second in volume after the U.K. It is the home of two of the largest producers in the world, Hunter's and Savanna, which incidently are both owned by the same company, Distell Group Limited. Together, they supply a good 90 percent of the market, but that other 10 percent is seeing interesting things happening, and we can now find a couple of dozen small to midsize craft makers that are filling the niche. We'll mention three of them here, who all make full-juice cider without use of concentrates, using apples grown in the Elgin Valley, near Cape Town, in the extreme south of the country.

Sxollie is an urban cidery founded in 2014 in Cape Town, resolutely modern in its approach to the process and marketing of cider. They make single-variety ciders from Granny Smith, Cripps Pink (another name for Pink Lady), and Golden Delicious apples, plus a perry from Packham's Triumph pear. They add no sugar, concentrates, or flavorings and keep a residual sugar from arrested fermentation. The ciders are carbonated for a light sparkle.

Windermere Cider has a different approach, Mark Stanford and André Le Roux having planted European bittersweet cider apples in their orchards by the end of the 1980s. They started a production by mid 1990s, introducing South Africa's first real craft cider, but this didn't really work out—the market wasn't ready then for such cider. Nonetheless, they kept on making cider, just in very small quantities. It was in 2012 that they started again on a larger scale, and now their main product is a full-fruit cider inspired by German Apfelwein with no added sugars, preservatives, or additives.

Everson's Cider is the work of William Everson, a wine maker who started to experiment with making cider in 2009. He makes his cider from a blend of dessert and culinary apples and ages it on wood. His process is also rather modern, with inoculated yeast and carbonation for sparkle. Back-sweetening is done with freshly pressed apple juice. He produces two ciders, one perry, and three flavored ciders.

I hope you have enjoyed this tour of our Cider Planet. . . . Before closing the book, however, I invite you to have a look at two subjects I discuss briefly at the back of the book in appendices A and B: The first is about the acidity–tannin balance point of different cider styles, and the second is about the types of glasses that are used for tasting and drinking cider.

Cheers from cold Quebec! And many fruitful travels around our Cider Planet.

Acidity–Tannin Balance Point

We examined in part I the basic traditional cider styles of Europe. They are all very distinct and come from long-standing traditions that have slowly evolved and also have seen some modernization during the last decades. It is interesting to plot on an acidity–tannin graph the balance point of those ciders.

The graph shows the approximate locations of these important cider styles in function of their average acidity and tannin concentrations. Also shown are the locations of cider apples of different classes as reference. We can highlight the following interesting features:

- The French styles (Breton and Norman) are those with the least acidity and most tannin, with the Breton style being slightly more bitter and the Norman style being slightly higher in acidity.
- The German and Spanish styles are those with the most acidity and least tannins, with the Spanish ciders usually having a bit more tannins than the German.

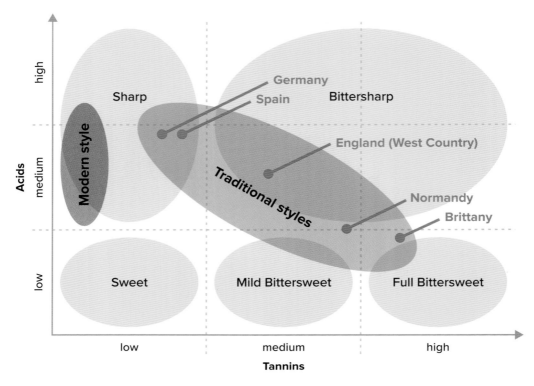

Figure A.1. Acidity–Tannin graph showing the balance point of cider styles.

- The English style of the West Country is somewhat intermediate and could be seen as the better balanced of the lot. The English eastern–style would be located at the same position as the German style with higher acidity and low tannins.

From all these styles, we can define a zone, which is shown in green on the graph, inside which all those balance points reside, and which we could consider the ideal zone for traditional cider styles. It shows that as the tannins increase in the blend, the acidity needs to decrease in order to maintain a pleasant flavor, and similarly, as the acidity increases, the tannins should decrease. A cider that would have as much tannin as a Breton cider, combined with as much acidity as a German cider, could be too intense to be pleasant to drink. Conversely, a cider with low tannins such as the German combined with a low-acidity cider such as the Breton could be somewhat bland, without much character.

The other factor to take into account is the amount of residual sugar in the cider. Generally speaking, the two French styles are those that traditionally contain the most residual sugar, while the German and Spanish ciders are generally dry or off-dry. And in England it is quite variable, although we more often see the craft ciders being dry to medium. It seems that the more tannin in the cider, the more residual sugar is required to balance the tannins and give a pleasant flavor. And in effect, we can have a cider that technically would be a semisweet, but still taste quite dry when there is a high tannin content.

Let us now look at where the nontraditional ciders would position themselves on this graph. Ciders of the modern style made with commercial apples would be more to the left on the graph than the German style, as they have very little content of tannins and usually a medium acidity, hence it appears as the zone in gray on the left of the graph. On the other hand, ciders of the traditional or heritage style from newer production regions could be anywhere inside the green region of the graph, some closer to where the German style is, others closer to the West Country or near the position of the two French style balance points.

Glasses for Cider

Recently, a cider producer friend asked my advice about cider glasses, as he wanted to choose a model of glass for tastings at his cidery. This made me think about all the types of glasses that I have used to drink cider—and there are quite a few. I made a picture of some glasses from my personal collection which, although not complete, does show the diversity that exists. We can see in figure B.1:

1. The INAO glass was created by the Institut national de l'origine et de la qualité as a standard tasting glass for wine. It is the most common type of glass used in cidery tasting rooms all over the Cider Planet. It is also used for judging at cider competitions. This glass works well for cider, although it is a bit small, and some find it old-fashioned.
2. The Spanish traditional glass for sidra (see chapter 4). This particular one is decorated for the Fiesta de la Sidra.
3. The CiderDays' "Cider Salon" glass is used for the tastings at the CiderDays festival in Massachusetts. It is in fact a fairly standard wine glass that also works well for cider.

Figure B.1. Cider glasses from author's own collection.

4. This small bowl is traditionally used for farm cider in Brittany, where we talk about *une bolée de cidre*. Its usage is now less common, as people often prefer more modern glasses.

5. This tasting glass from Angry Orchard in Walden, New York, is a shape somewhat similar to the INAO glass, but slightly larger.

6. Another glass from Angry Orchard, this model is intended to go with their Understood in Motion series of high-quality ciders. The shape is that of the renowned Teku beer glass, which is also used for cider service at the Joran Cidrothèque in Brussels.

7. The Austrian tasting glass, selected by the Most Barons and used by most cideries in the Mostviertel region (see chapter 8), is a beautiful glass. A similarly shaped glass is used for service at Le Sistrot, a cider bistro in Quimper, Brittany.

8. This glass is used for tasting at the CiderWorld fair in Frankfurt. I find it is a bit large for a cider glass.

9. The Gerippte is the glass for serving traditional Apfelwein in Germany (see chapter 5) and used in all cider bars in Frankfurt. These

are available in two sizes, 250 and 300 mL (8.5 and 10 oz.), the one pictured being the smaller size.

I wish to make it clear to the reader that I am no specialist on glasses. The main point that I want to make here is that there is yet no standard established for a cider glass, as we can see that all sorts of shapes and sizes are used—although some are traditional to a given region. If there is one type that may eventually emerge as a "standard cider glass," in a similar way as we have standard glass shapes for red wine, white wine, beer, and so on, I'd take a guess it would be based on the INAO tasting glass but slightly larger, somewhat like glass #5 in the photo. In effect the INAO glass has a full capacity of approximately 200 mL (7 oz.), and many find it a bit too small because it should be less than half filled when tasting. For example, at Le Sistrot, the standard serving for a glass of cider is about 120 mL (4 oz.), and this is too much for the INAO glass, which would then be more than half-filled. I can, however, see that glasses with similar shapes and proportions but with a capacity of 300 to 350 mL (10 to 12 oz.) would become a favorite for the service of cider. It should be noted that some manufacturers of fine glassware are starting to add cider glasses to their collections, and it will be interesting to see what they come up with.

You may ask which are my favorites from those in the photo? Well, I'd say the INAO tasting glass (#1) is probably the one I use most often for daily cider drinking, closely followed by the CiderDays "Cider Salon" glass (#3). However, my favorite is the Austrian glass (#7) for its elegance and delicacy, but since I don't want to break it I use it only on special occasions! What I have experienced is that a good cider will taste good in just about any glass, and a bad cider won't become good if served in a great glass. But, a nice glass does add a little something special, the pleasure of drinking in a quality glass, and this is not negligible. We can add that pleasant company and a good story about the cider or the apples also increase the pleasure of drinking. . . .

INDEX

Note: Page numbers in *italics* refer to photographs and illustrations. Page numbers followed by *t* refer to tables. Page numbers followed by n refer to footnotes.

hydraulic rack and cloth presses
    in Austria, 216
    in France, *23*, 117, 202
    in Germany, 180
    in traditional cider making, 23, *23*
    in the United Kingdom, 84
    in the United States and Canada,
        274, *275*, 281
hydropress-type presses
    for small producers, 23, 84
    in the United Kingdom, 84
    in the United States and Canada,
        274, *275*
Hyslop apple, 293

ice cider making
    in Canada, 246, 278–282, *279*
    PGI label for, 246
    in Sweden, 295
Idared apple, 250
IFPC (Institut Français des
    Productions Cidricoles), 96
IGP (Indication géographique
    protégée), 7
*The Illustrated History of Apples in
    the United States and Canada*
    (Bussey), 256n
Improved Foxwhelp apple, 227
INAO tasting glass, 310, *311*, 312
India, nascent cider production
    in, 299
industrial cider making
    in France, 90, *95*
    in Germany, 158, 159
    in Ireland, 288–89
    in the Nordic countries, 294
    practices of, 44–45
    in the United Kingdom, 60–62, 70
injection method (carbonated
    cider), 43
INRA (Institut national de la
    recherche agronomique), 107, 112
Institut Français des Productions
    Cidricoles (IFPC), 96
Institut national de l'origine et de
    la qualité, 310
integrated pest management (IPM)
    bush orchards, 70
    modern orchards, 19

intensive orchards
    orchard management, 19–20
    super spindle ultra-intensive
        management, *268*
International Cider & Perry
    Competition (Hereford Cider
    Museum), 62
International Cider Challenge, 62
Ireland
    Magners brand, 229, 288
    nascent cider production in,
        287–292, *288*, *291*
Irish Russet apple, 290
Isensee-Kiesau, Christine, 160
Italy
    Charmat method used in, 40
    nascent cider production in,
        284–87, *284*, *285*, *286*

Jaanihanso Siidrivabrik cidery, 292
James Grieve apple, 72
Japan, nascent cider production in,
    300–301, *301*
Jazz apple, 233
Jefferson, Thomas, 243, 253, 262
Jenkinson, Mark, 287, 289, 290, 291
Jersey family of apples, 74–76, *75*
Jersey Flenier apple, 74
Jodoin, Michel, 244, 257, 263, 265
Johnson, Mike, 69, 70, 84, 190
Jonagold apple, 72, 233, 250, 290
Jones, Tim, 227–28, *228*
Joran Cidrothèque, 311
Journal (Gilles de Gouberville), 91
Jubert, Jacques, 91, 92, 93
Judaine apple, 107
Judeline apple, 107
Judor apple, 105, 107, 112–13
juicing. *See* pressing
Juliana apple, 107
Jurella apple, 107

Kaiser Wilhelm apple, *163*, 171
Kalveram, Konstantin, 163,
    164, 165
Kaminsky, Matt, 265
Karpentin apple, 173
Katy apple, 72
Kaye, Adie, 165

Kazakhstan
    nascent cider production in,
        13–14, 297–99, *298*
    wild apple forests in, 8–13, *9*, *10*, *12*
keeving
    ancestral method combined
        with, 39, 86
    in Australia and New Zealand,
        241, 242
    belt press considerations, 24
    in Denmark, 294
    in France, 28, 37, 94, 117–18, 203
    in Ireland, 287
    principles of, 26, 28–29
    in the United Kingdom, 86, 195
    in the United States and
        Canada, 277
Kelterei (press house), 157
Kendell, Gail, 225
Kendell, James, 225
Kennedy's Late apple, 72
Kermerrien apple, 105, 113–14,
    113, 252
Kerr apple, 293
Khamzina, Banou, 9
Kingston Black apple, *81*
    description of, 82
    favored status by cideries, 227,
        228, 241, 245
    importance of, 72, 235, 251
kizkias (apple collecting tools), 149
Knight, Thomas Andrew, 26, 28,
    59, 73
Knollbirne pear, 214
Königlicher Kurzstiel apple, 173
Kopparberg cider, 294

labels of certification. *See*
    certification of origin labels
Labounoux, Paul, 95
Lady Williams apple, 236
Lafond, Pierre, 244, 278
Lagadec, Dominic, 133
Lagadec, Jon, 133
Lambig (distilled apple eau-de-vie), 89
Landlbirne pear, 214
Landsberger Renette apple, 173
Latin America, nascent cider
    production in, 301–4

Pomme de fer apple, 168

Pomme Raisin apple, 172

Pommes et cidre de Cornouaille (Gleonec), 104, 109

Le pommier à cidre (Warcollier), 94

Le Pommier à cidre et le cidre (Labounoux), 95

Pommiers à cidre – variétés de France (Boré and Fleckinger), 104, 111, 235

Pomologen-Verein (organization), 165

Pomologie du Finistère (Crochetelle), 104

Pomologie et cidrerie (Warcollier), 94

Pomona (Evelyn), 58, 65

Pomona Herefordiensis (Knight), 26, 28, 59, 71, 73

Porter's Perfection apple, 72, 82, 235, 251

Portugal, nascent cider production in, 295

Possmann cidery, 158, *164*, 175, *177*

Pound Sweet apple, 257

Power, Georges, 93, 104

pre-fermentation clarification (débourbage)
  description of, 30
  at Ferme de la Sapinière cidery, 118
  for perry, 217
  in the United States and Canada, 274

pre-fermentation processing
  in Australia and New Zealand, 240
  in Austria, 217
  in France, 117–18
  in the United States and Canada, 276

Preh *most*, 209

preservatives, for chemical stabilization, 34

Président Descours grafts, 102

presses
  early versions, *52*
  for perry, 194, 216, *216*
  twelfth- and thirteenth-century developments in, 53
  types of, 22, 23

pressing
  in Austria, 216, *216*
  in France, *23*, 117, *117*, 202

in Germany, 180

modern vs. traditional cider making practices, 22–24

in Spain, 150–54, *151*, *152*, *153*

in the United Kingdom, *69*, 84, 194

in the United States and Canada, 274, *275*, 281–82

The Principles and Practice of Cider-Making (Charley, tr.), 94

prise de mousse, 35

Les producteurs de cidre du Québec, 245

Pumpkin Sweet apple, 257, 258

pupitres (wooden racks), 36, *37*

Putley Trials (Big Apple Cider and Perry Trials), 62

quality marks, 7

Quebec, Canada
  craft cideries in, 244, 246
  ice cider making, 278–282, *279*
  regulations, 6–7, 279

Quebec Ice Cider, 246

Quebrada del Chucao cidery, 304

quince (*Cydonia oblonga*), 175, 304

rack and cloth presses. *See* hydraulic rack and cloth presses

racking, 26

Ragan, W. H., 260

Rambo (Rheinischer Winterrambur) apple, 173

Ramborn Cider Company, 159, 166

Raventze apple, *285*, 286, *286*, 287

Raxao apple, 144

Real, Laurence, 304

real cider, defined, 4

RECUPOM, 269

Redbyrd Bitter apple, 269

Redbyrd Orchard Cider, 267

Red Delicious apple, 232, 250, 303

Redfield apple, 263, 264–65, *264*

redflesh apples, 263–65, *264*

Red Foxwhelp apple, 80

Redlove apple, 300

Red Moon (Roter Mond) apple, 173

Red Sails cidery, *226*, 227, 232

Redstreak apple, 58–59, 73

Red Trierer apple, 171–72

Redwood Cider Co., 230

regional pommages, 17
  See also pommages; *specific regions*

Regona apple, 144–45

regulations, variability in, 6–7

Reikersdorfer (Most Baron), *210*

Reine de reinettes apple, 170, *171*

Reine des hâtives apple, 107

Reineta apple, 139–140

Rejuvenated Foxwhelp apple, 80

Rekorderlig cider, 3, 229, 294

remuage (riddling), 36–37, *37*, *38*, 40

René Guéret cidery, *95*

Renetta di Antey apple, 286

Republic of Ireland, cider making in, 287
  See also Ireland

residual sugar, 32, 309

Rheinischer Winterrambur (Rambo) apple, 173

Rheinische Schafsnase apple, 172

Ribston Pippin apple, 78

riddling (remuage), 36–37, *37*, *38*, 40

riddling aids (fining agents), 36

Rivera, Diego, 304

Robert-Dantec, Philippe, 98

Roman Catholic Church, orchard development, 51

Rome, ancient, cider making in, 49–53, *52*, *54*

Roosimaa, Alvar, 292

Rosé Cider, 248

rosé ciders, 248, 263, 265

Ross on Wye Cider & Perry Company, 69, 70, 84, 86

Rosstriebkellerei cidery, 161

Rote Pichlbirne pear, 213, *213*, 214

Roter Mond (Red Moon) apple, 173

Roter Sauergrauech apple, 172

Roter Trierscher Weinapfel apple, 171–72

Rouge de Trèves apple, 171

Rouge vigné pear, 201

Rouston, Tierney Schipper, 265

Route du cidre (France), 97

Royal Bath & West Show, 62

Royal Gala apple, 233, 303

Royal Guillevic cider, 99

Royal Society, 58

ABOUT THE AUTHOR

E_Bernier

Claude Jolicoeur is the author of *The New Cider Maker's Handbook*, which has been acclaimed worldwide as a major reference on the topic of cider making. In French, he has authored *Du pommier au cidre* (*From Apple Tree to Cider*) and collaborated to the collective work *La transformation du cidre au Québec* (*Cider Processing in Quebec*).

A mechanical engineer and research scientist by profession, he started in the late 1980s making cider as a hobby. Since then, he has accumulated vast experience, always searching to obtain the highest quality possible. His ciders have earned many awards at competitions, including Best of Show at the prestigious Great Lakes International Cider and Perry Competition (GLINTCAP).

Claude has traveled widely throughout the Cider Planet, is regularly invited to be a guest speaker or cider judge at international cider festivals and events, and actively participates in discussion forums such as the Cider Workshop. He currently works on the evaluation of wild native apples for the establishment of collections of high-quality cider apple varieties that are well adapted to the conditions of eastern Canada. He lives in Quebec City.